Black Protest
Issues and Tactics

Robert C. Dick

Contributions in American Studies, Number 14

Greenwood Press
Westport, Connecticut • London, England

Library of Congress Cataloging in Publication Data

Dick, Robert C
  Black protest; issues and tactics.

  (Contributions in American studies, no. 14)
  Bibliography: p.
  1. Slavery in the United States—Anti-slavery
movements. 2. Negroes—Colonization. 3. Negroes—
History—To 1863. I. Title.
E449.D53   322.4'4'0973   72-794
ISBN 0-8371-6366-8

Library of Congress Catalog Card Number 72-794
ISBN: 0-8371-6366-8 Cloth Edition
ISBN: 0-8371-8922-5 Paper Edition

First published in 1974
Paperback Edition 1976

Greenwood Press, Inc.
51 Riverside Avenue, Westport, Connecticut 06880

Manufactured in the United States of America

TO

BECKY, SHELLY, DANA, AND ALLISON

Sweet is the virgin honey, though the wild bee store it in a reed;
And bright the jeweled band that circleth an Ethiop's arm;
Pure are the grains of gold in the turbid stream of the Ganges;
And fair the living flowers that spring from the dull cold sod.
Wherefore, thou gentle student, bend thine ear to my speech,
For I also am as thou art; our hearts commune together:
To meanest matters will I stoop, for mean is the lot of mortal;
I will rise to noblest themes, for the soul hath a heritage of glory.

Anonymous verse from *Narrative of Sojourner Truth* (New York: Published for the Author, 1853).

Contents

Illustrations

Preface

Antebellum black spokesmen protested against slavery and the treatment of free Negroes in numerous rallies, meetings, conventions and organizational activities. Their rhetorical appeals were advanced in a multitude of forms such as speeches, pamphlets, petitions, and newspaper articles. Some messages were directed toward various types of white audiences, whereas others were designed for their own people.

This is a study of the ideas expressed in the rhetoric of northern black spokesmen of the period from 1827 to the Civil War, with minimal emphasis on biographical data of the individuals involved. It provides a perspective on the cultural history of Negroes by examining their rhetoric and setting forth the propositions and supporting arguments advanced by black spokesmen on major subjects affecting their people. Since there were conflicting viewpoints among black leaders, there is an attempt to scrutinize each position on the issues. As the circumstances of the blacks altered and changed, so did their rhetoric. Thus, the rhetorical changes that took place throughout the movement are emphasized. This is an exploration of the prevalent assumptions, values, and attitudes of black spokesmen as embodied in their discourses. It not only gauges the minds of the rhetorical agents but also indirectly explores the minds of the listeners and readers to whom their rhetoric was directed. In short, this volume is an overview of the intellectual history of blacks as a people in the antebellum period.

Whenever possible, the black spokesmen are allowed to speak for themselves via verbatim quotations. Naturally, a study of this sort is limited to those blacks who were able to articulate their ideas and whose ideas were recorded and are extant. There are listings throughout the book of blacks who often assumed leadership roles at meetings and organizational functions in the movement. Little is said about them, but it is hoped that their being listed will at least acquaint the reader with names of some black leaders who should be recognized and perhaps even stimulate interest in conducting more biographical research.

The appendices are devoted to sets of contrasting rhetorical discourses on some of the major issues concerning blacks. Eleven different antebellum blacks are featured, and there are brief introductions to more readily put the materials and spokesmen into perspective.

Acknowledgment of all those who have in some way helped with this work would be impossible. The idea for it began nearly fifteen years ago in a history class with Professor George Winston Smith at The University of New Mexico. It was given further growth at Stanford University in study with the late Professor David M. Potter in History and Professors Jon Ericson, Helen Schrader, and Naomi Wrage in Rhetoric and Public Address.

Thanks is extended to Stanford's History Department and their Department of Speech and Drama for jointly purchasing some needed microfilmed material. In addition, Professor Howard H. Bell, then of Texas Southern University, loaned me some important microfilmed material during my study at Stanford.

More recently, The University of New Mexico has provided vital assistance. Their Library Committee approved a special grant for purchasing Negro history materials. The UNM Research Allocations Committee subsidized my travel for personal study at archives and manuscript collections on black history. Finally, I am grateful for the leave granted me for the conducting of this project.

Valuable assistance was afforded me by numerous libraries.

Some of those most extensively used were: Boston Public Library, Harvard University Library, Henry E. Huntington Library, Historical Society of Pennsylvania Library, Library of Congress, Moorland-Spingarn Collection of the Howard University Library, Schomburg Collection of the New York Public Library, Stanford University Library, and the University of California Library at Berkeley.

For reading this manuscript and offering suggestions, appreciation is given Professors Phil McFarland of New Mexico State University and James Hoban of The University of New Mexico. Grateful acknowledgment is likewise extended to Professor Cullen Bryant Owens of The University of New Mexico, who furnished careful guidance and assistance from the outset of the project.

Finally, a special "thank you" must go to Mrs. Cathy Retzlaff and Mrs. May Polivka for typing much of the final manuscript.

Black Protest

Introduction

The period from 1827 to 1861 was one of America's most stirring eras of militant organized black protest. Although there had been notable black spokesmen as early as colonial times, those who emerged in this later period were more strident and intense than their predecessors. They strengthened the battle against slavery and sought to achieve justice for all their race. This was the first militant black crusade for freedom in America.

Three events mark the beginning of this early black crusade. The first of these was the founding of the Negro newspaper *Freedom's Journal* in New York City in 1827. Two years later in Boston, David Walker issued his fiery *Appeal*, a pamphlet urging slave rebellion written by a black man and addressed to the slaves. Finally, in 1830, the first National Negro Convention was held in Philadelphia.[1] All three phenomena represented an effort by blacks to speak more assertively and unequivocally for themselves. As Samuel E. Cornish and John B. Russwurm, editors of the *Freedom's Journal*, said in launching their first edition, "We wish to plead our own cause. Too long have others spoken for us. Too long has the publick [*sic*] been deceived by misrepresentation in things which concern us dearly."[2]

Many subjects involving slavery and the free Negro did demand the vital attention of black spokesmen during the late 1820s. They felt compelled to devise strategies to deal with the numerous exigencies of their people's unenviable situation. Frames of accep-

3

tance and rejection were determined by black leaders according to their values and philosophies. Kenneth Burke, a literary and rhetorical critic, has emphasized that "in the face of anguish, injustice, disease, and death one adopts policies."[3] A study of the policies adopted by representative black spokesmen and the strategies they advocated provides an insight into the intellectual and social history of their people.

EMERGENCE OF BLACK SPOKESMEN

As Negroes were mobilizing their rhetorical forces in the beginning of their militant protest movement, they faced the problem of determining how to produce a sufficient number of educated spokesmen from their own race. Though they received some assistance from philanthropic white colleagues in this struggle, only a minimal number of blacks had a college education and at the time most were considered fortunate to receive any kind of formal education at all.[4] Nevertheless, many of them knew the importance of learning the details of their condition, and through various means articulate, well-informed Negro spokesmen were developed.

One institution which encouraged and trained intelligent Negroes was the church; a review of the roster of leaders at the First National Negro Convention reveals a high percentage of ministers, including its President, Rev. Richard Allen. Black theologians were among their race's leadership throughout the movement, but their views probably dominated most during the 1830s; they advocated elevation of blacks in America, working within the law, and a clinging to hopes for the future and to other worldliness. Negro ministers assumed responsibility for instilling a spirit of faith and optimism in their people and assuring them that they would win respect and fair treatment from white society. They soothed and encouraged their downtrodden people during this period. Among the names that appeared most commonly at meetings and conventions of blacks in the thirties were the following ministers: Richard Allen, Amos G. Beman, Jehiel C. Beman, Samuel E. Cornish, Hosea Easton, David Nickens, Daniel A. Payne, J.W.C. Pennington, Charles B. Ray, Christopher Rush, Peter Spencer, and Theodore S. Wright. Their churches provided facilities for meetings and helped provide organizational unity for the black race.

Moreover, Biblical doctrines provided Negro spokesmen with many philosophical assumptions and a sense of "right." Representative of the feelings of these ministerial speakers was a statement by Rev. Theodore S. Wright, himself a Princeton Seminary graduate, when he said at an antislavery meeting, "Blessed be God for the principles of the Gospel. Were it not for those, and for the fact that a better day is dawning, I would not wish to live."[5]

In addition to the educational training through churches and the aid of some white philanthropists and agencies, Negroes aided their own education through the establishment of numerous libraries and literary societies; the societies often sponsored debates as a means of teaching members of their race to express themselves and to keep abreast of the issues affecting them. Such establishments were especially common in major cities like Philadelphia, New York, and Boston.

Negroes in Philadelphia got an early start in the use of debating societies as a means of preparing their students for the public forum. In 1833, the strides which Negroes were making in training their students were revealed by a correspondent for the *Genius of Universal Emancipation*. He reported that the "colored population" of Philadelphia had, "for the few years past, progressed in their moral intellectual, and general condition by establishing several libraries, reading rooms, and debating societies." After observing discussions at a debating society, he reported that the participants "displayed exceptional cogency and acuteness of reasoning."[6] Similar reports on excellent discussions and debates were made by observers in New York, Boston, Cleveland, Buffalo, and some eighteen other cities plus the District of Columbia.[7] As a result of all these agencies—debating societies, literary societies, libraries, church training, and some formal education—Negroes were getting prepared for the intensified rhetorical struggle that was to follow. Black spokesmen emerged in surprisingly considerable numbers during the movement.

NOTES

[1]These three developments were soon followed by such more commonly known events as the establishment of the New England Anti-Slavery Society, William Lloyd Garrison's founding of the *Liberator*, and Nat Turner's insurrection.

[2]*Freedom's Journal*, March 16, 1827, p. 1.

[3]Kenneth Burke, *Attitudes Toward History* (Boston: Beacon Press, 1961), p. 3.

[4]For a survey of the formal education of blacks in the antebellum period, see Carter G. Woodson, *The Education of the Negro Prior to 1861* (New York: G. P. Putnam's Sons, 1915).

[5]*Colored American*, July 8, 1837, p. 1.

[6]Cited in *Liberator*, June 1, 1833, p. 86.

[7]See *Liberator*, October 10, 1835, p. 162; and *Colored American*, July 8, 1837, p. 3, March 2, 1838, p. 3, and November 4, 1837, p. 2. An incomplete summary report of the states and towns featuring such establishments as Literary Societies and Debating Societies is given in the *First Annual Meeting of the American Moral Reform Society, Philadelphia, 1837* (Philadelphia: Printed by Merrihew and Gunn, 1837), p. 17.

Martin Robison Delany—Emigrationist

1

The Colonization
Controversy

Colonization was a most pressing issue demanding a response from black spokesmen early in their crusade for freedom; should Negroes leave the United States? The launching of the *Freedom's Journal*, the issuance of David Walker's *Appeal*, and the calling of the first National Negro Convention all came about at least partly in response to colonization, particularly to the plan of the white-sponsored American Colonization Society to export free blacks to the West Coast of Africa.

Freedom's Journal denounced colonization from the beginning. At the New York Anti-Slavery Society's Annual Meeting in 1836, Rev. Theodore S. Wright described in retrospect the spirit that prevailed among blacks during the period before the inauguration of *Freedom's Journal*. He explained that Negroes throughout the nation were nearly "unanimous" in their feeling that in America, *their* country, they were born, had toiled and suffered, and would die. They held meetings and drew up protests but could "not gain access to the public mind; for the press would not communicate the facts in the case [against colonization]; it was silent." Negroes "saw colonization spreading all over the land." Finally, "the united views and intentions of the people of color were made known, and the nation woke from slumber. The

Freedom's Journal . . . announced the facts in the case. . . . It came like a clap of thunder."[1]

The fourth and last article of Walker's *Appeal* was entitled "Our Wretchedness in Consequence of the Colonizing Plan." Finally, the Convention of the "Free Persons of Color," in September 1830, was called in part to protest against the American Colonization Society and to devise a plan for a settlement in Upper Canada for blacks who were forced to leave this country because of the oppressive laws in some states. The Convention, contrary to the wishes of colonizationists as blacks perceived them, contended foremost that "our forlorn and deplorable situation earnestly and loudly demand[s] of us to devise and pursue all legal means for speedy elevation of ourselves and brethren to the scale and standing of men."[2]

Another sign of the ubiquity of black anticolonization at this early stage of the crusade came in 1832. In that year, William Lloyd Garrison, who had been moderate concerning colonization just three years earlier, published a treatise, *Thoughts on African Colonization*, which strongly condemned the scheme; it contained a section on the "Sentiments of the People of Color." In addition to statements by individual blacks, the Garrison compilation featured declarations from mass Negro anticolonization meetings; in the year 1831 alone, such meetings were recorded in fifteen cities in eight states and the District of Columbia. It is evident, therefore, that Negroes were beginning their militant protest movement with a united front against African colonization.

AMERICAN COLONIZATION SOCIETY

What were the arguments of the white-sponsored American Colonization Society that blacks so strongly opposed? The Society, established in 1817, represented a diverse set of attitudes and motivations. P. J. Staudenraus rightly observed that "after fifteen years of proselytizing, the American Colonization Society had won a large measure of public approval. Many distinguished and influential men looked to colonization as the only practicable solution to the race and slavery questions."[3]

Despite the differences in attitudes and positions among colonization supporters, the managers of the American Colonization Society had some general unifying views. They felt that insurmountable forces were working that made it impossible for Negroes and whites to coexist amicably in the same social system. The managers considered it clear that the causes were "fixed, not only beyond the control of the friends of humanity, but of any human power. . . . This is not the fault of the coloured man, nor the white man, nor Christianity; but an ordination of Providence and no more to be changed than the laws of nature."[4] They stressed that "uncontrollable circumstances" forbade the elevation of Free Negroes on United States soil.[5] In using this premise, the Colonization Society was transcending some of the potential conflicts of its members by saying the circumstances "cannot be explained with reference to their face value alone."[6]

A more outspoken article in a colonization journal in New England attributed the uncontrollable circumstances to "racial feelings." It gave the common view that "almost all nineteenth century Americans" believed that Negroes were innately "different" if not actually inferior human beings; supposedly this belief was derived from the "silent though powerful voice of nature."[7]

Due to that common belief, the blacks encountered discriminatory social policies and laws. As at least a partial consequence, the Negro led a degraded life which in turn was used as more evidence of the "natural," "inevitable" difference that existed between the races. Blacks were not given employment or other opportunities, yet were cited for contributing to undesirable social and economic conditions. For instance, in a speech at the 1831 Annual Meeting of the American Colonization Society, Gerrit Smith, who was still a pro-colonizationist at the time, was quick to point out that Negroes in the northern states constituted about one-fortieth of the whole population, yet comprised about one-sixth to one-fourth of the convicts and paupers.[8]

Similar statistics were cited by Edward Everett of Massachusetts at the Society's next annual convention. He noted that about one seventy-fifth of the population of his state were Negroes while Negroes constituted about one-sixth of the convicts in that state's prisons. Everett admitted that there were many respectable and productive colored persons in his state, but "as a class, they are depressed to a low point on the social scale."[9]

After stressing the degradation which "must" accompany the retention of Negroes in America, the colonizationists at that 1832 convention made it clear that there should be no effort to encourage colored people to remain in America. To them, nothing could be more "unkind" than "to excite hopes in their minds never to be realized." It was equally cruel to entice Negroes to forego the rich inheritance in Africa "for the rights and privileges in this land which they can never attain."[10] These, then, were some of the basic opinions of the colonizationists which black leaders had to consider.

BLACK ANTICOLONIZATION ARGUMENTS

An important strategy followed by many black anticolonization spokesmen was the qualifying of their attacks on colonization. Instead of making a blanket indictment of all those who promoted emigration, Negro spokesmen acknowledged that some colonizationists were well-intentioned but unenlightened individuals who thought they were doing the right thing for the Negroes. After all, some blacks had also moderately favored colonization when the Society was in its planning stages, but most of them had subsequently turned away from it.

At the first National Negro Convention in 1830, the "Address" indicting African colonization was prefaced with the remarks, "Not doubting the sincerity of many friends who are engaged in that cause [colonization]; yet we beg leave to say, that it does not assist in this benevolent and important work [of bettering the Negro]."[11] Likewise in the 1831 National Convention, the Negroes referred to the American Colonization Society as an "august body of learning, talent, and worth" but begged them to desist from their operations.[12] Perhaps the most dramatic demonstration in the 1830s of the free Negroes' desire to objectively consider the views of their "well-intentioned but misguided friends" who favored colonization occurred at the 1832 National Negro Convention in Philadelphia. At the convention a debate was held between two invited guests, Reverend R. R. Gurley, Secretary of the American Colonization Society, and William Lloyd Garrison, who had become vehement in his denunciation of that Society. After the debate, the Negro delegates said they admired "the distinguished piety and Christian feelings with which he [Gurley] so solemnly portrayed that institution." Yet they asserted that Gurley only tended to more firmly rivet their solid conviction that the Society's doctrines were "at enmity with the principles and precepts of religion, humanity and justice."[13]

Similar assertions were made at local black anticolonization meetings. In Brooklyn, a statement denouncing colonization was drafted by a committee of three, including J.W.C. Pennington; it was prefaced: "We truly believe that many gentlemen who are engaged in the Colonization Society are our sincere friends and well-wishers."[14] A New Haven Negro meeting, with Henry Berrian presiding, resolved that "we believe some of them [colonizationists] our friends and well-wishers, who have not looked deeply into the subject."[15] A mass meeting denouncing the New-York Colonization Society was chaired by Samuel Ennals with Philip Bell serving as Secretary. The meeting's published address, composed by an unnamed committee of three, opened with the statement, "we believe many of those gentlemen are our friends, and we hope they all mean well."[16] Negro attacks on the general principle and policies of colonization, rather than on the individuals supporting it, were possibly given some credence by the conversion of such persons as Arthur Tappan, Gerrit Smith, and James G. Birney from colonization to immediate abolitionism during the early thirties.

Black anticolonization arguments at this early time had some expected emotional overtones. Probably the most common emotional appeal to white as well as black society was in the argument that Negroes were born here and this was the only country they considered home. It was only reasonable to assume that regardless of why or how their ancestors got here, they made this a home for forthcoming black generations. The delegates at the First Annual National Negro Convention emphasized that many of their fathers and some of their own number had fought and bled for the liberty, independence, and peace which was now enjoyed by the whites. They concluded that it would be "ungenerous" and "unfeeling" of whites "to deny us a humble and quiet grave in that country which gave us birth."[17]

However, the major task of blacks now was to refute the colonization philosophies. In doing so, they advanced the counter proposition that blacks and whites could indeed coexist in the American system. In support of that proposition, they argued that colonizationists could not prove that Negroes were inherently incompatible with whites. Since colonizationists were advocating a change, they were obliged to assume the burden of proving that the racial differences were "fixed" or insurmountable. The Colonization Society was attributing the insurmountable "force" to "providence," and this was an assertion that could not be easily proven regardless of how much it was supplemented by signs of degradation among Negroes. A representative argument of the times was presented at the 1832 National Negro Convention in the address "To the Free Coloured Inhabitants of the United States." The committee drafting the address consisted of Abraham D. Shadd of Delaware, William Hamilton of New York, and William Whipper of Pennsylvania. They had been told by R.R. Gurley at that

convention that there were causes which forbade their advancement as a race in this country "which no humanity, no legislation
and no religion can control." In response, they answered "believe
it not. Is not humanity susceptible of all tender feelings of
benevolence? Is not legislation supreme—is not religion virtuous?
Our oppressed situation arises from their opposite causes."[18]

The same argument was given at other Negro conventions of the
1830s. For instance, a challenge was issued the very next year to
the Colonization Society to prove their assertion of racial incompatibility. They said "no argument has been adduced other than
that based on prejudice, and that prejudice founded on difference
of color."[19] To refute this argument, Negroes were saying "we
ask for proof" of the inherent inability of races to co-exist.[20]

Negroes admitted that a prejudice against them did exist in the
United States but asked "is it unconquerable? Is it not in the power
of those gentlemen [colonizationists] to subdue it?" Instead of
inherent causes, black leaders asserted that what kept them down
was a want of human powers such as wealth, which they could not
accumulate "simply because we are not encouraged."[21]

In addition to asking for proof of so-called insurmountable
racial incompatibility, Negroes argued from past examples that no
race could be regarded as inherently inferior to another. At a New
York mass Negro meeting, some past examples were given of the
attainments of Indians and Negroes. They argued that the red man
was once thought uncivilizable, yet "our country presents a practical refutation of the vain assertion in the flourishing condition of
the Cherokees, among whom intelligence and refinement are seen
in somewhat fairer proportions than are exhibited by some of their
white neighbors."

In turning to Negro accomplishments, the meeting cited a white
historian, Alexander H. Everett, who proclaimed that "blacks
must be rewarded as the real authors of most of the arts and
sciences which give the whites at present the advantage over
them." He had asserted that when Greece and Rome were still

barbarous, the light of learning and improvement was emanating from Africa ''out of the midst of the very wooly-haired, flat nosed, thick lipped, and coal black race, which some are tempted to station at a pretty low intermediate point between men and monkeys.''[22]

The examples of the Cherokees and Negroes may have tended to disprove the argument of one race being inferior to another but they did not directly counter the colonization argument that the two races were incompatible regardless of whether or not one was inferior. If the analogy is acceptable, a later example given by two black leaders from New York, Samuel E. Cornish and Theodore S. Wright, did show that Jews, against whom there had been strong religious prejudice in Europe, were successfully adapting within that society. Cornish and Wright admitted that a strong prejudice against Negroes existed throughout American society. However, they argued that ''an *existing* state of things does not imply that it is to be *permanent*, much less perpetual.''[23] Not many years previously, they argued, there was a fierce prejudice throughout Europe against the Jews, but that bias was showing no signs of ''perpetuating itself. . . . it is rapidly giving way before the influence of a religious and philosophic age.'' Cornish and Wright asserted that the natural and peaceful adjustment was prohibited in the United States by *laws* which ''artificially'' withheld from blacks the stimulus to exert their faculties.[24]

Since many whites at this time believed that blacks were innately ''different'' if not ''inferior,'' Negroes had to deal with this belief if they wanted to verify the contention that they could amicably coexist here. Cornish and Wright argued that blacks should not be exiled *even if* they were decidedly inferior to whites. They argued that there were many large white families who from generation to generation had not produced a single individual qualified for any but the ''most humble'' occupation. Those white families may give no promise of ever rising above their past and present condition, yet those families should not be sent away.

Society has high places, low places, and innumerable intermediate places, "all of which ought to be filled and. . . , in a well adjusted social structure, will be filled—and in the most easy and natural way—if the members of the community are only left free to fall into the several niches for which they are fitted."[25]

The issue of whether or not the two races could coexist was left unresolved. The American Colonization Society did not deny that prejudice existed and readily admitted that an intangible "racial attitude" contributed to the "irreconcilability" of blacks and whites. Perhaps it was just as intangible for blacks to argue that the "racial attitude" *could* be overcome. Nevertheless, Negroes decided to oppose colonization, particularly the American Colonization Society, and presume that "our condition can be best improved in this our own country and native soil, the United States of America."[26]

In addition to arguing about potential coexistence, black spokesmen asserted that colonizationists discouraged Negroes in all pursuits in this country in order to encourage them to emigrate to Africa. Thus the very prejudice which Negroes were endeavoring to overcome was perpetuated by colonizationists. Negroes spoke out on this argument at all National Negro Conventions and at many local meetings of the early 1830s. The Brooklyn Address, drafted by Pennington and others, attacked colonization on this ground and cited colonizationists who were claiming that friends of blacks were wrong to say blacks could ever achieve equal rights in this country. If it was thought wrong to encourage blacks in this country, the Brooklyn Negroes inferred, then "may we not accept this as an assurance that they [colonizationists] will do all they can to prevent us from arriving to any degree of respectability at home, in our native land?" They concluded that Negroes should disassociate themselves from "such false sympathies and friendships. They are as foreign to us as the coast of Africa."[27]

Discouraging blacks from thinking they could elevate themselves in America appeared to mean inevitable further degradation

for those who chose to stay. At a New Bedford Negro anticolonization meeting, it was resolved that to achieve its purpose the
Colonization Society "teaches the public to believe that it is
patriotic and benevolent to withhold from us knowledge and
means of acquiring subsistence, and to look upon us as unnatural
and illegal residents in this country."[28]

It was difficult for Negroes to accept the idea that the colonizationist might be doing them a favor by encouraging their
degradation in America. Regardless of whether a colonizationist
with that view was acting cruelly or compassionately, the results
were the same; he was hurting the Negroes who chose to remain
and elevate themselves in America. It was hardly surprising, then,
that blacks were opposing those persons who they felt were unwilling to treat them as men while they were in their midst "but if
we will get out of their reach, they will begin their charity."[29]

Blacks further argued that if the colonizationists were to persuade many of the more intelligent and ambitious free Negroes to
emigrate, then a large portion of those remaining would be more
leaderless and apathetic. Such a situation would tend to further
alienate American whites from free Negroes. In the 1831 National
Negro Convention Address there was a reference to the fact that
the "best blood" of the race was threatened with being sapped for
the colonization cause.[30] Moreover, at a black protest meeting in
Pittsburgh under the chairmanship of John B. Vashon that same
year, it was resolved that Negroes in America were threatened
because the Colonization Society could export "the better informed part of the colored people."[31] At a Delaware black anticolonization meeting, the delegates were "well convinced" that
at the same ratio that the industrious part of their race would
emigrate, those who remained would become "more degraded,
wretched, and miserable."[32]

Another harm purportedly inflicted by colonization concerned
the slave. Whatever colonization might do for the free Negro, what
of his enslaved brethren? Black spokesmen claimed that coloniz-

ing free Negroes would only perpetuate slavery. By remaining in America, the free black people, especially if they were more knowledgeable, might at least set an example of the correctness of freedom for blacks. If they were gone, however, slavery would appear more natural and slaves could not be so easily reminded that freedom was possible. That argument was included in a report drafted at a Boston Negro meeting, by such leaders as John T. Hilton, James G. Barbadoes, and Reverend Hosea Easton. They said colonizationists were apparently fearful "lest the free colored people may whisper liberty in the ears of the oppressed."[33] Similarly, at a meeting in Columbia, Pennsylvania, the black delegates described colonization as a scheme for "riveting more firmly, and perpetuating more certainly the fetters of slavery." They further saw colonizationists as being "only anxious to rid themselves of a population whose presence, influence, and example, have a tendency (as they suppose) to produce discontent among the slaves, and to furnish them with incitement to rebellion."[34]

Aside from opposing colonization because they felt the Society feared they might incite slaves, free Negroes also felt morally obligated to remain close to their brethren in slavery. After the National Negro Convention was temporarily discontinued in 1835, there was some semblance of national Negro unity through the American Moral Reform Society. That Society was created at the National Negro Convention of 1834 and officially met in conjunction with the convention the following year. For the remainder of the decade, the AMRS was essentially a Pennsylvania-based organization directed by such black leaders of that area as William Whipper, Robert Purvis, and James Forten. It emphasized a moral commitment by the free Negro to the slave when it suggested that colonization by free blacks would be tantamount to desertion of their bonded brethren. At their 1837 Convention, the AMRS members resolved never to voluntarily separate themselves from the slave population in this country. They believed that since slaves were their brethren by ties of "consanguinity," there was "more virtue in suffering privations with them [slaves] here, than in enjoying fancied advantages for a season."[35]

In a final major proposition during the 1830s, Negroes asserted that the Colonization Society's objective of evangelizing the natives of Africa was inconsistent with their treatment of free blacks in America. The main argument used to substantiate this claim was that the Colonization Society refused to educate the Negroes whom they sent to civilize and teach the natives. Negroes submitted that the persons whom the Society claimed were ignorant and degraded in America could not miraculously metamorphose themselves when landing on the coast of Africa. The Conventional Board President of the 1834 National Negro Convention, William Hamilton of New York, told the delegates he could not see how the inconsistency of the Society could be reconciled; at times the Colonization Society represented blacks as the most degraded class in the community. They were seen as ignorant, idle, a nuisance, and a drawback on the resources of the country. "But as abandoned as we are, in Africa we shall civilize and christianize all that heathen country."[36]

A New Haven Negro anticolonization meeting had earlier declared that it was an absurd and invidious plan to send "a ration of ignorant men to teach a country of ignorant men."[37] Thus, the missionary goal of the Colonization Society was considered impracticable if not hypocritical. The idea of sending a parcel of uninstructed uncivilized people to Africa to teach the natives was considered "mockery and ridicule in the extreme."[38]

As the thirties drew to a close, no new arguments were added to the black anticolonization repertoire. Negroes remained so united in opposition to the scheme that racial leaders spent less time in specifically protesting it. Instead, they encouraged their people to elevate themselves in this country. Despite the colonization movement's subsiding during this period, blacks still held occasional anticolonization meetings in New York, Pennsylvania, and

New England, the three largest centers of Negro leadership of the time.

In December 1838, a call was issued in New York for a meeting among Negroes to reaffirm their disapproval of colonization. Although New York Negroes had "at all times" publicly and privately expressed their dislike for colonization, they still wanted their opposition to go on record. They especially wanted to oppose colonization's "pecuniary" appeals and fight efforts to increase existing prejudice in order to apply "indirect coercion." Included in the names of those calling the meeting were Philip A. Bell, Samuel E. Cornish, William P. Johnson, Charles B. Ray, Charles L. Reason, David Ruggles, Christopher Rush, and James McCune Smith. To punctuate their opposition, a large anticolonization meeting was held in New York City on January 8, 1839.[39] There was also a black anticolonization meeting in Philadelphia in early January attended by such persons as James Cornish and Robert Purvis and chaired by James McCrummell. The meetings in New England reiterated that blacks owed it to their "self-respect," to their "enslaved brethren at the south," and to "bleeding Africa" to protest colonization.[40]

Negro arguments during this decade were primarily concerned with the morality and principles of the colonization scheme. Although many white abolitionists centered arguments on the cost and logistics of shipping a nation of blacks to Africa, the free Negroes focused on the "rightness" of colonization philosophies and policies.

Colonization, African or otherwise, was a subordinate concern of black spokesmen of the 1840s. At their meetings and conventions and in their speeches during the decade, they concerned themselves with their educational, economic, social, and political elevation in America and with the antislavery cause. They passed perfunctory resolutions that denounced the Colonization Society, regardless of the "purity" of motives with which some blacks thought it may possibly have been founded.

BLACK EMIGRATION DEBATED

In the 1850s many free blacks adopted favorable new attitudes toward the idea of emigrating, particularly to Central America. This resorting to emigration can be chiefly attributed to frustration, despair, and increasing uneasiness about potentialities for elevating blacks in the American system. The states and territories had regularly enacted proscriptive legislation against them. Black efforts had failed to achieve adequate educational or economic opportunities. The major political parties had not extended them recognition, and blacks were subjected to widespread prejudicial treatment and even to abusive mobs. On a national level, blacks were greatly distressed by passage of the Fugitive Slave Law as part of the Compromise of 1850. In the Fugitive Slave Law, the government had provided federal officers a fee for returning escaped slaves to bondage. In May of 1854, the Kansas-Nebraska Act repealed the Missouri Compromise and opened Northern territory to slavery. Finally, in 1857, the blacks were dealt perhaps the most severe blow of the era by the United States Supreme Court's Dred Scott decision. In this case, Justice Taney's court denied citizenship to American Negroes.

At this time, a new, impatient, and vocal minority of black leaders were fighting the philosophy of those who had articulated the representative anticolonization arguments that had been so widely accepted among blacks for more than twenty years. The new spokesmen included such men as Martin R. Delany and Nathan Cole of Pennsylvania, W.C. Munroe and William Lambert of Michigan, Charles H. Langston and W.H. Day of Ohio, James Whitfield and J. Theodore Holly of New York, and H. Ford Douglass, then of Louisiana. This group also contained a larger representation from the western states. Instead of concentrating so much on faith in principles and morals, the new black emigrationist breed was more concerned with the realities of the moment. In 1852, Martin Delany reflected the shorter patience of some members of the new generation; he said that "the colored people to-day are not the colored people of a quarter of a century ago, require very different means and measures to satisfy their wants and demands, and to effect their advancement."[41]

Delany gave the first thorough case for black emigration in his 1852 publication *The Condition, Elevation and Destiny of the Colored People of the United States*. This was followed by a National Colored Emigration Convention at Cleveland in August 1854; this convention attracted some 140 delegates from nine free states, three slave states, and Canada. The small but vocal group of black emigrationists insisted on looking at the "reality" of the situation and concluded that the black had no future in the United States. Delany gave the foundation of the new emigration perspective when he argued, "We speak logically and politically, leaving morality and right out of the question—taking our position on the acknowledged popular basis of American Policy; arguing from premise to conclusion. We must abandon all vague theory, and look at *facts* as they really are."[42]

He looked at the blacks' position in the American body politic and concluded that they had no viable part in it. In Delany's opinion, blacks were "politically not of them, but aliens to the laws and political privileges of the country. These are truths —fixed facts, that quaint theory and exhausted moralising are impregnable to, and fall harmlessly before."[43] His argument about "fixed" facts had a shade of the old white colonization belief in an "insurmountable" "fixed" barrier, but the difference was that Delany attributed the fixed facts to the realities of the U.S. governmental structure. At the 1854 Colored Emigration Convention, Delany and eleven other delegates issued a lengthy statement, endorsed by the convention and included in the published minutes, contending that "when the condition of the inhabitants of any country is fixed by legal grades of distinction, this condition can never be changed except by express legislation." The statement said it was "the height of folly" to expect such express legislation except by the force of some irresistible internal pressure. They asserted that blacks did not have the power, numerically or otherwise, to effect the necessary political pressure.

This position was directly in conflict with their black predecessors who had believed that legislation could be effected because "humanity was susceptible of all tender feelings of benevolence." The real conflict was over whether or not society would voluntarily *give* blacks the place that had been denied them in the political system. The convention statement argued that "the rights of no oppressed people have ever yet been obtained by a voluntary act of justice on the part of the oppressor." It asserted that Christians, philanthropists, and moralists may "preach, argue, and philosophise as they may to the contrary; facts are against them."[44]

The emigrationists gave examples of political rights having been gained by either force or superior numbers; even the colonies demonstrated force in dealing with the British governmental structure. Black emigrationists admonished Negro "political leaders and acknowledged great men" for telling their race to "be patient, remain where we are; that there is a 'bright prospect and glorious future' before us in this country."

In refuting the argument that Negroes would ultimately win their political rights in America, black emigrationists gave a review of the history of their race since their arrival in this country. If Negroes were expected to obtain equality by *earning* it, then they had already earned it long ago. Delany devoted an entire section of his treatise to "Claims of Colored Men as Citizens." Negroes, he said, had worked hard as "skillful cultivators" since they had been brought here. In colonial days, the Indians had proved unable to develop an agricultural economy beyond what was necessary on the small plots by their living quarters. Even then, white men in the South depended on and were sustained by the industry of Negroes. Negroes provided labor for public roads and highways and even such public works as wharves, docks, ports and all pertinent improvements. Delany maintained that if evidence of industry and interest did not entitle blacks to equal rights and privileges in our common country, then indeed, nothing could justify the right of any portion of the American people to liberty.

Nevertheless, the majority of black leaders were urging their people to work hard, for God would ultimately set them free. A black leader of the old school, William J. Watkins of New York, clashed with emigrationists, saying that "sorrow and darkness may continue for a night, but joy shall come forth in the morning." Watkins rebutted emigration criticism by admitting that blacks would "remain in America but not 'tamely submit to the lash'." Instead, they would fight the good fight, believing God would soon say, as of His oppressed people of old, "I have seen the affliction of my people and am come to deliver them."[45]

This philosophy was disputed by Delany, when he said that the dependence on divine intervention was doing the colored people "incalculable injury." Emigrationists believed that success in life did not depend on religious character but that laws governing worldly temporary affairs benefitted equally the "just and the unjust. Any other doctrine than this, is downright delusion." *Moral theories* about the brighter day tomorrow had been used by blacks for too long; the *practical* application of principles, or "the thing carried out, is the only true and proper course to pursue."[46]

Emigrationists admitted that blacks might eventually arrive at equality in the American political system if they were willing to completely lose their identity and assimilate into white society. The leaders at the Emigration Convention passed resolutions opposing that alternative. They vowed ever to "cherish our identity of origin and race, as preferable in our estimation to any other people."[47] Besides not wanting to wait that long for rights, Negro emigrationists realized that as a race they could not gain greatness or a place in posterity by losing their identity. Black emigrationists wanted the Negroes as a "people" to attain greatness. They said to their people, "the truth is, we are not identical with the Anglo-Saxon or any other race of the Caucasian or pure white type of the human family, and the sooner we acknowledge this truth, the better for ourselves and posterity."[48]

Another emigrationist argument was that Negroes needed to leave their present environment if they were ever expected to elevate themselves. Due to circumstances beyond either their control or natural ability, the blacks were too far behind Caucasians in America to elevate themselves in this country. Like so many emigrationist arguments, this sounded similar to the white colonizationist arguments which their race had strenuously opposed for many years. The important difference was that black emigrationists specified the *causes* of the circumstances which *blacks* did not have the power to control. Blacks believed that to compete with the mighty odds of "wealth, social and religious preferences, and political influences" of this country at its advanced stage of existence was unrealistic. Thus, they thought "a new country, and new beginning" was the only "true, rational, political" remedy for their disadvantaged position.[49]

Under the existing circumstances in America, talented Negroes were confined to such menial tasks as barbering or being waiters in hotels. Under "unfettered" circumstances, those people would rise to their capacities and not reconcile themselves to servile pursuits.

Black emigrationists were obliged to answer the attacks that other members of their race had directed against colonization over the years. In regard to the issue of blacks being born here and therefore wishing to die here, H. Ford Douglass gave a harsh analogy that perhaps reflected the cold realism of some black emigrationists. After J.M. Langston had used this appeal at the 1854 Emigration Convention, Douglass responded that it was a "poor argument" that had grown stale. He said "there is just as much force in a Black man's standing up and exclaiming after the manner of the 'old Roman'—'I am an American citizen,' as there was in the Irishman who swore he was a loaf of bread because he happened to be born in a bake oven."[50] Yet even while maintaining warm memories about their childhood homes and pleasant domestic relations, the black emigrationists were compelled to "take another view" of the colored man's political realities.

Emigrationists also had to decide whether or not their leaving the country of their enslaved brethren would indeed perpetuate slavery. As a chief spokesman for emigration, Delany argued that the best way to free the slave was for the freeman to elevate himself, and if he could not elevate himself in this country he should go elsewhere. One major conviction was that it accomplished no good for the degraded slave to have the free Negro remain in forced degradation. In fact, J.M. Whitfield, a leader in the 1854 Emigration Convention, explained that if free Negroes demonstrated they could capably advance and assume higher offices in Central America, where the opportunity is afforded them, it could "excite the colored people of this country" and "be the only thing sufficiently powerful to remove the prejudices which ages of unequal oppression have engendered."[51]

The black emigrationists, who were ostensibly attempting to be so realistic, were apparently also being narrow in their advocacy. They were endorsing the old colonizationist views about the inability of blacks to elevate themselves in America yet they were admitting that "the mass of the colored people in this country must ever remain here, and can never, by any possibility be brought to emigrate *en masse*."[52]

With the knowledge that the mass of colored people must remain, it was questionable strategy to impress upon the minds of society, either blacks or whites, that blacks in America were destined to have a degraded existence. The black anticolonizationists were at least attempting to instill optimism in those many Negroes who would have to stay. Moreover, at least they were not giving white oppressors the impression that blacks were resigning themselves to degradation without thinking there was even a possibility for elevation in America.

Just as had been feared by Negro anticolonizationists of the old school, some of the better informed black spokesmen emigrated instead of remaining and setting a good example of black potential in America's predominantly white society. Even before the Fugitive Slave Law was passed in 1850, Henry Highland Garnet, a famous Negro leader of the forties, had told Samuel Ringgold Ward, a black Liberty party colleague, that he favored colonizing to "Mexico, California, the West Indies, or Africa, or wherever it promises freedom and enfranchisement."[53]

When the 1850 Law caused more widespread depression among Negroes, many did decide to take exile. Soon after the Law's passage, Bishop Daniel A. Payne of the AME Church indicated that his courage in fighting the American system was wearing thin. He moaned, "we are whipped, we are whipped and we might as well retreat in order."[54] By the end of 1851, the legislation had taken its toll of Negro leaders. Frederick Douglass, who had become a famous black editor and orator by this time, lamented the loss of such "strong men" as Jermain W. Loguen, William Wells Brown, Henry H. Garnet, Alexander Crummell, Samuel Ward, and Henry Bibb, all of whom were out of the country. Douglass complained that "we protest all this—and especially the despair in which it has plunged our people."[55]

Earlier in 1851, Frederick Douglass had issued a plea for some of his colleagues such as Garnet, Brown, and Crummell to "come home and help Samuel R. Ward, C.L. Remond and Amos G. Beman rouse the slumbering conscience of this nation to our wrongs."[56] However, between this plea and the one in November, the situation had worsened as Samuel Ward also left the country and Charles Remond had temporarily become less prolific in his protest oratory.

During the early 1850s, anticolonizationist Negroes were holding conventions on both the federal and state level as a means of drawing attention to and speaking out for their rights. In 1853, Negroes held a National Convention in Rochester, and despite intervening setbacks, or perhaps because of them, the Negro

Convention effort was intensifying. In 1854, the Emigration Convention formalized the basic split among Negro leaders as to a *modus operandi*.

The last National Convention held by Negroes before the Civil War, in Philadelphia in 1855, was not as large as the one in 1853 and did not devise future programs. It was plagued by the split some had made on emigration and by the collapse of some of the substantial plans that had been made at the 1853 Convention. There were numerous local conventions during the time which passed resolutions protesting colonization. In Ohio, where the National Emigration Convention was later held, the 1852 State Convention strongly opposed *African* colonization. The Committee on Emigration, including such enthusiastic black emigrationists C.H. Langston and H. Ford Douglass, submitted a report that was "indefinitely postponed" by the overall Ohio Convention. The report had urged a national emigration convention of colored men for the "settlement of our people, and the establishment of an independent nationality."[57]

The philosophy that Negroes should not emigrate, which was still subscribed to by the majority of black leaders who made their views known during the period, was very similar to the anticolonization attack given during the first part of the movement. At a colored citizens meeting in New York in January 1852, J.W.C. Pennington urged the Negro people to reenact those many resolutions which were formulated by Negroes in the past and recorded in Part II of Garrison's *Thoughts on African Colonization*. He said the arguments given by Negroes at meetings such as those in Philadelphia, Boston, and New Haven were still valid. In addition, when he was Chairman of the Committee on Colonization at the 1853 National Negro Convention, Pennington submitted a report urging that delegates get their local communities to resolve confirmation of "the several addresses of blacks recorded by Garrison over twenty years previously."[58]

The 1851 and 1852 New York Conventions vowed never to

forsake their brethren to perpetual slavery. With the slaves they were "bound bone of our bone, and flesh of our flesh."[59] Black anticolonizationists also attempted to counter the "facts" of black emigrationists with their faith in their future in America. In the 1853 National Convention Address, the delegates were "encouraged to persevere in efforts adapted to our improvement, by a firm reliance upon God, and a settled conviction, as immovable as the everlasting hills, that all the truths in the whole universe of God are allied to our cause."[60] Negro anticolonizationists did not rebut attacks made on their *moralizing* and *philosophizing* about the future of their people in America. In their estimation, no explanation or excuse was needed for their willingness to accept faith as a premise from which to conclude that a continued fight would result in victory.

AFRICAN CIVILIZATION SOCIETY

The blacks were dealt the devastating blow of the Dred Scott decision in 1857, and the religious optimism about the elevation of blacks in America was not as outward or enthusiastic as it had been previously. Moreover, the sphere of Negro action was not as organized as it had been during the preceding fifteen years. No national Negro conventions were held during the period, although there were state and regional meetings. In 1858, for instance, Negroes held state conventions in Massachusetts, New York, and Ohio. The most widely attended Negro meeting of the period was a New England Convention in 1859 which attracted delegates from New York, New Jersey, Pennsylvania, Illinois, and the New England states. The prevalent attitude of most Negroes during the period was one of increased bitterness, and they made a more pragmatic attempt to elevate themselves however they could in a society that did not legally recognize them as citizens. A description of the frustrated hopes of dedicated and faithful black leaders was made in the policy statement of the *Anglo-African Magazine* in its opening edition in January 1859. The New York-based magazine, edited by Thomas Hamilton, explained its role as that of a foundation under the crumbling hopes of the Negro people. In addition to providing an exposé of the condition of the blacks, the new magazine pledged to uphold and encourage the "now depressed hopes of thinking black men in the United States—the men, who, for twenty years and more have been active in conventions, in public meetings, in societies, in the pulpit, and through the press, cheering on and laboring to promote emancipation, affranchisement [sic], and education."[61] Those men were seeing only negative laws and the denial of citizenship as the apparent result of their efforts and sacrifices.

However, the idea of Negro emigration was dying down among black spokesmen. The last antebellum effort to encourage black emigration was made by the African Civilization Society, founded in 1858 with Henry H. Garnet as President. Unlike the American Colonization Society and its affiliates, the African Civilization Society was not designed for ridding America of Negroes. According to the Civilization Society's Constitution, it was not designed to encourage general emigration but to aid only such persons as may be "practically qualified and suited" to promote the development of Christianity, morality, and the general improvement of Africa. Those emigrating would be carefully selected and recommended so they could indeed promote civilization.

As might be suspected, this organization, with a philosophy that did not conflict with the popular black goal of elevating free Negroes in America, gained adherents among certain blacks who were previously opposed to colonization. The African Civilization Society, by casuistically stretching its philosophy to allow for continued optimism among blacks remaining in America, was able to gain as officers such men as Bishop D.A. Payne, Jeremiah Asher, and William Whipper as well as their earlier emigrationist enemy, Martin R. Delany. The organizational Headquarters for this disparate group was in New York.

A raison d'être of the Society, as stated in its Constitution, was the "principle of an African Nationality, the African race being the ruling element of the nation, controlling and directing their own affairs."[62] This principle would demonstrate the Negroes' ability to think and act for themselves; they wanted to prove they were capable of running their own government without the white supervision that they were suspected of having from abolitionists in America. Negroes were determined to effectively exercise their innate abilities.

Another related argument was that bringing civilization to Africa would cut off the slave trade at its source. That argument was fundamental to the Society and was stressed by Garnet in a speech at a meeting of colored citizens in Boston. He explained that the object of his Society was the "immediate and unconditional abolition of slavery in the United States and in Africa, and the destruction of the African slave-trade *both* in this and that country."[63]

Earlier that year (1859) Garnet had had a dispute with Frederick Douglass over the efficacy of his Society and had emphasized his argument for stopping the slave trade. In a letter to Douglass, Garnet asked: "What objection have you to an organization that shall endeavor to check and destroy the slave-trade, and that desires to co-operate with anti-slavery men and women of every grade in our own land?"[64]

In his Boston speech, Garnet also emphasized that he opposed the view of the American Colonization Society which held that America was not the home of the colored man. "I say it *is* the home of the colored man, and it is my home (applause). The American Colonization Society says the colored man cannot be elevated in this country. I believe nothing of the kind."[65]   To the above arguments, which were more fundamental to the case for the Civilization Society, Garnet added the contention that Africa was rich in trade, commerce, and resources which the Negroes of America could acquire for themselves if they could only rid themselves of the predisposition against colonization that had been generated among them through the years. In his case for emigration, Garnet said that the resources of Africa were opening and white men were daily filling their pockets while "laughing at us poor colored people" who are arguing among ourselves and destroying the character of every man who does not agree with us."[66]

Like Delany and the other black emigrationists before him, Garnet's Society was represented by a vocal minority of the Negro race. Most Negroes were occupied with trying to maintain a daily subsistence and did not seriously consider emigration. They had heard attacks on colonization by their leaders for years; the prospects were risky and speculative at best. At least in the United States they were semi-free and had some security in knowing what lay ahead on a short-term basis. They also had many friends and relatives in slavery and they were not certain whether their leaving would help or hinder the bondsman.

On the other side were those definitely opposed to the arguments for emigration which had been advanced by the African Civilization Society. A representative articulate enemy of colonization schemes, be they black or white, was Frederick Douglass. Douglass refuted Garnet's assertion that African slave trade should be stopped at the source, Africa. To the contrary, Douglass argued that the African slave trade could better be stopped if capable Negroes remained in America. Negroes had the choice, said Douglass, of dissuading the Southern slavetraders or the uncivilized African chieftains. He asserted that the former would be easier, as the savages on the west coast of Africa had sold captives into bondage for ages. They would not be able to understand and accept the American Negroes' moral and economic ideas as readily as the slavetraders of Maryland and Virginia. Douglass concluded, therefore, that he personally was "less inclined to go to Africa to work against the slave-trade, than to stay here to work against it."[67]

As a refutation of the argument that Negroes could prove their self-reliance and govern themselves in Africa, Douglass argued that Negroes could better stay in the United States and prove their abilities by deeds and in speeches to American audiences. He wondered whether American whites would pay any attention to the self-government of Negroes way over in Africa, but he had no doubt that Negroes would have direct confrontations with white audiences by remaining at home. There were approximately four million slaves in the United States who were stigmatized as an inferior race, fit only for slavery, incapable of self-care or self-elevation. To Douglass it seemed plain that *here* was the place and the blacks were the people to meet and put down these conclusions concerning his race. "Certainly there is no place on the globe where the colored man can speak to a larger audience, either by precept or example, than in the United States."[68]

Douglass maintained that blacks needed to settle down in America and get to work, and not be distracted by glancing over their shoulder at emigration. That same argument was given by William C. Nell of Boston through the columns of the *Weekly Anglo-African*. Nell asserted that the African Civilization Society was "creating dissention among them [the Negro people] and diverting their activities and means from what should be cardinal with them—the abolition of slavery in the United States, and the elevation at home of colored Americans."[69]

As we have seen, blacks showed strong opposition to the colonization scheme in the early part of their movement. Black opposition to the gradualism of colonization was consonant with the immediate abolition doctrine preached by the soon-to-be-formed New England and American Anti-Slavery Societies. Many of the white immediate abolitionists, including William Lloyd Garrison, changed over to the anticolonization philosophy already held by their black counterparts.

As the movement progressed, a minority of blacks gave up on America and conceded what the majority of black spokesmen had long denied, i.e., that Negroes were not an inherent part of the

American system. While this minority was realistic in viewing past mistreatment of blacks, it was dampening the hopes for black elevation to equality in America. Most black emigrationists chose to locate in South and Central America, whereas white colonizationists promoted the shipping of blacks to Africa.

The majority of blacks who chose to remain had numerous motivations: a love for their native country, an unwillingness to leave numerous free blacks behind because of logistic necessity, a feeling that emigration would mean deserting their bonded brethren, faith in their ultimate salvation in this country, or a combination of these factors. Regardless, most black leaders attempted to instill patience and optimism in their people while fighting for them to remain and elevate themselves in their native land, America.

NOTES

[1]*Liberator*, October 13, 1836, p. 165. An irony of the times was that while a vast majority of Northern Negroes were opposed to colonization, John B. Russwurm, co-editor of *Freedom's Journal*, soon consented to emigrate to Liberia. After he expressed approval of the colonization scheme, his correspondence to R. R. Gurley of the American Colonization Society states that he was "persecuted" by outstanding people of his own race. Russwurm's letter to Gurley on May 7, 1829 is in the American Colonization Society Mss., Library of Congress.

[2]*Constitution of the American Society of Free Persons of Colour, for Improving Their Condition in the United States. Also the Proceedings of the Convention with Their Address to the Free Persons of Colour in the United States, Philadelphia, 1830* (Philadelphia: J. W. Allen, 1831), p. 9-10.

[3]P. J. Staudenraus, *The African Colonization Movement, 1816-1865* (New York: Columbia University Press, 1961), p. 188.

[4]*The Fifteenth Annual Report of the American Society for Colonizing*

the Free People of Colour of the United States (Washington, D.C.: James C. Dunn, 1832), p. 17.

[5]*The Sixteenth Annual Report of the American Society for Colonizing the Free People of Colour of the United States* (Washington, D.C.: James C. Dunn, 1833), p. 25.

[6]Burke, *Attitudes Toward History*, p. 224-25.

[7]*The Colonizationist and Journal of Freedom* (Boston: Published by Geo. W. Light, 1834), p. 101-7.

[8]*The Fourteenth Annual Report of the American Society for Colonizing Free People of the United States* (Washington, D.C.: James C. Dunn, 1831), p. xiii.

[9]*The Fifteenth Annual Report of the American Colonization Society*, p. xii.

[10]Ibid., p. 18.

[11]*First National Negro Convention, Philadelphia, 1830*, p. 10.

[12]*First Annual Convention of the People of Colour, Philadelphia 1831* (Philadelphia: Published by Order of the Committee of Arrangements, 1831), p. 15.

[13]*Second Annual Convention for the Improvement of the Free People of Color, Philadelphia, 1832* (Philadelphia: Martin & Boden, Printers, 1832), p. 33.

[14]*Liberator*, July 2, 1831, p. 107.

[15]Ibid., August 13, 1831, p. 130.

[16]*Resolutions of the People of Color, at a Meeting Held on the 25th of January, 1831. With an Address to the Citizens of New York, in Answer to those of the New York Colonization Society* (New York: n.p., 1831), p. 3.

[17]*First Annual Convention of the People of Colour, Philadelphia, 1831*, p. 15.

[18]*Second Annual Convention for the Free People of Color, Philadelphia, 1832*, p. 35.

[19]*Third Annual Convention for the Improvement of the Free People of Colour, Philadelphia, 1833* (New York: Published by Order of the Convention, 1833), p. 35.

[20]*Liberator*, February 12, 1831, p. 1.

[21]Ibid., p. 1.

[22]Ibid., p. 1.

[23]Samuel E. Cornish and Theodore S. Wright, *The Colonization*

Scheme Considered (Newark: Printed by Aaron Guest, 1840), p. 8.

[24]Ibid., p. 13.

[25]Ibid., p. 11.

[26]*Liberator*, August 20, 1831, p. 134.

[27]Ibid., July 2, 1831, p. 107.

[28]"A Voice from New Bedford," in William L. Garrison, *Thoughts on African Colonization*, Part II (Boston: Printed and Published by Garrison and Knapp, 1832), p. 50.

[29]Rochester black anticolonization meeting, in *Liberator*, October 29, 1831, p. 1.

[30]*First Annual Convention of the People of Color, Philadelphia, 1831*, p. 15.

[31]*Liberator*, September 17, 1831, p. 150.

[32]Ibid., September 24, 1831, p. 1.

[33]"A Voice from Boston," in Garrison, *Thoughts on African Colonization*, Part II, p. 17.

[34]*Liberator*, August 20, 1831, p. 134.

[35]*First Annual Meeting of the American Moral Reform Society, Philadelphia, 1837*, p. 23.

[36]*Fourth Annual Convention for the Improvement of the Free People of Colour, New York, 1834* (New York: Published by Order of the Convention, 1834), p. 5.

[37]*Liberator*, August 13, 1831, p. 130.

[38]Ibid., July 2, 1831, p. 107.

[39]Ibid., January 8, 1839, p. 1. The Convention Call was in *Liberator*, December 21, 1838, p. 203.

[40]Ibid., December 14, 1838, p. 199. John T. Hilton also argued for the Boston Negroes against colonization, in *Liberator*, November 1, 1839, p. 175.

[41]Martin Robison Delany, *The Condition, Elevation and Destiny of the Colored People of the United States* (Philadelphia: Published by the Author, 1852), p. 8.

[42]Ibid., p. 157.

[43]Ibid., p. 158.

[44]Ibid., p. 59.

[45]M. F. Newsom (ed.), *Arguments Pro and Con on the Call for a National Emigration Convention, by Frederick Douglass, W. J. Wat-*

kins, and J. M. Whitfield (Detroit: Tribune Steam Presses, 1854), p. 12-13.

[46]Delany, *Condition of the Colored People*, p. 39-41.

[47]*National Emigration Convention of Colored People, Cleveland, 1854* (Pittsburgh: Printed by A. A. Anderson, 1854), p. 27.

[48]Ibid., p. 40.

[49]Delany, *Condition of the Colored People*, p. 205.

[50]H. Ford Douglass, *Speech of H. Ford Douglass in Reply to Mr. J. M. Langston before the Emigration Convention at Cleveland, 1854* (Chicago: Printed by Wm. H. Worreld, 1854), p. 15.

[51]Newsom (ed.), *Arguments Pro and Con*, p. 9.

[52]Ibid., p. 12.

[53]From the *Impartial Citizen*. Cited in *North Star*, March 2, 1849, p. 1.

[54]Frederick Douglass, *Life and Times of Frederick Douglass*, 1892 Edition (New York: Collier Books, 1962), p. 279. Also in J. Saunders Redding, *They Came in Chains* (Philadelphia: J. B. Lippincott Company, 1950), p. 119.

[55]*Frederick Douglass' Paper*, November 27, 1851, p. 2.

[56]Ibid., July 31, 1851, p. 2.

[57]*Proceedings of the Convention of the Colored Freemen of Ohio, Cincinnati, 1852* (Cincinnati: Printed by Dumas and Lawyer, 1852), p. 9.

[58]*National Colored Convention, Rochester, 1853* (Rochester: Printed at the Office of Frederick Douglass' Paper, 1853), p. 57.

[59]*National Anti-Slavery Standard*, March 27, 1851, p. 1; and *Liberator*, March 5, 1852, p. 1.

[60]*Colored National Convention, Rochester, 1853*, p. 18.

[61]*Anglo-African Magazine*, I, January 1859, p. 3.

[62]*Constitution of the African Civilization Society* (New Haven: Printed by Thomas J. Stafford, 1861), p. 4.

[63]*Weekly Anglo-African*, September 10, 1859, p. 3.

[64]*Douglass' Monthly*, February 1859, p. 19.

[65]*Weekly Anglo-African*, September 10, 1859, p. 3.

[66]Ibid., September 17, 1859, p. 1.

[67]*Douglass' Monthly*, February, 1859, p. 19.

[68]Ibid., p. 19.

[69]*Weekly Anglo-African*, September 10, 1859, p. 3.

Courtesy of Special Collection, Fisk University Library

William Wells Brown—Disunionist

(Copyright, 1927, The Associated Publishers, Inc.)

2

Blacks in America's Governmental System

Negroes began their rhetorical battle without the knowledge of their legal status in America, yet they strongly endorsed the general principles and spirit of the Declaration of Independence and the Preamble of the United States Constitution. Even the first line of their first convention's "address" in 1830 proclaimed belief in the principles of the Declaration of Independence. The next year, at the First Annual Convention, black leaders urged that the Declaration of Independence and Constitution of the U.S. be read regularly at future meetings, believing that the "truths contained in the former document are incontrovertible" and that the latter "guarantees in letter and spirit" to every freeman born in this country all the rights and immunities of citizenship.[1] However, the belief by blacks in the principle that they were citizens and their actual legal treatment were discordant factors. A prevailing Negro sentiment, as expressed in a New York Negro meeting, was that "the time will come when the Declaration of Independence will be felt in the heart, as well as uttered from the mouth, and when the rights of all shall be properly acknowledged and appreciated."[2]

CIVIL OBEDIENCE

Once they took the position that blacks were included in the American governmental system, Negro spokesmen gave the reasons why they thought the inclusion should be automatically conceded. The overriding reason submitted was that they were God's children and thus their birth in this country afforded *natural* rights.

This belief in natural God-given rights was vividly propounded by Negro leaders of Rhode Island, including George C. Willis and Alfred Niger, who drafted an open letter to President Andrew Jackson pleading for recognition of their rights. They explained to Jackson that blacks had established meeting houses, school houses, literary societies and benevolent associations throughout New England. Their sentiments and conduct, even amidst deeply rooted prejudices and disadvantages, had gained the esteem and friendship of "such persons as regard the principles of truth and justice." Yet they demanded their rights on higher grounds than sentiments of conduct; they demanded recognition because they were part of God's family of man. They asserted, "We will not believe that we and our beloved children are not human beings and are not made of the same blood as the people of other nations and different complexions."[3] Blacks argued that whites *should* recognize their rights on the basis of nature alone. In an address presented at a Brooklyn mass meeting, Reverend H.C. Thompson said, "brethren, we are not strangers; neither do we come under alien law. Our constitution does not call upon us to become naturalized; we are already citizens."[4] Nevertheless, Thompson knew the extent of American prejudice that made citizenship much less than an assumed fact with most whites. Negroes were not thought to be *men* and therefore were denied their so-called God-given rights.

Another reason for inclusion in the system was that blacks' forebears had fought alongside white revolutionaries to gain freedom for the colonies. Therefore, they had earned the liberties expressed in the fundamental political documents written during revolutionary times. They argued that any native born person whose fathers "fought, bled, and died" in defense of the new system should be a recognized part of that system.[5] At a Harrisburg, Pennsylvania meeting in 1831, the Negroes resolved that it was their duty to be true to the constitution of their country. We "are satisfied with the form of government under which we now live; and, moreover, we are bound in duty and reason to protect it against foreign invasion. We always have done so, and will do so still."[6]

This military bravery and fidelity was mentioned to whites consistently in the movement. Blacks recalled the bravery of Negro soldiery in the Revolution and the War of 1812. General Jackson had issued a Proclamation in high appreciation for Negro services in the Battle of New Orleans. Yet the military sacrifice by blacks had not gained the liberty for themselves that they had helped defend for others. In a later address before a meeting of the American and Foreign Anti-Slavery Society, Negro Reverend Samuel R. Ward alluded to the fact that "at the battle of Bunker Hill, a Negro mounted the ramparts and discharged his musket at the enemy no less than fourteen times, and yet in the celebrated picture of that battle, he is represented skulking behind a white man."[7]

By subscribing to existing symbols of authority, blacks were able to praise the words of the founding fathers and even challenge contemporary white lawmakers to live up to the principles of their own patriotic ancestors. Later in the movement, the blacks endorsed a resolution designed to place their oppressors in a paradoxical situation; it was introduced by Henry H. Garnet and stated that "the Declaration of Independence is not a lie" and the fathers of the Revolution "were not base and shameless hypocrites."[8]

Although in the 1840s there arose some Negroes who held the Garrisonian anti-Constitution viewpoint, there was nearly unanimous support of the Constitution during this preceding decade. Blacks vowed support for the spirit of America's basic documents and asserted their right to recognition as equal citizen partakers of those documents, but they were far from being treated as such. Not only was there the institution of slavery in southern states, but northern states and territories placed exclusive limitations on Negro civil rights, including denial of the franchise everywhere but Maine, Massachusetts, New Hampshire, Vermont, Pennsylvania, and New York. Pennsylvania disfranchised blacks in 1837 and New York had restrictions on the Negro vote. Nevertheless, a large majority of blacks remained obedient and loyal to specific state and federal laws as well, regardless of how much they disagreed with them. The major exception was laws pertaining to fugitive slaves; throughout the movement, Negroes refused to return escaped brethren to bondage.

The *Freedom's Journal* reflected the pattern in 1827 by saying "in our discussion of political subjects we shall ever regard the Constitution of the United States as our political star."[9] Later, when the first Negro Convention was held in 1830, the delegates vowed to pursue all *legal* means for their elevation to the scale of men.

Local Negro groups followed suit in vowing civil obedience. For instance, the Constitution of the Colored Antislavery Society of Newark, formed in 1834 with Reverend Henry Drayton as President, pledged to effect immediate abolition by "all honest means sanctioned by law, humanity, and religion." It also vowed to correct public opinion about the blacks' situation and obtain for them "equal civil and religious privileges with white inhabitants of the land."[10]

More arguments favoring civil obedience were given as the movement progressed, but the chief effort at the time was to show the fidelity of Negroes to the laws of *their* country. They thought that legislators would be spiritually awakened by the phenomenon of an oppressed people devising plans for their elevation within the system by "moral suasion alone." The parting advice of the 1832 Convention Address was "Be righteous, be honest, be just, be economical, be prudent, offend not the laws of your country."[11] A guiding creed for the times was to "be obedient to the laws of our common country; honour and respect its lawmakers."

The general commitment to obey the laws was *not* to be interpreted as an approbation of them. Blacks were saying that *God's* laws were right in stressing equality and that manmade laws that denied equality were wrong. They would, however, obey the latter while at the same time praying for such laws to be rescinded. William Whipper of Pennsylvania wrote a "Declaration of Sentiments" at the 1834 Convention calling on blacks and whites to remember that "under whatever pretext or authority these laws have been promulgated or executed, whether under parliamentary, colonial, or American legislation, we declare them in the sight of heaven null and void, and should be immediately abrogated." Concerning the so-called Constitutional legality of slavery, Whipper declared that no people's "patriotic" appeals for liberty and justice possessed more hallowed claims on the "interposition of Divine Providence" than the Negroes'.[12]

With the power of the federal government to enforce slavery, there was no earthly retaliatory force blacks could see to combat it, so they thought obedience to manmade laws that endorse slavery was their only alternative. In addition, they used *moral suasion* to change powerholders' sentiments and hoped for God's intervention.

From the outset, though, Negro leaders encouraged their people not to obey fugitive slave laws, and they made this evident to white oppressors. In a situation wherein one had to choose between man's law of returning his brethren to bondage and "God's law" of letting them go free, black spokesmen urged the latter along with suffering whatever consequences might come from the law. William Whipper presented a resolution at the 1835 National Convention that said the Negro's "duty to God and to the principles of human rights'' so far exceeded his allegiance to those laws that return a slave to his master. The delegates supported the resolution which further recommended that black people disobey those laws and ''peaceably bear the punishment.''[13] Black leaders had no ethical alternative to transcending to a higher authority in this instance.

SUASION BY DEEDS

Perhaps the most compromising reason why blacks remained obedient to discriminatory laws was that they knew their race had been oppressed for so long that their human qualities were not elevated enough for some white lawmakers to comfortably recognize them. Thus, they were compelled to *prove* their title to equality under law. Even David Walker's *Appeal* asserted that in order to ''prepare the way'' for the Lord's interposition, the blacks had ''to prove to the Americans and the world that we are MEN, and not *brutes* as we have been represented, and by millions treated.''[14]

As their chief means of proving their manhood during the thirties, the blacks performed deeds to elevate themselves in the white observer's eyes. They established schools, mutual benefit societies, libraries, literary societies, and various multipurpose organizations which spoke volumes in their behalf. Much of their rhetoric was devoted to reassuring Negroes of their natural capabilities. Hard work and clean righteous living would improve their lot in life and gain recognition by those who needed persuasion. With civil laws and social attitudes working against them, blacks were reminded that their road to recognition as worthy men was extremely rough. Negroes were regularly denied education in colleges, advancement into different branches of business, or entrance into mercantile houses and manufacturing establishments. In fact, they were even turned away from common labor jobs and work as cartmen and porters.

Yet black spokesmen complimented their own people for making significant strides *despite* the discrimination against them. For instance, colored residents of Ohio were able to make steady progress in the face of that state's racial persecution. At a large gathering of Negroes at Chillicothe, Ohio, Reverend David Nickens gave a typical speech of encouragement to his people. In 1832 he said, "ten years ago, it entered the heart of some of our worthy colored citizens . . . to form a combination to remove the moral gloom, and ameliorate the condition of our rising race." The effect had been seen and admired by "every strict observer in the town." Therefore, he demanded abolition of the "prejudiced and slanderous assertion that imbecility of the Africans renders them incapable of improvement."[15]

Hence, it can be seen that the precedent for Negro mutual aid societies was established even before the upsurge of militant protest, and racial spokesmen were able to refer to the accomplishments of these earlier acts by blacks as evidence of their worth. One of the earliest of these organizations was a Boston society called the "African Members," which was formed in 1796 for the "mutual benefit of each other."[16] Renewed emphasis was given by Negroes in Boston during the 1830s to elevating themselves morally, mentally, and economically. This emphasis was referred to by a Negro woman, Mrs. Maria W. Stewart, in a speech at the African Masonic Hall of Boston in 1833. As was common among black leaders speaking to their own people, she stressed their progress under the adverse circumstances, saying, "had we as a people received one half the early advantages the whites have received, I would defy the government of these United States to deprive us any longer of our rights." Now all the blacks had to do was continue striving to raise themselves by virtuous ambition. She wanted to erase false comments that "we are not capable of becoming like white men and that we can never rise to respectability in this country."[17]

In addition to local activities, there were regional and national efforts in cooperation with white philanthropists and teachers to establish manual labor schools and colleges for more classical education for blacks.

SUASION BY WORDS

A period of transition began in 1835 with a gradual change of strategy as Negro leaders broadened their attack to include sharp denunciation of discrimination against their race, especially the denial of civil rights. This meant that Negro discourse had to appeal to whites for understanding and assistance.

The year 1835 marked the last of the preliminary National Negro Conventions. On a national scale, the colored spokesmen relied more on white organizations as an outlet for their appeals. This is not to say that the intensity of Negro work decreased, or that their leadership was lacking. Such an implication was made by the *National Reformer* in discussing activities of "free colored people" during the five years following their general convention in 1835. The *Reformer* said that

> ever since that period they [blacks] have lost their representative character . . . Their attention has been directed to the subject of education. . . .
> They are now capable, by their moral and intellectual ability, of giving a powerful impetus to the cause of universal emancipation. With but few exceptions, their organized powers lay dormant.[18]

The work that black spokesmen saw for themselves as necessary at this time was not a concentration on a national racial organization for emancipation of slaves but on organizations in which whites could have their attention drawn to the needs and accomplishments of free blacks.

It might also be falsely assumed that Negro leaders' power was

lessened to the point of being rubber stamps for their white co-
workers during this phase of the movement. Distressed by what he
thought had been too much submission by blacks, Martin R.
Delany wrote that from the time white abolitionists attended the
National Negro Convention in 1831, Negroes, "with their hands
thrust deep in their breechespockets, and their mouths gaping
open, stood gazing with astonishment, wonder, and surprise, at
the stupendous moral statues of our Anti-Slavery friends and
brethren."[19]

Instead of standing by in idle wonderment, black leaders
pleaded with white society to let their race have its part in the
American system. Garrison, one of the "stupendous moral
statues," soon opposed the Constitution as "an agreement with
Hell." Some black moral suasionists also took that view, but the
majority of Negro spokesmen pledged loyalty to that document, a
position they had assumed before Garrison emerged.

During the latter part of the 1830s, Negroes appealed to whites
through petitions for franchise rights, particularly in New York
and, after 1837, in Pennsylvania. The petition campaign was used
extensively in the overall abolitionist movement, and a resumé of
that use is given by Barnes and Dumond. They demonstrate that
Congress' denial of a hearing on the petitions in the last part of
1836 gave rise to petitioning the Federal Legislature on the principle of the "constitutional right of petition." Thousands who were
inimical to the object of petitioners furthered the petition campaign
with their signatures, preferring that the object of the petitioners
should be attained rather than that sanctuary of all rights should be
violated.[20] Petitions came to the Federal Congress in large quan-
tities from New York, Pennsylvania, Massachusetts, Ohio, and
other northern states. Many came from antislavery societies which
had the active participation of Negroes. However, much of the
work of Negroes in New York and Pennsylvania was directed
toward petitioning the respective state legislatures for the elective
franchise. Independent petitioning by Negroes was not so evident

in Garrisonian New England nor in the far western states that were more sympathetic to slaveholding.

New York and Pennsylvania had their own unique problems with the franchise. The State of New York had a constitutional stipulation that a Negro could vote if he owned $250 worth of property, and Pennsylvania abolished the black vote in 1837. Thus, the black petition campaign in those states was directed toward the proposition that voting requirements should be equal for all races. Negroes from all over New York prepared and sent petitions to their state legislature. Black leaders such as T. Van Renslear and W.P. Johnson circulated petitions around the state and took them personally to Albany after receiving the signed ones in the mail in New York City.[21]

At Philomathean Hall in New York City in December 1837, measures were adopted for preparing petitions. On the committee of ten chosen to draw up the petitions were included the more commonly known names of Charles Reason and Reverend Henry H. Garnet.[22] Blacks of that area were following the philosophy later articulated in 1839 by Philip Bell, a local black newspaper editor, that "while we have separate and distinctive rights to contend for, we must use separate and distinctive means . . . The petition for the restoration of these rights must come from ourselves."[23]

Negro spokesmen made it known that only through the efforts of their own people could they be assured of having their unique constitutional grievances heard. The pleas of Negroes might be indirectly relayed to some legislators but that was a secondary method of obtaining a hearing. Direct action was needed and it was urged by Samuel Cornish in the *Colored American*. As senior editor, he wrote that young men of New York City must "talk *less* and DO MORE, or the subject of their political rights will never be properly presented before our State Legislature." He urged them to obtain even more signatures and send suitable agents to Albany.

In his opinion, the practice of "meeting and spending idle hours speechifying" needed to be supplemented with the contribution of funds and the "efficient" presentation of their case to white society. Otherwise, the entire subject of legal rights for blacks "will be a hopeless one . . . for years to come."[24]

In an effort to get their arguments presented before the state legislature, New York Negroes formed the "Association for the Political Improvement of the People of Color." Their strategy was to unite the people of color in the state and keep agitating the lawmakers. They vowed to petition session after session; if denied at one session, they would apply to the next with petitions that were "worded in language decorous, courteous and dignified. We must weary the legislature with our prayer, even as the partriarch Jacob wrestled with the angel until he obtained the blessing."[25]

An editorial in the *Colored American* also suggested that petitioners should be consistent; they should not call legislators unjust tyrants. Instead, they were urged to "be steady, patient and persevering in your petitions. Let your language be temperate, courteous and dignified. Let your motto be to agitate! agitate!! AGITATE!!!"[26]

Black New York petitioners realized that the newly emancipated slaves were not elevated to the point of voting when the black property requirement was put in the New York Constitution in 1821. Yet the requirement was made of all Negroes, strictly on the basis of color, regardless of background or intellectual qualifications.

Black leaders conveyed the point that since 1821 their race had *earned* the right to equal voting requirements by making themselves intellectually competent. That argument was presented in "The Address of the Convention of Colored Citizens of New York" in 1840. One of the convention's objectives was to decide upon the best appeals to present to the state legislature for enfranchisement. Alexander Crummell drafted and delivered the address. He noted that in all parts of the state "from Montauk to Buffalo, literary and debating societies and clubs" existed among black people in city, town, and village. Their schools and associations were continually sending forth a host of youth with strong determination and the ability to serve their "proscribed" race.

However, it was not because of their deeds and training alone that they asked for the elective franchise. "We would not fall into the error of basing rights on grounds so untenable . . . We base our claim upon those common and yet exalted faculties of manhood. WE ARE MEN."[27]

In Pennsylvania, while the 1837 Constitutional Convention was being held to rescind the black franchise, Negroes in all parts of the state presented that convention with petitions arguing for retention of their right to vote. The most thorough statement of grievances by Pennsylvania Negroes was the *Appeal of Forty Thousand Citizens*, a pamphlet issued after a large meeting of blacks at a Presbyterian Church in Philadelphia on March 14, 1838. The *Appeal* was first presented as a report to the meeting by Robert Purvis, chairman of the committee that had drafted it in advance; other members of the committee were James Cornish, J.C. Bowers, Robert B. Forten, J.J.G. Bias, James Needham, and John B. Burr. After it was read, the *Appeal* was unanimously adopted, published, and circulated in a fruitless attempt to defeat ratification of the new disfranchisement clause. The *Appeal* said, "we love our native country, much as it has wronged us . . . We are PENNSYLVANIANS, and we hope to see the day when Pennsylvania will have reason to be proud of us, as we believe she has now none to be ashamed! Will you starve our patriotism?"[28] In their *Appeal*, Pennsylvania Negroes took a legal position similar to that which Lincoln later took on the Dred Scott decision when he abided by the ruling without fully agreeing with its validity. Negroes abided by the Fogg vs. Hobbs decision, the recent test case that denied black enfranchisement in their state. They thought the court was wrong and wanted the voters to defeat the proposed

Constitution in order to affirm that they also objected to black disenfranchisement.

Just as New York Negroes were tolerant of the expectation of preparing newly emancipated slaves for the franchise, Negroes of Pennsylvania could understand why paupers might be temporarily deprived of the vote. Foreigners and paupers could justifiably wait "because a little time or labor will make it theirs."[29] But the Negroes argued that disenfranchisement of an entire class on the basis of *color* was undemocratic.

As was also done earlier by Negro petitioners in Pennsylvania, they showed that blacks were sustaining themselves through mutual beneficent societies. They had paid more into the public treasury than they had received for support of the poor. Furthermore, the petitioners pointed to various schools, literary societies, and other assets of blacks in Philadelphia, Pittsburgh, York, West Chester, and Columbia. They also argued that if Negroes were treated as *men* in the handling of title-deeds, contracts, notes of hand, and other such things, it was only consistent for them to have the vote.

In addition to numerous arguments concerning specifics of the Pennsylvania controversy, the black petitioners gave arguments of a national nature that foreshadowed some of the more detailed and refined black rhetorical appeals of the future. They argued that they were citizens of the United States *as well as* their home state. In regard to the federal government, they noted that no color specifications were made in the Articles of Confederation in reference to free citizens and "on the adoption of the present Constitution of the United States no change was made as to rights of citizenship."[30]

Moreover, blacks were subjected to "taxation without representation." Just as importantly, they were being deprived of the franchise without each person being given the "due process of law" in a situation where each black should be accused of abusing his suffrage and tried accordingly. Finally, according to their constitutional rights, the government was tearing away from Negroes the power of consent, "a tyrranical usurpation which we will never cease to oppose."[31]

The petitions in both New York and Pennsylvania were the beginnings of a longer and broader struggle by blacks to become a part of America's legal structure. They contained verbal appeals to supplement and draw attention to the lawful efforts at elevation being made by the black race.

DISUNION

During the 1840s, there was less unanimity among black leaders in supporting the Constitution, but a strong majority retained their loyalty and faith. In fact, that devotion characterized most blacks throughout their crusade. Dwight Dumond has said that Negroes "fought for their own rights to remain in the United States, and through it all they were a thousand times more loyal to the Constitution than white men many times their numbers both North and South."[32]

There were, however, new conflicting lines of thought devised by Negro leaders in the forties. In addition to espousing the idea that Negroes should retain loyalty and fidelity to the Constitution, some black spokesmen advocated that as long as they were in practice ignored by the Constitution, they should reciprocally be indifferent to it if not ignore it entirely. Still others were declaring that the Union as established by the Constitution should be dissolved.

The most common proposition presented by Negroes to both black and white audiences was that Negro elevation could be most effectively achieved by continued support of the Constitution. Adherence to this proposition was avowed at the only National Negro Conventions of the decade in 1843, 1847, and 1848 and at State Conventions of Colored Citizens in Connecticut, Maine, Michigan, New Hampshire, New York, Ohio and Pennsylvania.

This proposition was supported with the argument that the Constitution granted Negroes equal rights which are illegally denied by interpreters and enforcers of the law. In New York, the 1840 Negro Convention lauded "the spirit of the Constitution, and the designs and purposes of its great originators."[33] The 1843 Michigan State Negro Convention resolved that racially discriminatory laws of that state were in "violation of the Constitution of the United States."[34] Or, more encompassingly, Samuel H. Davis, Chairman *pro tem* at the 1843 National Convention, stated in his opening address that blacks were endeavoring to secure rights which were "unjustly, and, we believe, unconstitutionally denied us in a part of the Union."[35]

By this time, though, the Negro people needed more than assurances that the Constitution was right in principle and only wrongly interpreted. If it was not being interpreted or enforced correctly for them, what good did it do to continue praising its spirit and purpose? In response to that question, pro-Constitution black spokesmen said that change or reform would be effected by working within the system. The 1843 National Negro Convention recognized the legal oppression of blacks but resolved that "God-fearing men can make the government of our country well pleasing in His right."[36]

One way to make the government "pleasing in His right" was to challenge the constitutionality of existing laws. For instance, in the early 1840s, when free Massachusetts Negro seamen were restricted from entry into Southern port cities, the black *and* white political activists challenged the constitutionality of such restrictions. J.W.C. Pennington expressed his enthusiasm about New England's hiring two legal agents, one to go to Charleston, South Carolina and the other to New Orleans, Louisiana. In a letter to Thomas Clarkson, Pennington explained that "the business of those agents is to test the Constitutionality of those Southern laws by which the colored seamen of Mass[achusetts] are imprisoned by appealing their case."[37]

It was resolved at a meeting of colored citizens in Oberlin, Ohio that "we hereby, each to each pledge ourselves to support the other in claiming our rights under the United States Constitution, and in having the laws oppressing us tested."[38] By vowing to have the constitutionality of laws tested, the majority of blacks were actively *using* the system. At the 1845 New York Colored Suffrage Convention, the majority promoting active work within the constitutional framework included Theodore S. Wright, Henry H. Garnet, and Samuel R. Ward. In his speech on the 1793 Fugitive Slave Law, J.W. North told the convention that "the Constitution was not at fault for the law. . . . If the Constitution be *now* wrong, how can it be made right, except by *acting politically* under the Constitution as it is?"[39]

However, there were some blacks at this time who refused to maintain loyalty to any document under which they were in actuality so frequently excluded and oppressed. They assumed it was folly to submit to "legal" oppression and appear to willfully give support to the Constitution or any laws while getting nothing in return. Negroes with this attitude advocated a proposition that they should *ignore* the Constitution; since they got nothing from it, they would give nothing to it. They especially did not want to give it their endorsement.

At the 1844 New York Negro Convention, there had been a resolution passed that stated blacks had "never forfeited it [franchise] by an opposition to law, and have always been and are now willing to bear the burdens of the State." There was a small group that voted against the resolution. James Hall explained the minority viewpoint, saying that the resolution "intimated that we were willing to bear the burdens of the state, without possession of the rights of citizenship."[40]

The 1844 American Anti-Slavery Society's meeting featured a disunion resolution with which several Negro delegates took issue. They suggested that the Constitution be *ignored* instead of violently attacked or dissolved. The best known Negro adherent of that viewpoint was Thomas Van Renslear of New York. The Convention reporter for the *National Anti-Slavery Standard*, the official organ for the Society, recorded Van Renslear's statement: "We do not wish to tear up anything. We merely say we will have nothing to do with the government; and as regards the Constitution, that we will have nothing to do with that instrument."[41]

Being an active disunionist, Charles Lenox Remond, who was the first renowned black abolitionist orator from Massachusetts, advised his people to at least ignore the Constitution. In 1841 he had encouraged disobedience of the laws of the land. After reprimanding blacks for being "quite too indifferent" in their views, he proclaimed: "Let every colored man, called upon to pay taxes to any institution in which he is deprived or denied its privileges and advantages, withhold his taxes, though it costs imprisonment or confiscation. Let our motto be—No privileges, no pay."[42] At the Cazenovia Anti-Slavery Society Convention in 1847, he defended civil disobedience, saying, "The government does not protect my rights, and I will not support such a government. Show me a Constitution which protects the rights of all men and I'll sustain that."[43] There is no record that Remond's actions of withholding taxes matched his rhetoric.

The strategy of advocating ignorance or nonsupport of the Constitution that, as interpreted, did not protect them, was apparently unique to the few blacks using it. Perhaps whites would be less inclined to sit back and do nothing with this strategy being used on them than they would if they knew blacks were willing to support the government regardless of reciprocal treatment. On the other hand, being loyal under even adverse circumstances could elicit more sympathy from white lawmakers, and the whites might respond out of a sense of goodness and humanity.

Another proposition concerning the Constitution, presented by both black and white Garrisonians, was that the Union as established by the Constitution should be dissolved. Like the preceding proposition, this was advocated by only a minority of the delegates to black conventions and most black mass meetings during the period.

The primary concern of many Garrisonian Negroes was agitating against slavery. In response to the Supreme Court's interpretation of the Constitution, especially in the 1842 Prigg vs. Pennsylvania decision which declared the Fugitive Slave Act of 1793 constitutional, Garrison's opposition to the Constitution was intensified. One of the earlier abolitionist proposals of disunion was issued by the Board of Managers of the Massachusetts Anti-Slavery Society at that Society's Annual Meeting in 1843. The Board said, in reference to the Prigg decision, "the whole tone of the decision is marked by the assumption that the preservation of slavery, and not liberty . . . was the guiding purpose of the framers of the Constitution." They regarded the Constitution as a "lie" that placed the foot of the slavemaster on their necks. With one voice, they exclaimed "LET THE CONSTITUTION PERISH."[44]

Then, at the 1844 Annual Meeting of the American Anti-Slavery Society, Garrison formalized his dissolution pledge by saying: "Henceforth . . . until slavery be abolished, the watchword, the rallying cry, the motto on the banner of the American Anti-Slavery Society shall be 'NO UNION WITH SLAVEHOLDERS'."[45] The Society set out to field as many "able and uncompromising advocates of immediate and unconditional emancipation, a free government, and a true independence" as its means would allow.

There were several well-known Negroes of the time who adopted the Garrisonian doctrine. Among those traveling and lecturing on that theme were Charles Lenox Remond, Robert Purvis, and two former slaves who soon became famous, William Wells Brown and Frederick Douglass. At the 1844 meeting of the American Anti-Slavery Society, in contrast to the anti-disunion appeals of New York Negro James McCune Smith, Charles Lenox Remond gave full support to the Garrison appeal for "no union with slaveholders.'' Remond stated that ''from the time the question of dissolution was first 'mooted' in Boston'' he had given it his ''hearty support'' and to this time he had not changed his sentiments.[46] The Eastern Pennsylvania Anti-Slavery Society, which preached dissolution, also had some black officers. Robert Purvis, a strong disunion advocate in the late 1840s, was elected President of that Society in 1847.[47]

Much fame and attention was attached to the escaped slaves who were so uncompromising and vindictive toward the Constitution that had condoned the ''wicked'' institution which they had personally experienced. In his tours of western New York, Brown vigorously advocated disunion. He reported that he ''sounded the tocsin of Disunion'' into the ears of his listeners. ''I am more than ever convinced that the watchword of the American Anti-Slavery should be the watchword of all Abolitionists.''[48]

Black orators used one major argument in support of the ''tocsin'' of disunion. They argued that remaining in the Union prostituted their principles by forcing them to support proslavery elements. The escaped slaves, William Wells Brown and Frederick Douglass, gave strong vindictive pleas with surprisingly similar emotional intensity and content. In his address to the 1847 meeting of the American Anti-Slavery Society, Douglass said:

> I have no patriotism. I have no country . . . The only thing that links me to this land is my family, and the painful consciousness that here there are three millions of my fellow-creatures, groaning beneath the iron rod of the worst despotism ever devised . . . I cannot have any love for this country or for its Constitution. I desire to see its overthrow as speedily as possible, and its Constitution shivered in a thousand fragments.[49]

In 1849 and the four following years, William Wells Brown was in the British Isles preaching the same doctrine. A typical speech by Brown in London sounded nearly identical to Frederick Douglass':

> I have no Constitution, and no country. I hate her [America's] hideous institution, which has robbed me of my dear mother, which has plundered me of a beloved sister and three brothers . . . At all events, I hate that portion of her Constitution. I hate, fervently hate, those laws and institutions of America which consign three million of my brethren and sisters to chains for life.[50]

The escaped slaves were particularly unwilling to work gradually to "reform" the Constitution. In their minds, if not completely in reality, their brethren in slavery were brutally mistreated prisoners of a constitutionally protected war.

Anti-Constitution blacks were especially common around Boston, eastern Pennsylvania, and western New York. One agency with an unusual preponderance of notable black members was the Western New York Anti-Slavery Society. William Wells Brown spent much of the forties as a lecturing agent for that organization.[51] In 1847 alone, black officers of this society included Recording Secretary William C. Nell, and Executive Committee Members Charles Lenox Remond, Frederick Douglass, and William C. Nell.[52]

Even though black advocates of disunion were not philosophically representative of the majority of their race, they received a relatively great amount of attention at the time. Most were professional speakers who traveled extensively on lecture tours and had their discourses printed regularly in abolition newspapers under the auspices of the disunion-oriented American Anti-Slavery Society, i.e., the *National Anti-Slavery Standard* and *Liberator*.

Their invectives were counterbalanced by such pleas as that of the 1849 Connecticut Negro State Convention. That Convention's delegates included such names as S.M Africanus, Jehiel C.

Beman, Amos G. Beman, and Henry Foster. In the heart of Garrisonian New England, they pleaded that blacks had "always been eminently loyal and true citizens, and that too in the face of the strongest incentives for disaffection."[53]

PRAGMATIC LEGAL VIEWS

In the early 1850s, the black emigrationists contradicted the mainstream of Negro thought and foresaw no future for their race under the U.S. Constitution. While emigrationists denounced their prospects in America, the persevering majority of blacks were developing more specific cases for their inclusion as citizens under the Constitution. This was done in two national conventions of the period in 1853 and 1855. They examined the numerous individual clauses that pertained or *should* pertain to them. State Negro Conventions also vowed support of the Constitution but disagreed considerably over the wisdom of doing so and expressed some concern as to the Constitution's realistic meaning for Negroes. The desperation and uncertainty of delegates to the 1851 Ohio State Convention was shown in a speech by Charles H. Langston in which he urged his brethren to *use* the Constitution to their full advantage regardless of its meaning. He hoped that "the colored men will vote, or do anything else under the Constitution, that will aid in effecting our liberties, and in securing our political, religious, and intellectual elevation."[54]

A large factor in the Negro controversy over the Constitution was the increasingly famous Frederick Douglass' switch from Garrisonianism. Douglass showed signs of a change in his views on the Constitution when in February 1849 he admitted in a letter published in his *North Star* that if the Constitution were "strictly construed according to its reading, it is not a pro-slavery instrument." Nevertheless, he held, as he always had, that the original intent and meaning of the Constitution, given by its framers and subsequent court interpretations, made it a proslavery document.

Thus, he still could not bring himself "to vote under it, or swear to support it."[55]

Douglass had to take into account several considerations concerning the above position. One, he admitted that the law of the land worked for slaveholders and against antislavery advocates. Two, he had apparently accepted the Supreme Court's interpretations as unavoidable in previous years. He thought, however, that it might be more profitable to *use* the Constitution to fight slavery, instead of conceding its meaning to the side of his enemies. Likewise, he thought the Supreme Court should be encouraged, regardless of its views on slavery, to see the antislavery leanings of the Constitution. Perhaps he also feared alienating prospective supporters by attacking their Constitution. A review of Douglass' strategy in switching positions was given by Philip Foner:

As Douglass saw it, national necessity compelled him to accept an interpretation of the Constitution which might not be evident in the document itself. Realizing the importance of having the Constitution fight for him, he interpreted it in a way most convenient for the anti-slavery crusade. The Garrisonians, by their insistence on an interpretation which the slaveholders shared, no matter how apparently correct that interpretation might be, not only played directly into the hands of their enemies, but created enmity for themselves. Whatever the average Northerner felt about slavery, he did not believe that his country was built upon falsehood and iniquities. While the Garrisonians announced their determination to destroy the Constitution and the Union to end slavery, Douglass decided to use both in the struggle against "a system of lawless violence; that was never lawful and can never be made so."[56]

Much to the dismay and skepticism of the Garrisonians, Douglass announced his formal change of opinion toward the Constitution at the annual meeting of the American Anti-Slavery Society in May 1851. In explaining his decision, Douglass said that when he escaped from slavery in the late 1830s, he was brought directly into contact with a class of abolitionists who regarded the Constitution as a slaveholding instrument. He felt "bound, not only by their superior knowledge . . . but also because I had no means of showing their unsoundness."[57] However, he explained that by a course of "reading and thought" he came to the conclusion that the Constitution, inaugurated to establish justice, "could not have been designed at the same time to maintain and perpetuate slavery."

Since Douglass was becoming recognized as one of the outstanding black leaders of the time, it was significant that his views on this and other issues began correlating more closely with those of other leaders of his race. He had been President of the 1848 National Negro Convention and was Vice President of the 1853 Convention. His extensive participation in the movement as an editor and orator made him singularly influential. During his transition, Douglass was subjected to the persuasive anti-Garrisonian Constitutional view of such black intellectual leaders as Samuel R. Ward. Douglass and Remond debated Ward over the meaning of the Constitution at an Anti-Slavery Mass Convention of Abolitionists of New York in Syracuse in January 1850. Douglass spoke with "great force, eloquence and wit" on behalf of the view of the American Anti-Slavery Society. Remond also made stirring appeals about the "utter derogation of his rights by the American Constitution."

Samuel Ward, on the other hand, took the view that predominated among his race. He had no palliation to offer for the "practical construction" which had been put upon the Constitution. Yet, as the reporter for the National Anti-Slavery Standard put it, Ward regarded "the Constitution itself as an Anti-Slavery instrument."

In describing Ward's oratorical abilities, the reporter said he "spoke for nearly an hour, holding the crowded house in breathless attention, or anon convulsing with merriment." He added that "these three addresses, by Douglass, Remond and Ward—three colored men—it is safe to say, afforded as fine an intellectual repast as our readers have listened to for many a year."[58]

In April 1850, another black, Henry Bibb, spoke to a meeting of the "Citizens of Boston" at Tremont Temple. He was there "in the name of Liberty and of the Constitution of the United States" to discuss principles that had been "trampled on and violated under the name of law and the Constitution. He was convinced that "all we have to do is correct the public sentiment [and] get the Constitution and the people right."[59]

The next year, 1851, W.H. Day argued with emigrationist H. Ford Douglass at the Ohio State Convention on the meaning of the Constitution. Day explained that he and H.F. Douglass agreed on the proslavery *action* of this government and on the aid which the U.S. Supreme Court had given slavery by their "illegal decisions." However, he submitted, "*that* is not the Constitution." Day noted by analogy that men have used the Bible in attempting to justify the worst iniquities. "Do we, in such a case, discard the Bible . . . or do we not rather discard the false opinions of mistaken men in regard to it?"[60]

In 1857, long after he had changed his view on the document, Frederick Douglass attacked the "misinterpreters" of the Constitution. Douglas drew an analogy between the Bible and the Constitution as W.H. Day had done. Douglass argued that there is no evidence that the Bible is a bad book just because those who profess to believe the Bible are bad. He said, "the slaveholders of the South, and many of their wicked allies at the North, claim the Bible for slavery; shall we therefore, fling the Bible away as a pro-slavery book? It would be as reasonable to do so as it would be to fling away the Constitution."[61] The above defense of the Constitution by Douglass was an effort to justify his position at the

American Anti-Slavery Society's annual meeting just after the Dred Scott decision was rendered in 1857.

A much more extensive argument given to support an antislavery interpretation of the Constitution was that a "literal" interpretation of the Constitution held out a ray of hope for the Negro whereas admission of a proslavery interpretation left no reasonable possibility for change. In effect, black spokesmen were saying "why *not* hope that someday the document will be given what we claim to be a literal interpretation?" Black emigrationists argued that there were "fixed legal distinctions" which inherently excluded Negroes, and those barriers could not be broken except either by force or a "voluntary" charitable act of the oppressors. In opposition to emigrationists, black "literalists" denied that "fixed legal distinction" existed. They argued that their rights did not depend solely on the charity of whites but on a correct interpretation of a document which literally inherently included them, i.e., they were "fixed" equally in the system.

Among the Constitutional clauses which Negroes frequently cited was the one regarding "due process," as it said that all *persons* in the United States were entitled to that right. At the 1851 Ohio State Convention, W.H. Day referred to the "due process" clause, along with others, and argued that he had to assume, from a literal interpretation, that he was entitled to its protection. He told the delegates that their business was with the Constitution; if it said "establish justice," it meant that. If it said no person shall be deprived of "life, *liberty*, or property, without the due process of law," he supposed it meant that, too, and he planned to avail himself of the benefit of that right. He said that coming as he did from the midst of three millions of men in chains, he would consider "every instrument precious which guarantees me liberty":

I consider the Constitution the foundation of American liberties, and wrapping myself in the flag of the nation, I would plant myself upon that Constitution, and using the weapons they have given me, I would appeal to the American people for the rights thus guaranteed.[62]

A mass meeting of "Colored Citizens" in Philadelphia in 1850 was generally united in support of specific Constitutional provisions for the Negro. The meeting denounced the Fugitive Slave Bill as being "at variance with the principles of the Constitution." More specifically, they referred to Article 1, Section 9 on habeas corpus and proceeded to demand application of Article 5 of the Amendments, which guaranteed the "due process of law."[63]

Probably the most representative use of the "literal" Constitutional interpretation argument occurred at the 1855 National Negro Convention. The "Address to the American People" by James McCune Smith said: "We claim that we are persons not things, and we claim that our brethren held in slavery are also *persons* not things; and that they are held in slavery in violation of the Constitution which is the supreme law of the land." It further asserted that the slaves and freemen were denied "due process" and that the "right of people to be secure in their persons shall not be violated." Charles Lenox Remond and Robert Purvis opposed the address because it disclaimed the "proslavery character" of the Constitution. Nevertheless, behind the advocacy of Messrs. Smith and Frederick Douglass, the address was adopted.[64]

Another clause for which blacks demanded literal interpretation was the one saying the persons born in the United States are citizens thereof. Negroes argued that their natural nativity gave them full rights of citizenship. At the beginning of their demand for literal interpretations of the Constitution, the Ohio Negroes said at their 1851 Convention: "Fellow Citizens—the 5th Clause of 1st section of Article 2d of the United States Constitution, recognizes the principle that *natural birth gives citizenship*."[65] The majority of freemen of Ohio reaffirmed their argument at their 1853 Convention despite the growing disillusionment of some delegates who were to help host the National Emigration Convention at Cleveland in 1854. Likewise, the 1853 National Convention reiterated all the old arguments claiming citizenship, i.e., birth, hardship and trials, and "courage and fidelity by our ancestors in defending the liberties and in achieving the independence of our land."[66] To give more literal and precise challenge to the old citizenship claims, Frederick Douglass stated deductively that "the Constitution knows but two classes: Firstly, citizens, and secondly aliens. I am not an alien, and I am therefore, a citizen."[67]

Other clauses in the Constitution cited by Negroes during the period included the provision of habeas corpus, the provision to guarantee a republican form of government in all states, and the provision to promote the general welfare.[68] On the whole, black rhetoric of the times was taking on a new characteristic. No longer were Negroes content to rely on general statements about the way in which the Constitution abstractly or in principle granted equal rights to all races. Instead, they were giving more specific citations of clauses, more explanation of why and where such clauses applied to them, and more challenges for adversaries to show where and why they should *not* presume inclusion in the system. As Samuel Ward stressed at the mass Anti-Slavery Convention at Syracuse, "the very terms of the Constitution are hostile to the idea of slavery. No 'service of labor' can be 'due' from a slave. The plain language of the Constitution is against slavery."[69] The two most broadly supported alternatives to a loyal pleading for a literal interpretation were (1) denouncing the Constitution and urging dissolution, and (2) denouncing the Constitution and urging emigration. The arguments countering colonization were discussed in Chapter One. Ward answered dissolutionists by saying: "We are asked, what should be done while we are securing a proper interpretation of the Constitution? But I ask HOW they will dissolve the Union?—and I wait their pleasure for a reply."[70]

The minority of blacks who advocated dissolution suggested that disunion had more advantages to it than waiting patiently for an interpretation that might not come. In 1850, before Frederick Douglass assumed Ward's position that the Constitution was anti-slavery, Douglass argued that slavery would more likely get abolished if all the white North was not obligated to defend the institution. Responding to Ward at the Syracuse debates, Douglass said:

> I wish to see it [the Union] dissolved at once. It is the union of white people of the country, who can be summoned in their whole military power to crush slavery, that perpetuates slavery. Dissolve the Union, and they [slaves] will raise aloft their unfettered arms, and demand freedom, and, if resisted, would hew their way to Liberty, despite the pale and puny opposition of their oppressors. In view of the opposition of this Union, I welcome the bolt, whether from the North or the South, from Heaven or from Hell, which shall shiver the Union to pieces . . . Let this unholy, unrighteous union be dissolved.[71]

Douglass was suggesting that dissolution might require the initiation of physical violence by the unarmed unorganized slaves. Such a bloodbath might have served some function as a rhetorical threat to white observers of the controversy. Otherwise, the advisability of such a recourse was strongly opposed by most black leaders of the time. Although the "solution" of dissolution was undesirable, the "problem" seemed inherent in the existing Constitutional system. As black emigrationists had suggested, a legal system that asserted a right to hold men as property appeared beyond the power of blacks to reform. To expect a voluntary act of liberation was "futile," yet the current legal power of white oppressors was intolerable whether it be "admitted as a 'necessary' part of the National Compact, the provisions of the Missouri Compromise, the detestably insulting and degrading Fugitive Slave Act, or the more recent Nebraska-Kansas Bill."[72]

At the height of his Garrisonian rhetoric, Frederick Douglass had argued that several clauses made the Constitution "literally" proslavery, and they entrenched the institution so solidly that any reliance on "theory" against the insurmountable odds created by those clauses was naive. Douglass indicted Article 1, Section 2, which determined legislative representational apportionment by "adding to the whole number of *free* persons, including those bound to service for a term of years and including Indians not taxed, *three fifths of all other persons*." He knew that some people were saying that the "all other persons" used in the clause related *only* to aliens, but he argued that a Constitution which so carefully pointed out one class of persons for exclusion, such as "Indians not taxed," would presumably not be silent regarding another class which it meant also to exclude. He said, "we have never studied logic, but it does seem to us that such a presumption would be very much like an absurdity."[73] He regarded the three-fifths clause as one of the most important because it gave the slave system a dominant representation in Congress. Other clauses exposed by Douglass included Article 5, Section 8, which gave Congress power to suppress insurrections; Article 1, Section 9, which provided for a continuation of the slave trade until 1808; and Article 4, Section 4, which guaranteed Federal protection against domestic violence.[74] After giving his thorough and precise reasons why he thought the Constitution afforded a protective impenetrable bulwark for slavery, Douglass concluded that "it is a compact demanding immediate disannulment."[75]

Once again, in the Syracuse debates, Douglass said the Constitution was literally proslavery. Ward had argued that Article 4, Section 2 of the Constitution was not literally applicable to fugitive slaves, and Douglass refutatively submitted that the clause was "irresistibly clear" in its proslavery meaning:

Let us look at it. What are the words? Is not a slave a person? The very name "slave" implies "person," . . . Is he "held?"

Yes. Does he "serve?" Yes. Does he "labor?" Yes. Under the "laws" of those States? Yes. So far the slave is fit, amply, completely described.[76]

Douglass' refutation took him to a crux in the debate between proslavery and antislavery interpreters of the Constitution. In countering the idea that nothing is "due" from the slave, Douglass asserted that "we are not under a system of morality. There is a difference here between morality and law. It is to be 'due' according to the 'laws' of the State."[77]

Yet destruction of the Union was not really the only means of combating the Constitution, even if it was inherently unjust. Those who claimed we had an antislavery Constitution were also saying that *lawmakers* were subject to "moral suasion" and laws could be changed as moral convictions changed. As reformers, they wanted to give the Constitution the antislavery interpretation which they hoped would eventually be given it by morally persuaded justices. That antislavery judicial interpretation could not be achieved unless those wanting it continued working within the system. The Garrisonians, regarding the system as too corrupt to work within, felt that it was not only immoral to support the system but that their support only perpetuated slavery.

There was another proposition that tended to bridge the gap between the proslavery-antislavery Constitution factions in black leadership. It contended that Negroes should *use* the Constitution for their own elevation regardless of their respective views toward it. Charles H. Langston had attempted to settle the difference between William H. Day and H. Ford Douglass at the 1851 Ohio Negro Convention by asserting that the Constitution could be used to the political advantage of blacks under any circumstance. At that same Convention, Langston reminded the disputants that "whether the Constitution is pro-slavery, and whether colored men can consistently vote under that Constitution, are two very distinct questions. I would vote under the United States Constitution on the same principle (circumstances being favorable) that I would call on every slave, from Maryland to Texas, to arise and assert *liberties*, and cut their masters throats."[78] This expedient viewpoint was emphasized by Frederick Douglass in 1851 when he urged that blacks should not be restricted in their means of protest, especially against slavery. Douglass thought the question of the "constitutionality or unconstitutionality" of slavery involved the solution to other vital and important questions. If disunionists persisted, they would be "restricted in their instrumentalities to pen and tongue," whereas the opportunity awaited them to use the powers of the Constitution and government against the institution of slavery.[79]

Throughout the first half of the fifties, the majority of black spokesmen saw little alternative to at least *using* the Constitution in a civilly obedient manner. As Frederick Douglass exclaimed to a racially mixed Rochester audience in 1855, the restoration of slave rights "can be accomplished" within the framework of the Constitution. To dissolve the Union, to him, was about as wise as it would be to "burn up this city, in order to get the thieves out of it."[80]

CONSTITUTIONAL ARGUMENTS AFTER THE DRED SCOTT DECISION

There was less praise from Negroes for the U.S. Constitution in the period from 1857 to the Civil War. The Dred Scott decision strongly suggested that testing black rights of citizenship had failed and the race was outside the government's structure as seen by the Supreme Court. At a Negro meeting in Philadelphia in April 1857 just after the Dred Scott decision was made, Robert Purvis urged that his people quit quibbling over the so-called literal meaning of terms in the Constitution. He wanted them to look at the facts and then figure the odds of persuading white political powerholders to believe that the Constitution meant anything different from the document it had been interpreted to be throughout the history of the country. The Dred Scott decision had "affirmed" that under the Constitution Negroes were "nothing," and could be nothing but an alien, disfranchised, and degraded class. Purvis' resolution, which passed the Philadelphia meeting with no debate, contended that to attempt to prove that there is no support given to slavery in the Constitution and essential structure of American government, was to "argue against reason and common sense, to ignore history, and shut our eyes against palpable facts." Purvis further accused the white abolitionists who supported the Constitution of playing legal theoretical games which black spokesmen should not play. It ill became "the man of color whose daily experience refutes the absurdity, to indulge in any such fantasies."[81]

A month later, the American Anti-Slavery Society held its annual meeting at which Purvis refuted the "literalists" in more detail and with greater scorn. He called the doctrine of the anti-slavery character of the American Constitution "one of the most absurd and preposterous that was ever broached." He said:

It is so contrary to history and common sense, so opposite to what we and every man, and especially every coloured man, feel and know to be the fact, that I have not the patience to argue about it . . . I know, sir, that there are some fine phrases in the Preamble about "establishing justice" and "securing to ourselves and our posterity the blessings of liberty." But what does that prove? Does it prove that the Constitution of the United States is an anti-slavery document? . . . If those fine phrases make the Constitution anti-slavery then all the Fourth of July orations delivered by proslavery doughfaces, and Democratic slave-breeders at the South, all these are anti-slavery documents . . .

I have no particular objection, Mr. Chairman, to white men, who have little to feel on this subject, to amuse themselves with such theories, but I must say that when I see them initiated by coloured men, I am disgusted.[82]

Purvis' *ad hominem* attacks on abolitionists having a different philosophy had more in common with Garrisonians, usually white Garrisonians, than with other abolitionists of either hue. However, frustration and disappointment were running particularly high among Negroes after the Dred Scott decision.

A resolution was passed at the 1858 Ohio Negro Convention declaring that "if the Dred Scott dictum be true exposition to the law of the land, then . . . colored men [are] absolved from all allegiance to a government which withdraws all protection."[83] The President of the 1858 Ohio Convention was Charles H. Langston; less than a year later, Langston was convicted as a member of a party that forcibly freed a recaptured fugitive slave, John Price, from where he was being held in Oberlin, Ohio. In his famed speech given in the courtroom during his trial at Oberlin, Langston confirmed his personal misgivings about the Constitution, saying he knew "that the courts of this country, that the laws of this country, that the governmental machinery of this country, were so constituted as to oppress and outrage colored men."[84]

Despite the doubts expressed, mostly in Ohio and Pennsylvania, there were many Negroes, including a majority at the New England and New York Conventions, who continued arguing that the Negro was a citizen. Perhaps the most thorough case supporting Negro citizenship was presented by George T. Downing of Rhode Island two years before he was elected President of the 1859 New England Negro Convention. Downing's case was not an emotional one based on general principle, nor was it based primarily on the literal phrasing of the constitutional clauses. Instead, it was a refutation of Justice Taney's decision based on historical references that "demonstrated" the meaning of the law of the land. His arguments were given in editorial form in the *Evening Post*. In his introduction, he said:

Judge Taney and his court declare that it is "true that every person and every class and description of persons at the time of the adoption of the Constitution, regarded as citizens of the several States, became citizens of this new political body." I will give a case as sufficient; more must be given to prove that "black men" were so regarded at the time of the adoption of the Constitution.[85]

To support his demonstration of Negro citizenship, Downing argued that Negroes of Massachusetts were regarded as citizens before adoption of the Constitution. He referred to Paul Cuffe, son of a native African, who was born in this country. In 1778, Cuffe had refused to pay his personal tax to a Massachusetts collector unless he was allowed to enjoy the complete rights of citizenship. The matter reached the legislature, and a "declaration went forth, previous to the adoption of the Constitution, securing to 'black men' all the privileges belonging to other citizens, and they have enjoyed them ever since."[86]

Downing further argued that Negroes were regarded as citizens in the debates on the adoption of the U.S. Constitution. In the records of the debate upon the Federal Constitution of June 11, 1787, Mr. James Wilson proposed in the matter of "equitable ratio of representation" the words: "In proportion to the *whole* number of *white* and other *free* citizens, which must have referred to *black* citizens; then you will observe by referring to the Constitution, that all distinctions as to complexion in the matter of citizenship was rejected."[87] The motive behind the framers' rejection of Mr. Wilson's wording cannot be determined. At worst it transpired because they wanted to suppress or avoid the issue of whether or not Negroes of that time were considered citizens.

To further his case against Taney, Downing noted that the state of Rhode Island, one of the thirteen original states, regarded him as a "natural-born citizen." Since the Constitution stated that "the citizens of each State shall be entitled to all the privileges and immunities of the several States,'' he was qualified for those privileges. After several arguments showing persons given citizenship privileges, including holding public office, who were not citizens at the time of adoption of the Constitution, Downing was "forced to accept Judge Story's declaration that 'every citizen of a state is *ipso facto* a citizen of the United States'.''[88]

Downing's final argument was not directly concerned with dates but it did affect the citizenship subject and shed doubt on the validity of the Dred Scott decision. He argued that Negroes were conceded to be citizens on passports and other contracts issued by the Federal Government. All such references constituted what he called "official acknowledgement of the fact that there can be coloured citizens of the United States.'' Passports were cited by number and quoted where they referred to their colored holders as citizens of the United States. Copies of the passports for Robert Purvis, William Wells Brown, and Rev. Peter Williams were produced. Downing also referred to the naturalization proceedings of George deGrass and John Remond, father of Charles Lenox Remond, and in each case the respective party was declared "a citizen of the United States.''

Regardless of the cogency or weakness of the arguments used concerning Negro citizenship, the decision had been made by the Supreme Court. Negroes could only use their arguments to change opinions of the populace and particularly the politicians. In appealing from the legally powerless position in which the decision had placed blacks, Downing, in a tone that implied an unfortunate alternative, said:

How can we put down an arbitrary power . . . from which there is no appeal? We might invoke the spirit of 1776; but let us first try what shame will do. Let Rhode Island, let the North be consistent in all its political relations with the coloured men in their midst. This, I think, will effect a bloodless victory for right and the country; and attach us even more strongly.[89]

The argument that passports constituted official acknowledgment of Negro citizenship was also used by other blacks, such as William Wells Brown. At the 27th Anniversary Meeting of the American Anti-Slavery Society, Brown spoke of his own citizenship and that of Robert Purvis as being declared on their passports.[90] Such a move was peculiar in that Brown was a dissolutionist who cursed the very document under which he claimed citizenship. The apparent inconsistency did not bother Brown, who wanted every advantage and legal opportunity from the Union he hated. At the same meeting, Robert Purvis spoke with strong vindictiveness, saying, "For such a government, I, as a man, can have no feeling but of *contempt, loathing*, and *unutterable abhorrence*!" He called the Dred Scott dictum "a fair sample of the cowardly and malignant spirit that pervades the entire policy of the country."[91] Yet, like Brown, Purvis asserted his citizenship under the document he denounced.

Downing's view came closer to reflecting the true feelings of Negroes, however, as was implied by his election to the presidency of the most widely attended black convention of the period, the New England Convention of 1859. At that convention, Negroes not only urged petitioning for repeal of the Dred Scott decision but pledged to work under the Constitution to achieve the election of the Republican Presidential ticket.

Throughout the movement, then, the predominant theme among blacks was to retain loyalty to the American legal system. They demonstrated obedience to all civil statutes except those asking them to return fugitives to slavery. In this situation, most blacks chose to disobey the law and assist their escaping brethren in attaining liberty. They felt these manmade laws were so much in conflict with God's law they should disregard the former and suffer the legal consequences.

When the white moral suasionists, predominantly from New England, advocated the dissolution of the Union under the Constitution, blacks faced a dilemma. They respected and admired the great moral suasionist William Lloyd Garrison as a person but the majority of blacks at conventions and other meetings pledged their support for the Constitution. Since black moral suasionists such as William Wells Brown, Charles Lenox Remond, Robert Purvis, and, until he changed philosophies, Frederick Douglass were so renowned, it is easily forgotten that their views represented only a small number of their people.

Even during the crises of the 1850s, most black spokesmen remained civilly obedient and claimed the Constitution was principally a nondiscriminatory antislavery document which they could use as a weapon in their fight for freedom. To the end, most blacks retained an undying faith that their true inherent place in America's government would someday be acknowledged and appreciated.

NOTES

[1]*First Annual Convention of the People of Colour*, Philadelphia, 1831, p. 4-5.

[2]*Liberator*, February 12, 1831, p. 1.

[3]*Emancipator*, July 27, 1833, p. 51.

[4]*Liberator*, July 2, 1831, p. 10.

[5]*Liberator*, August 13, 1831, p. 130.

[6]"A Voice from Harrisburg," in Garrison, *Thoughts on African Colonization*, II, p. 41.

[7]*Annual Report of the American and Foreign Anti-Slavery Society, 1850* (New York: Published by the American and Foreign Anti-Slavery Society, 1850), p. 23.

[8]*National Convention of Colored People and Their Friends, Troy,*

1847 (Troy, New York: Steam Press of J. C. Kneeland and Co., 1847), p. 14.

[9]*Freedom's Journal*, March 16, 1827, p. 1.

[10]*Emancipator*, May 27, 1834, p. 3.

[11]*Second Annual Convention for the Improvement of the Free People of Color, Philadelphia, 1832*, p. 36.

[12]*Fourth Annual Convention for the Improvement of the Free People of Colour*, New York, 1834, p. 28. Also in *Colored American*, June 9, 1838, p. 61.

[13]*Fifth Annual Convention for the Improvement of the Free People of Colour, Philadelphia, 1835* (Philadelphia: Printed by William F. Gibbons, 1835), p. 18.

[14]*Walker's Appeal with a Brief Sketch of His Life by Henry Highland Garnet, and also Garnet's Address to the Slaves* (New York: Printed by J. H. Tobitt, 1848), p. 42.

[15]*Liberator*, August 11, 1832, p. 126.

[16]Ibid., August 4, 1832, p. 124.

[17]Ibid., May 4, 1833, p. 72.

[18]Cited in *Emancipator*, March 12, 1840, p. 184.

[19]Delany, *The Condition of the Colored People*, p. 24-25.

[20]Gilbert H. Barnes and Dwight L. Dumond (eds.), *Letters of Theodore Dwight Weld, Angelina Grimke Weld, and Sarah Grimke, 1822-1844*, I (New York: D. Appleton-Century Company, Inc., 1934), p. xi.

[21]*Colored American*, March 11, 1837, p. 3.

[22]Ibid., December 16, 1837, p. 1.

[23]Ibid., November 2, 1839, p. 4.

[24]Ibid., December 16, 1837, p. 3.

[25]Ibid., July 14, 1838, p. 1.

[26]Ibid., March 15, 1839, p. 29.

[27]*Emancipator*, December 10, 1840, p. 1. Also in *Massachusetts Abolitionist*, January 14, 1841, p. 1.

[28]*Appeal of Forty Thousand Citizens Threatened With Disfranchisement to the People of Pennsylvania* (Philadelphia: Printed by Merrihew and Gunn, 1838), p. 4.

[29]Ibid., p. 4.

[30]Ibid., p. 5.

[31]Ibid., p. 18.

[32]Dwight L. Dumond, *Antislavery: The Crusade for Freedom in America* (Ann Arbor: University of Michigan Press, 1961), p. 326.

[33]*Emancipator*, December 10, 1840, p. 1.

[34]*State Convention of the Colored Citizens of the State of Michigan, Detroit, 1843* (Detroit: Printed by William Harsha, 1843), p. 23.

[35]*National Convention of Colored Citizens, Buffalo, 1843* (New York: Piercy and Reed, Printers, 1843), p. 4.

[36]Ibid., p. 16.

[37]Letter in Ms. Collection at Henry E. Huntington Library.

[38]*North Star*, January 12, 1849, p. 2.

[39]*National Anti-Slavery Standard*, September 11, 1845, p. 58.

[40]*Fifth Annual Convention of the Colored Citizens of New York, Schenectady, 1844* (Troy, New York: J. C. Kneeland & Co., Printers, 1844), p. 7-8.

[41]*National Anti-Slavery Standard*, May 16, 1844, p. 199.

[42]Ibid., May 27, 1841, p. 1.

[43]Ibid., March 25, 1847, p. 1.

[44]Ibid., May 11, 1843, p. 194.

[45]Ibid., May 16, 1844, p. 198.

[46]Ibid., p. 198.

[47]*Liberator*, September 10, 1847, p. 147.

[48]*National Anti-Slavery Standard*, August 29, 1844, p. 50.

[49]*Liberator*, May 21, 1847, p. 82, and *National Anti-Slavery Standard*, May 20, 1847, p. 202.

[50]*National Anti-Slavery Standard*, November 8, 1849, p. 1.

[51]For a review of William Wells Brown's anti-Constitution preaching see William Edward Farrison, *William Wells Brown: Author and Reformer* (Chicago: The University of Chicago Press, 1969).

[52]*North Star*, January 8, 1848, p. 2.

[53]*Connecticut State Convention of Colored Men*, New Haven, 1849 (New Haven: William H. Stanley, Printer, 1849), p. 16.

[54]*State Convention of the Colored Citizens of Ohio, Columbus, 1851* (Columbus: E. Glover, Printer, 1851), p. 11.

[55]*North Star*, February 9, 1849, p. 3.

[56]Philip S. Foner, *Frederick Douglass* (New York: The Citadel Press, 1969), p. 141.

[57]Frederick Douglass, *My Bondage and My Freedom* (New York: Miller, Orton and Mulligan, 1855), p. 397.

[58]*National Anti-Slavery Standard*, January 31, 1850, p. 142.

[59]*Liberator*, April 12, 1850, p. 60.

[60]*State Convention of the Colored Citizens of Ohio, Columbus, 1851*, p. 10.

[61]Frederick Douglass, *Address on the Dred Scott Decision* (Rochester: Printed at the Office of Frederick Douglass, 1857), p. 19.

[62]*State Convention of the Colored Citizens of Ohio, Columbus, 1851*, p. 10.

[63]*Liberator*, November 8, 1850, p. 178.

[64]*Colored National Convention, Philadelphia, 1855* (Salem, N.J.: Printed at the National Standard Office, 1856), p. 30.

[65]*State Convention of the Colored Citizens of Ohio, Columbus, 1851*, p. 22.

[66]*Colored National Convention, Rochester, 1853*, p. 11.

[67]*Frederick Douglass' Paper*, November 24, 1854, p. 1.

[68]For examples of Negro claims to application of the rights of habeas corpus and a republican form of government in all states, see *Colored National Convention, Rochester, 1853*, p. 10; *Colored National Convention, Philadelphia, 1855* (Salem, N.J.: Printed at the National Standard Office, 1856), p. 31; and *Frederick Douglass' Paper*, December 7, 1855, p. 2.

[69]*National Anti-Slavery Standard*, January 31, 1850, p. 142.

[70]Ibid., p. 142.

[71]Ibid., p. 142.

[72]*National Emigration Convention of the Colored People, Cleveland, 1854*, p. 25.

[73]*North Star*, March 16, 1849, p. 2.

[74]Ibid., p. 2.

[75]Ibid., p. 2.

[76]*National Anti-Slavery Standard*, January 31, 1850, p. 142.

[77]Ibid., p. 142.

[78]*State Convention of the Colored Citizens of Ohio, Columbus, 1851*, p. 10.

[79]*Frederick Douglass' Paper*, July 25, 1851, p. 2.

[80]Ibid., March 23, 1855, p. 2.

[81]*National Anti-Slavery Standard*, April 11, 1857, p. 2.

[82]Ibid., May 23, 1857, p. 1.

[83]*Convention of the Colored Men of Ohio, Cincinnati, 1858* (Cincinnati: Moore, Wilstach, Keys and Co., Printers, 1858), p. 6.

[84]National Anti-Slavery Standard, June 25, 1859, p. 1. The speech was reprinted in pamphlet form, and also appeared in such newspapers as the Columbus *State Journal* and the Cleveland *Leader*.

[85]*Evening Post* quoted in *National Anti-Slavery Standard*, March 28, 1857, p. 2.

[86]Ibid., p. 2.

[87]Ibid., p. 2.

[88]Ibid., p. 2.

[89]Ibid., p. 2.

[90]*National Anti-Slavery Standard*, May 26, 1860, p. 4.

[91]In *Speeches and Letters of Robert Purvis*, published by Afro-American League, n.d., compilation in the Schomburg Collection.

Samuel Ringgold Ward—Third Party Advocate

3

Role of Blacks in Political Parties

With some notable exceptions, blacks from the outset favored using political parties and, in the few places where it was granted them, the elective franchise to elevate themselves in America. For instance, in Massachusetts, where Negroes had the voting privilege, they met in 1834 to evaluate candidates. The assemblage of Negroes at Boston expressed opposition to the Jackson Administration and unanimously decided to endorse "the whole Whig ticket." William Lloyd Garrison was skeptical of the black group's decision and in his newspaper he asked Negroes to examine all candidates carefully and "from them all select such names of persons as you know or believe are most kindly disposed toward you as a people."[1] Negro concern with the franchise was expressed in speeches, discourses, and petitions at black and white meetings and conventions during their antebellum crusade for freedom.

THE ABOLITIONIST SPLIT

In the latter part of the 1830s, there was a division in abolition ranks, particularly between the Garrisonians and those abolitionists who wanted to achieve reform politically within the system. One of the first signs of Negroes' growing concern over this schism was in the dispute over five clergymen's "Clerical Appeal" indicting Garrison's methods. The clergymen were not against the principle of abolition but opposed Garrison's incendiary attacks on many of America's institutions. Some Boston Negroes immediately held a meeting severely criticizing the churchmen for attacking Garrison. Consequently, the editors of the *Colored American* stated that "it was not expected of us that we should take sides with any party of friends, and enter combat with another party engaged in our behalf." They explained that their sympathies were "with our dear friend Garrison," *but* they hoped "never again to see an instance in which any of our brethren shall unite in censuring and denouncing any, even the least among our abolition friends." The editors urged unity behind the "NOBLE CAUSE" and worried about the loss incurred by brother contending against brother. They used the biblical phrase later made famous by Lincoln that "a house divided against itself cannot stand."[2]

In the following year, 1838, there was a general Negro approval of the founding of the "Political Association" for the "political betterment" of the race in New York. The group seemed to show a logical connection between the moral suasionists, who wanted to effect change by appealing to the minds and consciences of people, and the political activists, who wanted to use political parties and other governmental machinery in achieving reform. Both groups believed in petitioning, and there was little outward objection at first to using the vote. When the Association was established, it was addressed by soon-to-be Liberty party black men such as Philip A. Bell and Thomas L. Jennings. Likewise, the staunch Garrisonian moral suasionist, Charles Lenox Remond, then of Salem, Massachusetts, spoke to the group attending the first meeting.[3] A few Negroes from New England, western New York, and eastern Pennsylvania later became opposed to political activity even to the point of objecting to *voting* under the Constitution, but the wall of white abolitionist unity had started to crumble in the late thirties while black spokesmen presented a somewhat more solid conciliatory front.

In May 1839, there appeared at the Annual Meeting of the American Anti-Slavery Society another sign of Negro desire to maintain unity between political activists and Garrisonians. The breach between white abolitionists was widening at the time and there was an important vote on the role of politics in the Society. They voted on whether or not members should retain the regular utilization of the franchise. While it cannot be said that Negroes voted the way they did only to preserve unity among abolitionists, that was probably a major consideration. The black delegates, including all but two from Garrison's home state of Massachusetts, voted to keep the use of the vote as an objective for members of the organization. The delegates voted eighty-four to seventy-seven to uphold the resolution that "this society still holds, as it has from the beginning, that employment of the political franchise, as was established by the constitution and laws of the country, as to promote the abolition of slavery is of high obligation—a duty which as abolitionists we owe to our enslaved countrymen groaning under legal oppression."[4]

By that time, Garrison was firmly opposed to the trend toward political participation and urged that the abolitionists of the country not take the organization's vote as "representative of the true feelings of the majority of abolitionists." Nevertheless, the affirmative vote was decisive and indicated the desire of black freemen to have all abolitionists work within the existing political framework, using all potential means for elevating their race. Voting against the resolution were W.P. Powell and Nathan Johnson of Massachusetts. All the rest of the Negro delegates from the other states represented at the convention supported it. They included Nathaniel A. Borden of Massachusetts, a strong admirer of Garrison; Charles Lenox Remond, then of Maine; Charles W. Gardiner of Pennsylvania; Amos G. Beman of Connecticut; and

Alexander Crummell, Theodore S. Wright, Henry H. Garnet, and J.F. Raymond, all of New York.[5]

In 1840, the annual American Anti-Slavery Society meeting was held in New York City; three hundred members of the convention representing eleven states withdrew and formed the politically-oriented American and Foreign Anti-Slavery Society. Members of this new society constituted the core of the Liberty party which was also formed in 1840. Negroes were forced to choose between the factions, and they found it harder to maintain a conciliatory role. Most blacks still tried to maintain loyalty to all abolitionists and attempted to support activities of both camps wherever possible. There was general restraint by blacks from involvement in *ad hominem* attacks on white abolitionists of either faction. Remaining in the Garrison faction were several New England Negroes such as Charles Lenox Remond, William C. Nell, William P. Powell, James G. Barbadoes, and John T. Hilton. The Pennsylvania leadership of the American Moral Reform Society, William Whipper and Robert Purvis, were also in agreement with Garrison that too much involvement in politics destroyed the purity of the movement.

However, the new politically inclined organization got strong support from Negro leaders, especially from New York. Theodore S. Wright and Samuel Cornish were on the first Executive Committee of the American and Foreign Anti-Slavery Society. The next year, 1841, the Executive Committee included four Negroes, three of whom, Samuel Cornish, Christopher Rush, and Charles B. Ray, were from New York. J.W.C. Pennington was from Connecticut.[6] Despite the division in organizational affiliation, there was still evidence of Negro efforts to keep abolitionists united. In a letter to James G. Birney and Henry B. Stanton, white members of the new organization, Charles B. Ray said:

If the colored people of this City [New York City], or any section of this country, do manifest less warmth of feeling than formerly towards *Mr. Garrison* it is owing to our *Friends* having multipled who are equally active, and equally efficient with *Mr. Garrison*, and as a necessary consequence our good feeling is scattered upon all, instead of being concentrated upon one, as when Mr. Garrison stood alone.[7]

While Negroes played a conciliatory role between the political and nonpolitical abolitionists, a majority of black spokesmen urged their people to use the franchise. The big issue among Negroes concerned *how* the vote would best be cast. One point of conflict concerned the purity of abolitionism espoused by parties and candidates for office. Politically inclined members of the American Anti-Slavery Society met in Albany on July 31, 1839, to determine political activities to be assumed. The meeting was attended by both blacks and whites and was controlled by soon-to-be members of the Liberty party. A resolution was passed stating that "we will neither vote for nor support the election of any man for President or Vice President. . . , or for Governor or Lieutenant Governor, or for any legislative office, who is not in favor of immediate ABOLITION OF SLAVERY."[8]

Most blacks attending the Albany meeting voted for the resolution. Henry H. Garnet, one of the first Negro members of the Liberty party, and Daniel A. Payne, a church official less directly committed to either group, both from New York, voted affirmatively. The only Negro negative vote was cast by Samuel Cornish, officially a delegate from New Jersey, who voted "no" because he thought abolitionists should vote regardless of whether or not candidates were for immediate abolition.

Even in Garrison's home state of Massachusetts, blacks were inclined not to be against politics per se but to defend Garrison as a person against anyone who might differ with him. Such a viewpoint was taken at an 1839 meeting of Negroes in Boston at which John T. Hilton was President and William C. Nell was Secretary. They did not come out in opposition to political activity but rather defended the character of Garrison. They passed two resolutions pertinent to the conflict of the time. One stated that the "bold and fearless stand taken by Garrison in our behalf" and the noble manner in which he carried out his "principles" demand "our unshaken confidence, which we pledge before high Heaven, if it requires us to wade through the deep waters, or the fires of affliction." Their second resolution denounced "every colored person who is an enemy to Garrison (if any there be) as a foe to liberty."[9]

The same defense of Garrison as an individual was given in a meeting of New Bedford Negroes chaired by Nathaniel A. Borden. They expressed a dislike and distrust for white leaders of the newly formed Massachusetts Abolition Society in saying that "we hold in utter abhorrence the 'Massachusetts Abolition Society,' recently formed by certain clerical, political jugglers, as a dangerous institution, and unworthy of our confidence and support."[10]

As indicated above, some Garrisonian Negroes, particularly in New England, were exceptions to the general tendency of their race to avoid *ad hominem* arguments. In the final analysis, the blacks were grateful to Garrison and were faced with either getting into Garrison-type personality conflicts or getting away from the persons involved and defending Garrison's political philosophy, with which many disagreed. They often chose to attack individuals rather than the franchise. To them, Garrison's "martyrdom" was more important than philosophies. Yet Garrison was propounding principles that were becoming less and less compatible with the "civil obedience" concept to which most Negroes adhered at that time. For example, Garrison persuaded a majority of the Massachusetts Anti-Slavery Society to denounce a proposed resolution which most blacks at that time would have supported. The rejected resolution said that it was the "imperious duty" of every abolitionist who can conscientiously exercise the elective franchise "to go promptly to the polls and deposit his vote in favor of some man, who, if elected will use his utmost constitutional power for the immediate overthrow of slavery."[11]

The dilemma facing blacks, especially those in the Boston area, was becoming increasingly evident. Throughout the country there was a growing dissatisfaction with the antigovernment, proslavery Constitution, and disunion principles of William Lloyd Garrison. There were increasing efforts by non-Garrisonians to get every antislavery man to cast a vote. Louis Filler described Garrison as thinking there was a "plot" to "stress the duty of abolitionists at the polls."[12]

When Reverend Jehiel C. Beman, a Negro from Connecticut, became an agent for the Massachusetts Abolition Society, Garrison immediately reacted on a personal basis and became "sorry to lose the good opinion that we formerly entertained of Mr. Beman. . . . He must know . . . that he is directly playing into the hands of the bitterest enemies with whom the Massachusetts Anti-Slavery Society and the *Liberator* have as yet to contend."[13]

The Massachusetts Abolition Society favored using the political instrumentalities toward which Garrison had such hostility. With their feeling of personal gratitude toward Garrison as a person on one side, and their belief of voting and generally working within the Constitution on the other, many blacks had extreme difficulty maintaining consonance.

THIRD PARTY CONTROVERSY

Although there was general agreement among blacks that the vote should be used, there were heated arguments over how best to use it. Most Negro spokesmen supported one or two antithetical groups. One group advocated that blacks should promote the establishment of a third party, and the other said that it would be more advantageous to vote for a candidate from one of the two major parties. Those blacks advocating a third party argued that voting for a third party was the only way to avoid voting for sin. Charles B. Ray and Philip A. Bell, now co-editors of the *Colored American*, supported a third party as the best of "three horns of a dilemma." They saw the alternatives as "either to vote against our principles, and sustain slaveholding in all [its] abominations, either not vote at all, or else come out and form a third political party." They had not always entertained a third party idea, but by 1839 they saw "no other course to be pursued."[14] They opposed both major parties on the assumption that it was wrong to vote for one candidate just because he was less sinful than another. As were so many Negro arguments of the time, this was based on an ethical, moral, or value judgment that had to be accepted or rejected on an *a priori* basis.

In justifying their refusal to endorse the less sinful of the two major candidates, Ray and Bell stated that abolitionists "have no right whatever to involve ourselves in a little guilt by sustaining the smaller sin, because other men will involve themselves in greater guilt by sustaining the greater sin."[15]

An additional argument favoring a third party was one refuting the charge that third party politics would cause the movement to degenerate from its moral base. Some opponents contended that moral purity could only be maintained by staying above political activities, but third party supporters contended that political activity within the system was not incompatible with morality and virtue. Just as petitioning could entail coalescing moral principle with political activity, commitment to third party did not necessarily mean descending from a spiritual or moral position. For example, one of the very first members of the Liberty party, Samuel Ringgold Ward, gave his view in a letter to the editor of a small town newspaper near Syracuse. Ward was complaining of the charge that Liberty party men were "discontinuing moral means, and using political instrumentalities *only*." He said, reprimandingly:

You are aware that the issue is false brother. You are aware that those of us who have lectured in your own village, have not shunned to declare the truth concerning slaveholding and prejudice . . . in a moral manner. . . . Nay in Cazenovia [New York assembling place for Liberty Party men] it was urged upon abolitionists to vote for the Slave, from moral and Biblical considerations *only*. Do you not know it? How can you say, or intimate, that we have ceased to use moral and spiritual weapons?[16]

Third party men felt their party could be *pure* in its antislavery functions, unlike the two major parties, and yet it would still be *using* the system to effect change. Thus, they were adding pure political instrumentalities to the other weaponry at their disposal. At the 1840 meeting of the New York State Anti-Slavery Society, the black and white delegates passed a resolution reflecting views of most Negroes in the country. They resolved that "politics rightly conducted are properly a branch of morals." The resolution concluded that those who refused to vote against oppression were, in effect, using "immoral action in its favor."[17] As the Liberty party developed during the 1840s, the black members refined their arguments supporting it.

In opposition to the establishment of a third party in the late thirties were those Negroes who held that the vote should be cast for one of the candidates of the two major parties, Whig and Democrat. One argument supporting this position was that voting for one of the two leading candidates was the only way to keep from in effect being disfranchised in an election, since a vote for a third party candidate was a vote "thrown away" instead of counting for a prospective winner. Thus, there was no practical alternative to voting for one of the two leading candidates. This argument was given by Samuel Cornish, the only black delegate who had opposed the resolution at the Albany meeting that endorsed only votes for "immediate abolitionists." He argued on the basis of practicality rather than moral principle and concluded that abolitionists would be a "small minority in all states, for years to come, and must be virtually disfranchised and politically of no account."[18]

A second "practical" argument was that abolitionists would gain strength by holding the balance of power between the two major parties. This balance of power could influence both parties seeking to win the abolition vote. Laws affecting blacks would be more generous as candidates competed for their votes in order to get elected. Cornish contended that abolitionists could "command the respect and control the influence of both parties, in legislating the policy of the nation."[19]

Even before the candidates might be induced to propose more attractive legislation to gain the power block, the abolitionists at least could for the interim prevent the worse of two evils, and that would be better than throwing one's vote out where it would not count. This argument, like the preceding one, was based on the assumption that abolitionists, black and white combined, could quantitatively constitute the balance of power. Cornish hypothesized a situation in which one candidate was much worse than the other and his election or defeat in a close election depended on abolitionist votes. He asked, "in such a case, would not abolitionists be bound to PREVENT THE GREATER EVIL by voting for the better man?"[20]

The political balance of power argument could be directed to white politicians outside the abolitionist ranks. Regardless of the extent of actual voting influence possessed by the coalition of black and white abolitionists, they were able to issue threats and inducements which had to be considered by white candidates. Greater consideration would have to be made in potentially close elections. An example of the issuance of such uneasy reminders was an editorial in the *Colored American* directed to Van Buren after he had been in office for two years. The coalition threatened to, "through the ballot-box, root out every vestige of administration from the Empire State, and at the end of four years, EXPULSE the Lord of the nation from his chair."[21]

After the 1838 election, Cornish told New Yorkers that a prevention of the greater evil "precisely was the case in the election of Governor in the State of New York [William H. Seward] last Autumn."[22] In another editorial after the same 1838 election, Cornish put the evidence into statistical terms for black and white voters and white candidates to see:

> We assert that there were 1500 abolition votes given in this city for Seward, and more than 1800 for Bradish. In the State, [Luther] Bradish [Lt. Governor] received more than 20,000 votes from abolitionists, and Seward more than 15,000. Their election has been effected by abolition suffrage; and should the Whigs find no better candidate for the Presidency of the United States in 1840 . . . the abolition votes will turn the victory the other way.[23]

A final argument for supporting an existing party was that the moral virtue of the abolitionist movement could only be retained if abolitionists refrained from engaging in politics beyond influencing candidates of one of the two existing parties. It was thought that moral strength lay in a lack of direct involvement. This argument attacked the third party concept and was a constructive defense of the status quo. As a part of his extensive elaboration of his case for the present system, Cornish said, "We are MORALLY abolitionists. . . . The very assumption of political measures . . . is a degradation of our cause." He thought Negroes ought to be conscientious politicians but they should let politics "grow out of conscious duty to God and slave, [and] always be subservient means in the prosecution of MORAL MEASURES, and never measures themselves in the prosecution of moral purposes."[24]

Further explication of that argument was given in Cornish's several editorials on politics in the *Colored American*. In each he stressed that "it is vain to hope that men will go to the polls and act with us, until they have seen slaveholding in some of its iniquitous forms, a sin against God, a moral encroachment upon the rights of men."[25] The job of protestors was first to get society "morally incensed" and urge officeholders to run on "principle" and not "pretense." *Then* the abolitionists, black and white, could look for political cooperation.

Finally, there was refutation of the Albany resolution, the resolution which said that abolitionists should vote only for candidates who favor immediate abolition. The case against this argued that the abolitionist was ethically compelled to vote for the better alternative rather than "throw his vote out." It was further argued that the expectation of purity in candidates was contradictory with other antislavery policies. The Cornishites were suggesting that true abolitionists should not directly engage in politics at all in order to maintain purity of their motives, and therefore the candidates they did support were not pure abolitionists. In attacking the Albany resolution, Cornish said, "How inconsistent! ! ! We want perfect political leaders, whilst we satisfy ourselves with imperfect moral and religious ones."[26]

Before a third party was established, blacks actually did what Cornish was suggesting. Many supported the lesser of two "evil" *parties*, the Whigs over the Democrats, assuming that individual candidates, like their party, were more representative of blacks. Just as some Massachusetts Negroes had met and resolved to support the entire Whig slate, New York colored freeholders in 1838 held a "respectable and numerous meeting . . . at Wilberforce Hall," at which John Fort was chairman and William Johnson secretary; they had held an earlier meeting at Masonic Hall. After some deliberation, they determined that "the colored citizens of New York be earnestly requested to vote the WHOLE WHIG TICKET."[27]

One cannot help but notice the element of practicality in Cornish's arguments and the idealism implied in the arguments of third party advocates such as Ray, Bell, Garnet, and Ward. Yet Negroes came predominantly to support a third party, and some supported Garrisonian nonvoting moral suasion appeals soon made popular by black orators such as Frederick Douglass, William W. Brown, and Charles L. Remond. There was a concern on all sides with the "moral" responsibilities of black abolitionists. Perhaps this reflected the influence of religion among Negroes during the time; Cornish, Ray, Garnet, and Ward were all ministers. The belief in the principles of "human dignity" was apparently more important to most blacks than the prospect of staying in the "mainstream" of American politics.

LIBERTY PARTY

Negroes were active in the Liberty party from its beginning. There was even a black delegate, John T. Raymond, at the first small nominating convention of the Liberty party at Albany in April 1840. Soon afterwards, the Liberty party and its nominees James G. Birney and Thomas Earle gained the endorsement of the *Colored American*. The 1842 New York Negro Convention also endorsed the Liberty ticket.

Perhaps the most prominent year of Negro involvement in Liberty party activities was 1843. At the party's Convention in Buffalo that year, black delegates included Henry Highland Garnet, Charles B. Ray, and Samuel R. Ward; Garnet and Ray were assigned to committees and Ward addressed the delegates.[28] Just two weeks earlier in Buffalo there had been a National Negro Convention in which it was resolved that "it is the duty of every lover of liberty to vote the Liberty ticket so long as they are consistent to their *principles*." Of an official registration of fifty-eight delegates, only seven voted against the resolution endorsing the Liberty party. Those speaking in opposition were C.L. Remond, W.W. Brown, and Frederick Douglass, who believed all parties are "verily and necessarily corrupt." Some supporting the resolution did so on the grounds that it did not mention any specific party, while other supporters interpreted the resolution as definitely adopting the "Liberty party."[29]

Black opponents of the Liberty party in the early forties were mostly Garrison supporters, and Garrison was still advising blacks to "scatter" their votes if they felt compelled to vote at all.[30] It was this very philosophy that strong third party men wanted to counter. At a Cazenovia Anti-Slavery Convention, Samuel R. Ward said that the "Liberty party was organized to prevent men from stultifying themselves in voting for slaveholders, under the scattering system." Ward believed that public opinion was not sufficient to abolish slavery without some legislative action.[31]

At the 1843 National Negro Convention, it was argued that slavery was only perpetuated by *either* voting for one of the two popular parties *or* not voting at all and thereby letting the two major parties oppress the Negro with impunity. Therefore, most delegates contended that the Negro was obligated to vote for the Liberty party. The Convention resolved that those who enjoy free suffrage and who use it to elevate slaveholders and their apologists to office are "practical opposers of the basest kind, and that those who, having the power to redeem their fellow-men, by their votes, and who refuse to do it, are in effect the same." At the same sitting, the delegates adopted a resolution, "without remark," that opposed the Whig and Democratic parties as being proslavery because both ruled that slavery legally existed; therefore, the delegates recommended to their brethren, who were qualified to vote, to support the Liberty party which had "abolition of slavery for its main object."[32]

As the 1840s continued, there emerged a strong number of blacks who advanced the proposition that Negroes should not patronize the Liberty party. Many of those taking this position were sympathetic with the Liberty party but saw outward support for that party as counterproductive for blacks who were fighting for the equal franchise in such states as New York, Pennsylvania, and Connecticut. If they pledged to vote in a bloc for any party, they might be seen as a threat to some persons in power; yet it was those persons in power to whom they were appealing in the respective states for franchise rights. By endorsing the Liberty party, they were in effect pledging to vote against both parties in power.

Although the 1842 New York Negro Convention endorsed the Liberty party, other conventions of that state during the period chose not to do so. At the 1841 Convention, the New York Negroes argued that they should not endorse the Liberty party because it was not the policy of black people to vote as a bloc. They appealed to their state legislature, saying:

> You may say that if the elective franchise be granted to the colored population they may, ''en masse,'' join one of the parties which divide the State, and thus fatally prejudice the interests of the others.
>
> Such an occurrence, we solemnly assure you, fellow citizens, in the nature of things can never happen; for from an extensive knowledge of them, we can assert, that they are divided in their views with respect to the politics of our country, the same as other classes of the community.[33]

The blacks of New York contended that their race would always ''be found mingling with different parties, as now found.'' In attempting to persuade legislators of New York that they would act as individuals, the 1841 Convention referred to the voting habits of Negroes in Massachusetts. There, for forty-nine years, the colored population had voted on an equality with whites, and the Bay State had produced a long list of able men selected by its equal electorate. To further their case with the example, New York blacks boasted that Negro voters in Massachusetts had never had corruption at the polls alleged against them.

The New York Negro Convention of 1844 was apparently mindful of the disadvantages of pledging bloc support for their favored Liberty party, for they did not publicly endorse any party. A letter from Theodore S. Wright to the Convention, published in the minutes, expressed the mood that must have existed among delegates. Wright said: "My confidence is in the principles upon which the Liberty party is based.—I believe they are just. But were it my happiness to be a member of the Convention I would not be anxious for its formal identification with this party." He advised against advocating the Liberty party unless an issue between it and one of the other parties was forced upon them, or unless "some action was proposed to the disparagement of the Liberty party."[34]

The strategy of refraining from endorsing a political party as a racial bloc became common in the forties. The National Negro Convention of 1847 gave no official endorsement to a political party. On the state level, the 1848 Pennsylvania Negro Convention warned in its "Appeal to Colored Citizens" that blacks should "look to *justice* of the people without distinction of *party*, *creed*, or *sect*."[35] That "Appeal" for the *franchise* was written by a committee which included such Garrisonians as William Whipper, Robert Purvis, and J.J.G. Bias.

The 1849 Connecticut State Negro Convention also decided against endorsing any political party; instead, the delegates wrote an "Address to the Voters of the State of Connecticut" which emphasized their lack of "distinction of sect in religion, or *parties* in politics."[36] Yet the Convention had Jehiel C. Beman, a Liberty party man, as its President, and they warmly received a speech by Henry Bibb, a black third party man.

While arguing for political equality, the New York Negroes were careful to avoid implying that this was a forerunner to social integration. Politically, they would "mingle with different parties," but civil integration and social integration were seen as distinct subjects. They argued in the 1841 New York Negro Convention that the former could exist without "fear" of the latter:

Men may be *politically* equal, and yet remain socially distinct; this grand problem it has been the glory of American institutions to demonstrate. The Jews, for example, downtrodden in every European nation, in our State enjoy *political* equality, and yet maintain their separate social identity. And the same is true for the Society of Friends. But there is a living and complete confutation of this objection in the State of Massachusetts, which rather than tax the colored men without granting them votes, so long ago as 1792 enfranchised her colored population; and no one can point to that State as *peculiar* for confounding what our objectors term social distinctions.[37]

In that convention, the New York blacks were giving the same argument that Booker T. Washington used some fifty-four years later in his "Atlanta Exposition Address" when he said, "In all things that are purely social we can be as separate as the fingers, yet one as the hand in all things essential to mutual progress."[38]

Despite some skepticism about Negroes supporting the Liberty party as a bloc, individuals such as Jermain W. Loguen, Henry Bibb, Henry H. Garnet, and Samuel Ward worked diligently, speaking for the new party from Michigan in the West to Connecticut in the East. Even William Wells Brown, a Garrison anti-Constitutionist, was caught up by the wave of political activity as he promoted a free suffrage convention at Geneva, New York in October 1845. Brown was not a Liberty party man as such, but wanted the blacks to use politics or anything else for their elevation.

The Liberty party had received over 63,000 votes in 1844,

whereas it had polled fewer than 7,000 votes in 1840 with the same candidate, James G. Birney. In a letter to J.W.C. Pennington, a black supporter at Hartford, Lewis Tappan, a white Liberty party officer, explained reasons for black supporters to be even more enthusiastic. Not only had the party fared well in Tappan's home state of New York but in Philadelphia alone the "Liberty Party votes more than doubled."[39] Before the next presidential election, Pennington joined Samuel Cornish and Charles B. Ray on the Executive Committee of the politically-oriented American and Foreign Anti-Slavery Society.[40]

In 1846 Gerrit Smith, a leader in the Liberty party, granted 120,000 acres of land to three thousand blacks in New York State. Smith deeded forty to sixty acres to designated colored people because they were the "poorest of the poor, and the most deeply wronged of our citizens." No small part of his motivation was to help overcome the fact that every colored man not owning a "landed estate to the value of $250, is excluded from this natural and indispensably protective right [of voting]."[41]

Those assisting in ascertaining qualified recipients included such well-known Liberty party men as Samuel R. Ward, Jermain W. Loguen, Theodore S. Wright, Charles B. Ray, and James McCune Smith. In encouraging fellow black recipients, Wright, Ray, and Smith exhorted, "Let no man henceforth say that the good people of the State of New York hate the colored man in his effort at self-advancement! Let us take courage brethren, and go on. The people will, in like manner . . . glory in the prosperity which two or three thousand additional tillers of the soil will bring to the Empire State."[42]

After the 1844 election, however, the Liberty party began declining. That party had committed itself to the single issue of abolishing slavery. Other politically-oriented abolitionists wanted more issues so they would have a broader voter appeal, e.g., they wanted to develop a platform dealing with such subjects as a national bank, the tariff, and public land distribution.

In June 1847, some Liberty party men met, drew up a nineteen plank platform to broaden their appeal, and nominated Gerrit Smith for President. Then, in October, the one-issue faction of the Liberty party met and nominated John P. Hale for President, ignoring their dissenters' earlier meeting. That same month the Negroes held a National Convention in which they did not endorse any political party or candidate. In fact, it was even debated whether or not the term "political action" should be added to "moral suasion" as an instrumentality in the "Report of the Committee on Abolition" that had been presented by Frederick Douglass. Amos G. Beman and Henry H. Garnet argued for including "political action" and William Wells Brown and Frederick Douglass favored mere "moral suasion" to "convince and convert the white people" to abolish slavery.[43] When the Report finally emerged from the committee to which it was referred, it had no mention of political action.

Nevertheless, political action was becoming common among blacks. In February 1848, there was a "great gathering of colored citizens at the Belknap Street Church in Boston. Garrisonian John T. Hilton was President and William Wells Brown, who was a renowned Garrisonian by this time, worked alongside Henry Bibb, a Liberty party man, in composing a resolution that "in the language of Wm. Lloyd Garrison, as contained in the Anti-Slavery Sentiments [1833], the people are under highest obligation to remove Slavery by moral and *political* action."[44]

One of the last major efforts by the Liberty party was its convention in June 1848. At that time, Gerrit Smith called another meeting at Buffalo to counter the one-issue abolitionists who had nominated Hale the previous October. The June meeting, called the "National Liberty Convention," featured notable participation by blacks. Henry H. Garnet was Vice President and a member of the Business Committee. Garnet delivered a speech and Frederick Douglass was called on to speak briefly despite his still being a Garrisonian disunionist at the time. More impressive was the fact that Samuel R. Ward was one of nine candidates for the vice presidential nomination. He was second in the final voting behind George Bradburn.[45]

The discontented members of the Whigs and Democrats, as well as Liberty party men, met in convention at Buffalo in August 1848 and the Free Soil party evolved. This new party was antislavery in principle, opposing slavery's expansion but conceding its legality where it existed. The Liberty party retained its pure abolitionist position that kept it closer to moral suasion than the new ''half loaf'' coalition could possibly have been. It continued with the support of a small number of blacks and whites, but most Negroes found it necessary to dilute their politics to the point of wishing the new free soil movement well.

FREE SOIL PARTY

A new political philosophy, free soilism, came into fruition in 1848 and retained attention of Americans for the remainder of the antebellum period. The Free Soil party, formed in 1848, was a main concern of most politically-minded antislavery men until the Republican party, another antislavery party supporting free soilism, was developed in 1854. In fact, the Republicans did not receive significant attention from blacks until the 1856 election. Free soilism in all its party forms recognized the legality of slavery where it existed, and accordingly could not elicit as much enthusiasm for its principles among blacks as the purer Liberty party did in the past, or as did varied incarnations of the Liberty party in the future.

Free soilism had its concept stressed in 1846, when David Wilmot of Pennsylvania proposed an amendment to a bill authorizing money to President Polk for acquiring territory from Mexico. The amendment would prohibit slavery in the territory; it passed the House but not the Senate. Democratic and Whig conventions early in the summer of 1848 came out strongly against the concept of the Wilmot Proviso. In August 1848, a convention was held among factions of the Whig, Democratic, and Liberty parties that at least had support for the Proviso in common. They nominated Martin Van Buren for President and Charles Francis Adams for Vice-President. S.R. Ward, Henry Bibb, and Captain Malvin were black delegates at the convention; Ward and Bibb addressed the gathering. Henry Garnet, Frederick Douglass, and C.L. Remond were also present;[46] Douglass and Remond attended despite their being Garrisonian in principle.

Loyal white Liberty party men such as Gerrit Smith, William Goodell, Beriah Green, and Julius Lemoyne were skeptical of uniting with the Free Soil party. In his later autobiography, Frederick Douglass described their rationale for reluctance. They had seen the Free Soil party as ''a step backward, a lowering of the standard.'' These men thought that the people should come to them, not they to the people. Douglass reflected that ''events, however, overruled this reasoning. The conviction became general that the time had come for a new organization which should embrace all who were in any manner opposed to slavery and the slave power, and this Buffalo Free-soil Convention was the result of that conviction.''[47] Even at the time, Douglass saw a strategic advantage to supporting the free soilists. He asserted, in August 1848, that *blacks* had some key choices. They could stand off and find fault with the Free Soil platform and thus ''play into the hands of our enemies.'' Or they could be oblivious, remain speechless and thus ''morally commit suicide.'' Instead of either alternative, he felt it a ''duty to pursue the course which will make us in some degree a terror to evil doers, and a praise to all that do well . . . [so] whatever influence we may possess . . . shall be given in the right direction.''[48]

Blacks had a major decision to make as to whether or not devotion to complete abolitionism could or would be sacrificed by backing a party that believed in free soilism. Free soilism carried the promise of greater numerical political support, but what of the *principles* of abolitionism?

The attitude that blacks should have toward free soilism was discussed at the Colored National Convention at Cleveland in September 1848. Considerable doubt was expressed over whether Mr. Van Buren was for "complete equality" even though he seemed like the candidate blacks should support for expedient reasons. Henry Bibb defended the "entire equality" position of the Buffalo Convention. Charles H. Langston of Ohio was in favor of the new movement but opposed a resolution saying the Buffalo Convention had "entire equality" as its object. Negroes at the National Convention finally agreed on a resolution that:

> While we heartily engage in recommending to our people the Free Soil movement, and the support of the Buffalo Convention, nevertheless we claim and are determined to maintain the higher standard and more liberal views which have heretofore characterized us as abolitionists.[49]

The blacks rejected two more laudable resolutions, the first of which recommended all blacks possessing the franchise should vote for the Free Soil candidates and the second saying blacks "hail with delight this great movement as the dawn of a bright and more auspicious day."[50] By this date, however, the delegates were generally convinced that political action was necessary and that slavery could not be "abolished alone through the instrumentality of moral suasion." The Free Soil party was seen as an expedient means of uniting antislavery factions. At the polls in November, Van Buren received about 300,000 votes from a total of nearly three million.

After the 1848 election, some leaders of the newly formed Free Soil party failed to continue pursuing the abolition cause. By March 1849, Frederick Douglass had become critical of the apparently unwarranted enthusiasm with which many antislavery men had jumped on the Free Soil bandwagon. Free soilism had "swallowed up the Liberty party press" which once spoke out much more strongly against slavery. The originators of the new party had been given extensive support because of the *crisis* or compelling exigence of the situation. Thus, the strategy of free soilism was, for many abolitionists, to lower standards and demands. "Many good men felt that here was the time, the place, and the platform upon which to work decisively against the monster of slavery, and they rushed into it."[51]

For the short time remaining in Samuel R. Ward's stay in the United States, he maintained his loyalty to the Liberty party. He argued that the higher principled Liberty party, advocating that all slavery was unconstitutional, was more important than numerical unity. It was reasonably certain to him that neither the Liberty nor Free Soil party would receive a large total of votes for a long time. What was to be gained or lost in supporting one party or the other? The free soilers might gradually gain support by "lowering" their standards and thus become a legitimate contender in future elections. On the other hand, it was difficult to vote for a party that was not pledged to abolish slavery where it existed in the South. Besides, blacks had a loyalty consideration in this case, just as they did when they disagreed with Garrison. Here they had high regard for Gerrit Smith, the Liberty party man who would not concede that slavery was constitutionally legal anywhere. The value of regarding principles above numerical gain was espoused by Ward in his "Address to the Four Thousand Colored Voters of the State of New York" published just after the Buffalo Free Soil Convention. He admitted that "it is not at all an unfavorable omen that men heretofore of opposite politics so far forgot their ancient animosities, as to unite in the nomination and support of Martin Van Buren. But can the colored voters of New York State support that nominee and join in that movement? I answer No!" He wanted New York blacks to vote according to their principles of abhorrence to slavery and their "desire for the enfranchisement of all colored men of the State." It only made sense to Ward for them to vote against the extension of slavery by voting against its very existence. He loyally advised them to "vote, in a word for the everywhere-known, outspoken, uncompromising, impartial, and truly-practical philanthropist, Gerrit Smith."[52]

In response to Ward, Frederick Douglass revealed in the columns of his *North Star* the practical strategy used by many blacks in supporting the Free Soil ticket in 1848. He explained:

The times create their own watchwords; and the watchword for one generation may not always be appropriate to another. We would as willingly fight the battle of liberty and equality under the banner of "Free Soil and Free Men," as under that of the Declaration of American Independence. "Deeds, not words," is our motto.[53]

Yet Douglass himself chose not to vote at all in the 1848 election as he still viewed the character of the American Constitution as proslavery. He could "as soon run [his] hands into a fiery furnace, as into the American ballot box." Ward and Garnet retained uncompromising loyalty to the Liberty party in 1848 but the colored citizens of their home base, New York City, resolved in a mass meeting prior to the election to support the Free Soil ticket.[54]

At the 1848 National Negro Convention, the future emigrationist, Martin R. Delany, proposed a substitute for the resolution endorsing the Free Soil party. His substitute resolution reflected his desire to use politics or anything else for racial betterment. It recommended that blacks in the several states "support such persons and parties alone as have a tendency to enhance the liberty of the colored people of the United States."[55] Despite efforts to the contrary, however, most blacks of the forties had a strong tendency to support one of the antislavery third parties.

Negro political action during the first half of the 1850s lacked the centralized organizational guidance of the preceding decade. Despite the political disagreements of the forties, there had been an endorsement of the Liberty party at the 1843 National Negro Convention and one of the Free Soil party at the 1848 National Convention. The 1853 Negro Convention favored the elective franchise and recommended that all blacks having the franchise should vote "only for such men, irrespective of party, as are known to be opposed to slavery and the Fugitive Slave Law."[56] This allowed unification around the antislavery principle regardless of whether or not the parties involved acknowledged legality of slavery where it existed. The last Negro National Convention of the decade, in 1855, made no mention of political parties or voting.

There were some scattered group endorsements of political parties on the local level during the period. For instance, Boston Negroes held "a series of meetings" in 1852 "under the auspices of colored citizens ranking with the Free Soil party." William C. Nell wrote descriptions of the meetings to Garrison and referred to such persons as J.C. Beman of Connecticut, Jermain W. Loguen and William J. Watkins of New York, and Rev. James E. Crawford of Rhode Island, most of whom gave speeches in support of the Free Soil party. As a gesture of their appreciation of Garrison's antislavery efforts, Nell included the observation that the group regarded the Free Soil party as a mere offshoot from the "old pioneer anti-slavery tree." They unanimously adopted a resolution of "unwavering confidence in the efforts of William Lloyd Garrison, and of sincere gratitude to him."[57] Other local meetings of blacks supporting free soilism were held in Illinois, Michigan, Ohio, as well as those states in the east where activities of freemen had taken place earlier in their freedom crusade.

After the movement had ended, Frederick Douglass retrospectively described the political changes that were taking place during the time. He saw political parties and their platforms as *means* to an end. Blacks adapted to those third parties without really changing their basic values or beliefs. After discussing his participation in the 1848 Convention of the Free Soil party, he wrote:

> It is nothing against the actors in this new movement that they did not see the end from the beginning—that they did not at first take the high ground. . . . Or that their Free-Soil party, like the old Liberty party, was ultimately required to step aside and make room for the great Republican party. In all this and more it illustrates the experience of reform in all ages, and conforms to the laws of human progress. *Measures change, principles never.*[58]

The dilemma facing Douglass was the same for all blacks, i.e., was it best for freemen to support higher principles or to work for greater numbers of political supporters? In March 1852, Douglass told the Rochester Ladies Anti-Slavery Society that "I am a 'Liberty Party' man and think I can give a more direct vote against slavery by acting with that party than by voting with any other."[59] Then, in September 1852, he announced his support for the Free Soil party. At the National Free Soil Convention in Pittsburgh, however, he cautiously reminded the free soilists of the importance of not allowing themselves to become infatuated with the prospect of great numbers of votes at the expense of diluting their sense of "right." He added that "the man who is right is a majority against the universe. Though he does not represent the present state, he represents the future state. If he does not represent what we are, he represents what we ought to be."[60]

Regardless of the relative impurity of free soilism in comparison to the Liberty party, Douglass went ahead and pledged support to Free Soil candidates, John P. Hale and George W. Julian. At the same time he warned them that if they should make any compromises with their existing stand, he would "drop them and take up such as are already in the field, by the action of a small division of the Liberty party."[61]

Douglass made the same kind of switch in the 1856 election. In January 1855, he praised the Liberty party and indicted free soilism in an address to the Rochester Ladies Anti-Slavery Society. Furthermore, in July he was highly skeptical of the newly-formed Republican party and hoped as it grew in "numbers" it would also grow "*in the knowledge of truth.*" In December, he believed the Republican party was antislavery but earnestly invited its members to "take a higher position [and] make no concessions to the Slave Power." However, in August 1856 Douglass' paper announced support for the Republican nominees for the nation's highest offices, Fremont and Dayton.[62] Then, after the 1856 election, Douglass became a "Radical abolitionist" once again.

While most blacks of the period were consistently free soilist, the highly respected Douglass continued to waver, perhaps in an attempt to lure larger numbers up to higher principles. Supposedly Douglass' shifts in policy were matched by a broadening in perspective. Such fluctuating moves are explained by Kenneth Burke, who says that a politician, unless he is opportunistic, changes policies while retaining unvaried principles: "A principle is eternal—a policy is its embodiment in a unique situation that never recurs in all its particularities."[63]

Since the upsurge of free soilism there had been a new consideration for all Negroes. The free soilists recognized slavery as being Constitutional where it existed. Those local black endorsements of the Free Soil party were given "despite" the party's not going "high" enough in its abolitionism. The real issue was: Is it advantageous to go ahead and compromise one's principles and vote for free soilism as a mere expedient? Answering "no" were black spokesmen such as James McCune Smith, Frederick Douglass (some of the time), and, until he left the country in 1851, Samuel R. Ward. One of their basic arguments was that free soilism was unsupportable because it acknowledged the legality of slavery in the South, thus diluting its abolitionism.

In September 1850, a convention of fugitive slaves at

Cazenovia, New York drafted a "Letter to the American Slaves," expressing their fear and discontent with the Fugitive Slave Bill passed earlier that year. They alleged that almost all abolitionists who could be trusted were members of either Garrison's American Anti-Slavery Society or the Liberty party. They said that other antislavery men such as free soilists were "grossly inconsistent" and hence not entirely trustworthy. "So inconsistent are they, as to vote for anti-abolitionists for civil rulers, and to acknowledge the obligation of laws, which they themselves interpret to be pro-slavery."[64]

The next year, Ward did more than generalize in arguing against the dilution of free soilers by citing the disappointment black and white abolitionists had in Van Buren in 1848 after they had decided to compromise their pure principles to support free soilism. He submitted that to "yield up, compromise, or hold in abeyance" any of their "great and vital principles, for the sake of making it easy for others to unite with us" would be detrimental to the long-range cause. Many people had hastened to support Van Buren, who believed in the legality of slavery and slave laws. Within "less than fourteen months of his nomination, and in less than ten months of his being voted for, [he] was a member of one of the most corrupt pro-slavery parties."[65]

In his address to the 1852 Free Soil Convention in Pittsburgh, Frederick Douglass "trusted" that the meeting would be a means of laying before the country the principles of the *Liberty* party. In indicting their acknowledgment of the legality of existing slave laws, he said "Slavery is such a piracy that it is known neither to law or gospel . . ." He told the convention that Martin Van Buren had merely gathered up votes here and there from compromising abolitionists and used the Free Soil party "as a fatling to be devoured."[66]

Another argument against free soilism was that it forces all federal troops to protect slavery by acquiescing to its "legal" existence in the South. Thus, free soilists inhibited abolitionists because "we cannot attack it [slavery] where it is not." Black and white Liberty party supporters, now going by the name of "Radical Abolitionists," wrote an open letter to "Radical Political Abolitionists"; the whites were William Goodell, Lewis Tappan, Gerrit Smith, Simeon S. Jocelyn and W.E. Whiting and the blacks were James McCune Smith and Frederick Douglass. They complained that the Free Soil party "denies the right of the Federal Government to touch slavery in the States; and, . . . it admits the Constitutional authority of every slaveholder to claim every State Government for his slavecatcher."[67] In contrast, the Liberty party was the only political party that insisted on the right and duty to "wield the political power of the nation for the overthrow of every part of American Slavery."[68]

Not only did free soilism admit the existence of slavery, blacks argued, but it perpetuated slavery and caused it to thrive. Free soilists claimed they wanted to put slavery on the road to "ultimate extinction," but the corruptness of slave states was regarded as having an evil influence on the free states bordering them. Thus, the idea that the influence of free states would naturally undermine and eventually overthrow slavery in the slave states was false. For instance, instead of Pennsylvania having an influence on Maryland, the latter influenced the former. Frederick Douglass, who opposed free soilism during the period from January 1855 to August 1856, complained that Maryland's influence was responsible for Pennsylvania whites mobbing and burning the property of abolitionists and for "converting her very halls of justice into slave prisons."[69] In short, by leaving slavery where it was, blacks argued that the peculiar institution could pollute free states. Additionally, by upholding the legality of the Fugitive Slave law, which free soilists intended to do, they forced Northern states to perpetuate slavery by being "slavenappers" for the Southern Power.

On the other hand, some black leaders argued that free soilism should be supported by their race so long as its candidates or parties were "basically" antislavery. "Basically" meant anything that was not proslavery to the extent that the Democrats and Whigs were. One of the least likely black spokesmen to argue this position was the Garrisonian Charles Lenox Remond. At an Anti-Slavery Society meeting in Essex, Massachusetts, Remond defended free soilism against those who thought it worse than not voting at all. A correspondent for the *Liberator* reported that Remond "took considerable exception to Mr. [Parker] Pillsbury's 'illiberal' remarks on Free Soilers. He held to the merit of that party, though he did not believe them pure." Remond argued that "we cannot *wait* the advent of a pure government; we must act under the present one, corrupt as it is." He wished that all men were free soilers, as he opposed people's isolating themselves. Yet to reaffirm his loyalty to his New England "martyr," Remond gave the "Garrisonians" the credit for being "the only even partially free men in the country."[70]

In more expedient terms, Remond was saying that abolition voters had to be governed at the polls not strictly by what was morally desirable but by what was politically achievable. As much as he may have thought and even preached a purer morality in the "off-season," Frederick Douglass gave Remond's argument support during the few weeks immediately preceding elections. In September 1852, for instance, Douglass attempted to justify editorially his decision to support the Free Soil candidates, Hale and Julian. He knew his decision would be criticized because free soilism did not fully represent all his moral convictions of what should be done by a political party. In countering this prospective argument, he explained that "the fallacy here is in the assumption that what is *morally* right is, at all times, equally politically possible. . . . The absurdity of the objection is seen in the fact that principle would make party action, or combined effort impossible, by requiring complete identity of opinion."[71] On the level of political practicality, he was arguing that a politically viable group had to recognize supporters' differences which result from "location, education, habits of thought, temperament, and mental development'' or it would leave no ground for factions to stand on.

The advantage of the ''Free Democracy'' [the name the Free Soil party gave itself in 1852] over the Liberty party, therefore, was in its politically practical power of uniting ''a very influential minority on a sound principle of universal application,'' i.e., the principle of opposing slavery. It could give to the good cause the ''energy derived from complete organization.'' Since there was no ''moral'' difference between free soil factions on their general opposition to slavery, they could be ''led by a fair view of the advantages of a united army against slavery to rally under one standard in the coming election.''

Thus, there was a point of agreement for most blacks, even for such Garrisonians as Remond of Massachusetts; no one would have to deny his antislavery view for the sake of political unity. Neither the Democratic nor Whig party was antislavery enough for them to support. The blacks who formerly acceded to supporting Whigs now could admit that the Whig party was not devoted to ''reformation of the American government;'' in fact, Whigs were not even for the ''repeal of that most shocking of all human enactments, the fugitive slave act.'' And, of course, the Democrats were deemed at least equally unworthy.

Upon this ground, blacks hoped a stronger antislavery political force might be built. Just because the free soilists recognized the legality of slavery where it existed was no sign they could not be made purer from within. Frederick Douglass believed the federal government had no more power to establish slavery than to ''establish a monarchy,'' but he also believed that free soilist recognition of slavery in the South ''ought not to be made a barrier against the union of the *Liberty party* men and Free Democrats, certainly not when it is remembered that the right of discussion is secured, and the means of enlightenment is at hand.''[72]

The case given against free soilism and in favor of purer abolitionism may have once served to strengthen the convictions of the few hardline Liberty supporters but it now stood the chance

of alienating prospective white allies. Those many blacks who
were supporting free soilism maintained higher principles than
many Free Democrats. They attempted to remain politically active
while retaining their self-respect and tried to identify with as many
values of Northern whites as their consciences would allow.

REPUBLICAN PARTY

As the black freedom crusade entered its final phase, free
soilism was still the center of political controversy. The Republican party, formed in 1854, was gaining in numerical strength as it
absorbed most of those who previously supported the Free Democracy. With the demise of the Whigs, the Republicans were now the
only major political opponent of the Democrats. John C. Fremont,
the 1856 Republican presidential candidate, had received over
1,300,000 votes of slightly over three million votes cast. It was
evident that Douglass had been drawn over to a formidable political entity when he announced for the Republicans in August of
1856.

With all the governmental actions against them in the 1850s,
blacks were acting out of greater political desperation. The 1857
Dred Scott decision was a catastrophic reminder that they were
politically powerless. From that point their political moves were
from the unenviable position of non-U.S. citizens. A new overriding strategy was to attack the Democratic party. Delegates to the
1858 Negro state conventions in New York and Ohio vowed that
the Democratic party must be defeated. New York delegates,
clinging to their principles, resolved that in endorsing the Republican party "we do not for a single moment endorse all the political
tenets of that party; we are Radical Abolitionists, and shall ever
remain so." That position was again taken by New York Negroes
at the same convention the following year.[73]

The biggest support given Republicans by blacks of the period
was at the New England Negro Convention held at Boston in 1859.

The "Call" for that convention was largely motivated by a Negro desire to gain political strength. The committee drafting the "Call" included the noted Garrisonian William Wells Brown as well as William C. Nell. They emphasized that the depressed condition of blacks in the Free States was attributable to their political weakness: "The national body politic sees in us nothing to fear, and no favors to court." At the convention itself a majority of delegates resolved to support the Republican party and recommended that colored voters press their claims upon the "Republican party, that if defeated, it may not be a fault of theirs."[74] They argued that so long as some states denied suffrage to Negroes the Republican party was losing potential support.

By this time, Frederick Douglass had permanently decided that his personal principles were against descending again to free soilism, but he still wanted the Republicans to defeat the Democrats. He said that "for one, Abolitionist though I am, and resolved to cast my vote for an Abolitionist, I sincerely hope for the triumph of the [Republican] party over all the odds and ends of slavery combined against it."[75]

Negro endorsements of the Republicans were strictly expedient ones, however, as the Republicans were not anxious to elevate blacks to civil equality or even citizenship. In fact, many Republicans were trying to erase the stigma of their "indiscriminate regard for the races." Lincoln had made his view clear on this issue in his debate with Stephen Douglas at Charleston, Illinois when he said "I am not, nor ever have been in favor of bringing about in any way the social and political equality of the white and black races." He had never favored making blacks voters or jurors or qualifying them to hold office or intermarry with white people. Climactically, he gave his Charleston statement a shade of the old view of the colonization society that "there is a physical difference between white and black races which I believe will for ever forbid the two races living together on terms of social and political equality."[76]

Through the period until the Civil War, blacks were treated

apathetically by the Republicans. Accordingly, Negroes modified their endorsements by saying they were abolitionists whereas Republicans needed some higher principles. Perhaps their restraint from supporting Republicans too strongly was actually advantageous for Republicans and consequently better for blacks in the long run. Republican indifference and even hostility toward equal citizenship for freemen caused many black and white abolitionists to be cautious toward them. James M. McPherson tells us that "Democratic efforts to pin the Negro equality label on the Republican party usually produced vigorous Republican denials."[77]

Yet with all the Republicans' political shortcomings, most blacks were ready to urge their election in 1860, and details of their case were most clearly expounded by Frederick Douglass. One argument for supporting Republicans was an encouragement of the secessionist attitude that matured after the 1860 election. Douglass contended that the threat by Southern states to secede from the Union if Lincoln was elected was a good reason to elect Lincoln.

Douglass was walking a strategic tightrope by even suggesting support of Republicans for that reason. The South, by threatening to secede, was hoping to frighten people away from the Republicans, and Douglass might also be frightening Northern whites away from the Republicans by wanting the South to secede upon Lincoln's election. Moreover, if Lincoln were elected, the secession threat could scare the North into appeasing the South in order to keep them in the Union. Such appeasement would most likely be at the expense of Negro rights and safety. Douglass could at least *hope* that the Southern states would follow through with their secession threat out of pride if nothing else; at least if the South seceded, the North would not be pledged to suppress slaves or even return fugitives. Douglass remarked: "The slaveholders know that the day of their power is over when a Republican is elected." He contended that all the mobs that gathered at Baltimore, Alexandria, and Wheeling, the threats of violence offered to Cassius M. Clay and his Republican associates in Kentucky, and the threats of secession in case of Lincoln's election were all "tolerable endorsements of the anti-slavery tendencies of the Republican party."[78]

Another argument was that the Republicans should be supported at the time because American society was not prepared for the purer and more principled abolitionism. Such a practical argument was submitted editorially in Douglass' newspaper just a month before the 1860 election. There was much antislavery work to be done, and in any case the Republicans had pledged for themselves enough to keep them busy during the four-year presidential term. Perhaps after those four years society would be ready for something stronger:

> Who cares whose road it is, if it will only help us on the way? We come to the practical point of divergence, we can jump off with all the passengers whom we can persuade to go along with us. . . .
> We simply say by such a vote these candidates are the best we can hope to elect in the present state of political culture in which we find the American people.[79]

This view was exclusively looking for what was best for the black race, but blacks were now excluded from the system of which they had loyally remained a part under the most adverse circumstances for years. The Republican party was the best *means* to help them arrive at their highly principled destination in their particular situation in 1860. In fact, just after Lincoln beat out Seward for the Republican nomination at Chicago in June 1860, Douglass surveyed the situation. It was a "sad fact" that the Americans were on a plane of morality and philanthropy "far below what the exigencies of the cause of human progress demand." He regretted that they persisted in approaching the "blood-cemented Bastille of oppression, by the slow processes of a cautious siege" rather than by the "brave and inspiring march of a storming party,'' but his strategy was to support the Republicans and he advised blacks to "submit for the present, and take with gratitude the little good thus proferred.''[80]

Blacks at the 1858 New York Convention had taken this submit-for-the-present attitude and urged Republicans to take a "manly stand" on Negro rights. Likewise, the delegates at the New England Convention stood ready to "acknowledge" whatever they determined was "faithfulness" exerted in their direction by the Republican leaders.

Finally, Negroes argued that they were not necessarily *for* the Republicans but were *against* the Democrats. Samuel Cornish, under the circumstances of the late 1830s, had not persuaded many Negroes to vote for Whigs as a lesser evil than Democrats. However, in the late fifties, when the Republicans gave them a purer alternative to Democrats, the strategy was given greater credence. New York Negroes at the 1858 State Convention in Troy resolved that "in the ensuing election . . . we can accomplish nothing . . . save the defeat and ruin of the so-called Democratic party.''[81] Thus they chose to unite behind the Republicans, believing that there was not a remote chance of electing their good friend Gerrit Smith as Governor on the Radical Abolition ticket. Every vote for Smith would supposedly be the same as one for the Democrat against the Republican, and they asserted the biblical adage that was so popular with them: "A house divided against itself must fall.''[82]

The above argument could be taken as an unjustifiable and ungrateful abandonment of Gerrit Smith by the New York Negroes. The *Louisiana Courier* made reference to the "ungrateful" New York blacks who had received land from Smith in his massive distribution of plots to Negroes but who were voting Republican:

Smith's nigger landholders sold his bounty and spent the money on brass rings, red waistcoats, onions, and whiskey, and, now that he has become for the second time the Abolition candidate for Governor of New York, the sable ingrates refuse *en masse* to vote for him! . . .

But the New York darkies don't want to "fro away" their votes. They want to fuse with the Black Republicans (as the Know Nothings tried to do at Syracuse), and so "unite all the elements of opposition to the slave-driving Democracy."[83]

Regardless of how disparaging or loaded were the words of such people as those speaking through the *Courier*, they were correctly analyzing and perhaps showing greater concern for the political strategy involved. Blacks who supported the Republican party *did* see the value of uniting and they did so despite the great respect they had for people like Gerrit Smith. Even if Negro voting and rhetoric made no difference in the outcome of the elections, they could take some solace from Republican victories in such important offices as the Presidency of the United States and the Governorship of New York in 1860.

There were some blacks in the country who argued that Negroes should not support Republicans. In the vanguard of those espousing that position were Robert Purvis of Pennsylvania, H. Ford Douglass, then of Chicago, and William Wells Brown, then of the Boston area. The Republican party was somewhat aloof to blacks on such questions as suffrage for Northern Negroes, and some Republicans had gone so far as to call theirs a "white man's party." For those and other reasons, some blacks rejected Republicanism despite their preference for it over the policies of Democrats. In his speech at the 1860 American Anti-Slavery Society meeting, Purvis proclaimed, "I would not be a member of the Republican party if it were in my power."[84]

Purvis attacked the philosophy of many Republicans as being colonizationist, in that they did not think the two races could coexist. He named several Republicans who advocated "voluntary" colonization, including Horace Greeley, who reportedly had said in the *Detroit Free Press* that he did "not like negroes" and heartily wished that not one individual of that race had ever been brought to America. Greeley wanted them "gradually, [and] peacefully" to draw off and form a community somewhere away from the United States. To Purvis, the Republicans were, because of the few he mentioned, guilty of following the "old spirit of African Colonization revived under a new name; it is the old snake with a new skin."

Another argument by Purvis was that the ultimate goal could be reached sooner by voting for weak Democrats. In contrast to William Seward's portrayal of the "irrepressible conflict," Purvis contended, "give us a weaker man; give us another James Buchanan, or Franklin Pierce, and we will have an irrepressible conflict that all men can see and understand."[85] Besides, Purvis could not vote for any party willing to continue letting slavery exist.

H. Ford Douglass was not only opposed to Republicans because they were willing to support slavery but extended the argument to express doubt that the Republicans as represented by Lincoln would even stop at leaving slavery where it was. He delivered a Fourth of July Oration at a meeting held under the auspices of the Massachusetts Anti-Slavery Society in 1860 in which he argued that he did not believe Lincoln's antislavery professions because Lincoln was on the side of the slave power. Douglass referred to the great debates in Illinois in which Lincoln responded to the question of whether he favored admission of slave states by saying, "So long as we owned the territories, he did not see any other way of doing than to admit those States, when they made application, WITH OR WITHOUT SLAVERY."[86] In Ford Douglass' opinion, Lincoln was preaching the doctrine and "stealing the thunder" of Stephen A. Douglas.

Another argument against voting Republican was that Republicans believed in keeping the Negroes on a basis inferior to whites. Since Republicans had spoken out against the political and social equality of Negroes as well as for the enforcement of slavery where it existed, such a well-known black leader as Rev. Amos G. Beman declared, "What hope for the slave, what hope for the free there is in the Republican party, as a party, is more than I can see."[87] Purvis and H. Ford Douglass both were repelled by the doctrines of inherent Negro inferiority expressed by this new group that styled itself the "white man's party."

So, from the outset of their crusade most blacks revealed a desire and willingness to use voting and the political system for effecting their elevation. When the white abolitionists split around 1840, most blacks, despite their respect for Garrison, gave their enthusiastic support to politically-oriented abolitionists who chose to work within the Constitution. They supported the Liberty party and many blacks later agreed to endorse the Free Soil party and the Republicans after that. Black leaders were highly pragmatic in their political choices while in no way compromising their principles. When free soilism emerged in 1848, many blacks stated they hoped the Free Soil party would rise to the higher principle of nowhere recognizing the lawful existence of slavery, yet they were willing to work alongside their "less pure" political colleagues. That same pragmatic position was shown in support of the Republican party which also propounded the less pure free soil philosophy. In fact, when their admired white politically-oriented colleague Gerrit Smith refused to "compromise his principles" to support free soilers, many blacks proceeded to do so anyway. A philosophic expression of the adaptive pragmatic attitude that Negroes had toward politics was expressed in an article signed "York" in an 1858 issue of the *Weekly Anglo-African*:

Man proposes, but God disposes, and the Republican party is building wiser than it knows. It is merely a *corps de reconnaisance* thrown out in advance of the main body of the army of freedom; and the positions it assumes are strategical, necessitated by the exigencies of the moment, but not indicative of the whole plan of attack. We do not belong to the corps, but are fighting on the same side, and before the campaign is over the Imperial Guard may yet be glad to recognize the Turcos as brother soldiers and companions in arms.[88]

NOTES

[1]*Liberator*, December 20, 1834, p. 203.
[2]*Colored American*, October 7, 1837, p. 3.
[3]Ibid., June 16, 1838, p. 66.
[4]*Liberator*, May 24, 1839, p. 82.
[5]Ibid., p. 82.
[6]*Massachusetts Abolitionist*, May 28, 1840, p. 59, and *National Anti-Slavery Standard*, March 25, 1841, p. 166.
[7]"Charles B. Ray to Henry B. Stanton and James G. Birney, May 20, 1840," in Dwight L. Dumond (ed.), *Letters of James Gillespie Birney*, I (New York: D. Appleton-Century Co., 1938), p. 578.
[8]*Liberator*, August 9, 1839, p. 127.
[9]Ibid., June 7, 1839, p. 91.
[10]Ibid., June 21, 1839, p. 98.
[11]Ibid., May 31, 1839, p. 87.
[12]Louis Filler, *The Crusade Against Slavery: 1830-1860* (New York: Harper Torchbook, 1960), p. 134.
[13]*Liberator*, February 28, 1840, p. 35.
[14]*Colored American*, November 16, 1839, p. 2.
[15]Ibid., November 9, 1839, p. 2.
[16]*National Anti-Slavery Standard*, September 10, 1840, p. 54.
[17]*Liberator*, October 5, 1838, p. 158.
[18]*Colored American*, August 31, 1839, p. 3.
[19]Ibid., August 17, 1838, p. 3.
[20]Ibid., p. 3.
[21]Ibid., November 18, 1838, p. 3.
[22]Ibid., August 16, 1839, p. 3.
[23]Ibid., November 17, 1838, p. 155.
[24]Ibid., April 30, 1838, p. 3.

[25]Ibid., November 16, 1839, p. 2.

[26]Ibid., August 24, 1939, p. 3.

[27]*Emancipator*, November 8, 1838, p. 112.

[28]For a review of some highlights of Negro involvement in politics during the period, see Charles H. Wesley, "The Participation of Negroes in Anti-Slavery Political Parties," *Journal of Negro History* 29 (January 1944), p. 32-74; also see Hanes Walton, Jr., *The Negro in Third Party Politics* (Philadelphia: Dorrance & Co., 1969).

[29]*National Convention of Colored Citizens, Buffalo, 1843*, p. 15-16.

[30]*Emancipator and Free American*, December 8, 1842, p. 127.

[31]*National Anti-Slavery Standard*, March 11, 1847, p. 25.

[32]*National Convention of Colored Citizens, Buffalo, 1843*, p. 25.

[33]*National Anti-Slavery Standard*, September 23, 1841, p. 1.

[34]*Fifth Annual Convention of the Colored Citizens of New York, Schenectady, 1844*, p. 21.

[35]*State Convention of the Colored Citizens of Pennsylvania, Harrisburg, 1848* (Philadelphia: Merrihew and Thompson, Printers, 1849), p. 17.

[36]*Connecticut State Convention of Colored Men, New Haven, 1849*, p. 21.

[37]*National Anti-Slavery Standard*, September 27, 1841, p. 1.

[38]Booker T. Washington, "Atlanta Exposition Address," in Arthur L. Smith and Stephen Robb (eds.), *The Voice of Black Rhetoric* (Boston: Allyn and Bacon, Inc., 1971), p. 98.

[39]Tappan's Letter to Pennington, November 6, 1844, is in Papers of Lewis Tappan, Library of Congress.

[40]*National Era*, May 18, 1848, p. 80.

[41]*An Address to the Three Thousand Colored Citizens of New York, Who are the Owners of . . . Land . . . Given to Them by Gerrit Smith, 1846* (New York: n.p., 1846), p. 4-5. Pamphlet in Moorland-Springarn Collection.

[42]Ibid., p. 20.

[43]*National Convention of Colored People and Their Friends, Troy, 1847*, p. 14.

[44]*National Anti-Slavery Standard*, February 10, 1848, p. 146.

[45]*National Liberty Convention, Buffalo, 1848* (Utica: S. W. Green, 1848), p. 3-5.

[46]*North Star*, August 11, 1848, p. 2.

[47]Douglass, *Life and Times of Frederick Douglass*, p. 276-77.

[48]*North Star*, August 18, 1848, p. 1.

[49]*Colored National Convention, Cleveland, 1848* (Rochester, N.Y.: Printed by John Dick, at the North Star Office, 1848), p. 14.

[50]Ibid., p. 15.

[51]*North Star*, March 23, 1849, p. 1.

[52]Ibid., September 1, 1848, p. 1.

[53]Ibid., p. 2.

[54]*National Anti-Slavery Standard*, November 8, 1849, p. 94.

[55]*Colored National Convention, Cleveland, 1848*, p. 8.

[56]*Colored National Convention, Rochester, 1853*, p. 40.

[57]*Liberator*, December 10, 1852, p. 1.

[58]Douglass, *Life and Times of Frederick Douglass*, p. 227 [Italics Mine].

[59]"To Mrs. S. D. Porter, President of the Rochester Ladies Anti-Slavery Society, Rochester, March 7, 1852," in Foner (ed.), *Life and Writings of Frederick Douglass*, II, p. 175.

[60]*Frederick Douglass' Paper*, August 20, 1852, p. 2.

[61]Ibid., September 10, 1852, p. 2.

[62]Ibid., March 23, 1855, p. 3; July 27, 1855, p. 2; December 7, 1855, p. 2; August 15, 1856, p. 1.

[63]Burke, *Attitudes Toward History*, p. 306.

[64]*National Anti-Slavery Standard*, September 5, 1850, p. 58.

[65]*Frederick Douglass' Paper*, September 29, 1851, p. 2.

[66]Ibid., August 20, 1852, p. 2.

[67]Ibid., June 8, 1855, p. 3.

[68]Ibid., p. 3.

[69]Ibid., August 24, 1855, p. 2.

[70]*Liberator*, August 15, 1851, p. 114.

[71]*Frederick Douglass' Paper*, September 10, 1852, p. 2.

[72]Ibid., p. 2.

[73]*Liberator*, October 1, 1858, p. 158; and *Weekly Anglo-African*, October 15, 1859, p. 2.

[74]*Liberator*, August 19, 1859, p. 132.

[75]*Douglass' Monthly*, September, 1860, p. 327.

[76]Don E. Fehrenbacher (ed.), *Abraham Lincoln: A Documentary Portrait Through His Speeches and Writings* (New York: The New American Library, 1964), p. 106.

[77]James M. McPherson, *The Struggle for Equality* (Princeton: Princeton University Press, 1964), p. 25.

[78]*Douglass' Monthly*, September, 1860, p. 327.

[79]Ibid., October, 1860, p. 344.

[80]Ibid., June, 1860, p. 276.

[81]*National Anti-Slavery Standard*, October 9, 1858, p. 2.

[82]Ibid., p. 2.

[83]*Louisiana Courier* in *National Anti-Slavery Standard*, December 11, 1858, p. 1.

[84]*Speeches and Correspondence of Robert Purvis*, p. 17.

[85]Ibid., p. 18-19.

[86]*National Anti-Slavery Standard*, July 14, 1860, p. 2. A rhetorical analysis of the speech is: Orville A. Hitchcock and Ota T. Reynolds, "Ford Douglass' Fourth of July Oration, 1860," in J. Jeffrey Auer (ed.), *Antislavery and Disunion* (New York: Harper and Row, 1963), p. 133-51.

[87]*National Anti-Slavery Standard*, May 12, 1860, p. 3.

[88]*Weekly Anglo-African*, October 1, 1859, p. 2.

Henry Highland Garnet—Revolutionist

4

Violence

A review of rhetorical appeals during the first decade of their militant protest movement indicates that almost all black spokesmen preached nonviolence. This is attributable in part to the highly religious values of black leaders and to their interpretation of the scriptures as being opposed to physical militance under any circumstances. Much credit can also be given to the faith blacks placed in the new white abolitionists of the thirties who were rhetorically violent but strictly opposed to physical bloodshed.

WALKER'S APPEAL

In 1829, before the emergence of the new brand of white abolitionists, David Walker introduced a stirring appeal to physical violence as a strategy to supplement the assertive words of *Freedom's Journal*, the newspaper for which he served as a Boston agent. His *Appeal* was probably issued as much as a threat to white slaveholders as anything else. Yet in order for it to circulate among free blacks, Walker tried to adapt to their existing values. He attempted to show that his advocacy of physical violence was compatible with religion. In his preamble Walker impressed upon his readers that "God works in many ways his wonders to perform."

He then proceeded to show how blacks had been reduced to the deplorable condition of slaves under white men's feet, and were held as descendants from tribes of "Monkeys" or "Orang-Outangs." He exclaimed, "O! My God! I appeal to every man of feeling—is not this insupportable! . . . Oh! Pity us we pray thee, Lord, Jesus, Master." [1] Walker tried to show that religion obligated blacks to attempt to escape from and to physically rebel against their white oppressors. "Are they not the Lord's enemies? Ought they not to be destroyed? They want us for their slaves, and think nothing of murdering us in order to subject us to that wretched condition—therefore if there is an *attempt* made by us, kill or be killed." To add pathos to his argument, Walker demanded, "Look upon your mother, wife and children, and answer God Almighty; and believe this, that it is no more harm for you to kill a man, who is trying to kill you, than it is for you to take a drink of water when thirsty." [2]

The *Appeal* further contained an attack on the "Preachers of Religion of Jesus Christ." Although Walker assured his religious brethren that he favored "pure and undefiled religion, such as was preached by Jesus Christ and his apostles," he attacked "Christian Americans" who got up patrols to drag and beat black people if they convened to pray and sing. Christian American preachers exhorted slaves to "be obedient to your masters." In contrast, Walker argued that the scriptures give no "distinction of color." Therefore, a wrathful God would stop those "taking His holy name in vain, PREACHERS and all. O Americans! Americans! ! I call God—I call angels—I call men, to witness that your DE-STRUCTION *is at hand*, and will be speedily consummated unless you REPENT." [3]

In addition to his religious appeals, Walker gave the practical argument that the blacks had little to lose by any action they took: "Can our condition be any worse?—Can it be more mean and abject? If there are any changes, will they not be for the better, though they may appear for the worse at first? Can they get us any lower? Where can they get us? They are afraid to treat us worse, for they know well, the day they do it they are gone."[4]

After his *Appeal* was released, the slaveholders held meetings throughout the South to discuss the pamphlet and its author. Georgia's Governor requested that the Mayor of Boston suppress the *Appeal*, but the Mayor simply affirmed Walker's right to express his thoughts. A company of Georgia men vowed to kill the young author and offered a reward of $1,000 for his head.[5] The next year, 1830, Walker was found dead near the doorway of his store.

In 1831, the kind of violence advocated by Walker was demonstrated in Nat Turner's bloody slave revolt in Southampton County, Virginia. The religious Turner's guidance of some fifteen slaves to chop and bludgeon several white families was confessedly motivated by a spiritual vision commanding him to lead a war of extermination.[6] Considering the rarity of black expressions of physical violence, it was ironic that the following letter, by a "Colored Philadelphian," appeared in the *Liberator* on the day before the Turner revolt:

> The time is fast approaching when the words "Fight for liberty, or die in the attempt," will be sounded in every African ear throughout the world; and when he will throw off his fetters, and flock to the banner which will be floating in the air with the words inscribed on it—"Liberty or Death."[7]

Walker's militant rhetoric and Turner's actions were strong forerunners of physical militance which did not begin intensifying and spreading until the 1840s.

NONVIOLENT RHETORIC OF THE THIRTIES

Blacks of this period remained consistent with their effort to live clean, moral, and civilly obedient lives by not countenancing the resort to physical force for the vindication of Negro rights. In the "Declaration of Sentiments," he wrote at the 1834 National Negro Convention, William Whipper rejoiced that blacks were thrown into a revolution where the contest was not for landed territory but for freedom; "the weapons are not carnal, but spiritual; where the struggle is not for blood, but for right; where the bow is the power of God, and the arrow is the instrument of divine justice; the victims are the devices of reason, and the prejudice of the human heart."[8]

As the title suggests, the American Moral Reform Society, a Negro organization, was opposed to violence of any kind. At their 1837 Convention in Philadelphia, at which James Forten, Sr., presided, the organization endorsed unqualified peace pleas by Pennsylvanians Frederick A. Hinton and William Whipper. Whipper told the convention he believed that whatever tends to the destruction of human life is "at variance with the precepts of the Gospel, and at enmity with the well-being of individuals of this society." In a resolution proposed by Frederick Hinton, there was to be no exception to the practice of peace because "the practice of the principles of peace, as exemplified in the life and character of our *Blessed Redeemer*, while on earth, is the most proper example for our people to follow."[9]

Black nonviolence was so generally accepted among freemen during the 1830s, that just one issue on the subject drew the bulk of controversy among racial spokesmen. There was intraracial debate over whether or not to resist pursuers of fugitive slaves. While it was fairly unanimous that blacks would disobey fugitive slave laws, there was some question about whether or not to fight slavecatchers. At the 1837 meeting of the American Moral Reform Society, the proceedings were suspended so William Whipper could present "An Address on Non-Resistance to Offensive Aggression." The address contained the basic arguments behind the nonresistance philosophy that was subscribed to by many blacks of the period. Rev. Samuel E. Cornish, editor of the *Colored American*, had attended the AMRS Convention and subsequently published Whipper's address in his paper. In his preface to the first installment of the address, Cornish said he hoped the readers would ''make the most of all the principles and arguments presented in favor of universal 'Peace'.'' However, Cornish confessed that he had ''yet to learn what virtue there would be in using moral weapons, in defence against a kidnapper or a midnight incendiary with a lighted torch in his hand.''[10]

Whipper gave much credence to man's superior gift of reason as opposed to violence and proceeded to cite scriptures from which rational men should draw inferences, e.g., ''love our enemies, bless them that curse you, pray for them that despitefully use you and persecute you,'' and ''Whomsoever shall smite thee on thy right cheek, turn unto him the other also.'' He concluded that it was reasonable to follow these dicta and proclaimed:

> I rest my argument on the ground that whatever is *scriptural* is *right*, and whatever is right is reasonable, and from that invulnerable position I mean not to stray for the sake of any expediency whatever. Therefore, every act of disobedience to the commands of Christian duty, is at enmity with our true interests and the welfare of human society.[11]

Although Whipper had advocated disobedience of *man's* law of returning fugitive slaves, he was saying that blacks should not engage in physical resistance of slavecatchers because that was disobeying *God's* law. To strengthen his position with facts, Whipper cited man's history of war. The attempt at physical redress from the beginning to the present day had cost mankind too dearly in ''sweat, blood and tears'' and was thus unreasonable. Whipper believed that people should avoid passions and ''seek for protection in something *higher* than human power. They must place their faith in Him who is able to protect them from danger, or will soon fall prey to the wicked artifices of their wicked enemies.'' However, the most pressing question for Whipper to answer was, what if someone physically attacks you? In response, he said:

> I will readily agree that it is the unbounded duty of every individual to defend himself against both the vulgar and false aspersions of a wicked world. But then I contend that his weapons should be his reasoning powers. That since a kind Providence has bestowed on him the power of speech and the ability to reason, he degrades his creator by engulfing himself in the turmoils of passion and physical conflict.[12]

To supplement his theories, which sounded somewhat ethereal when visualizing confrontation with an aggressor, Whipper gave the examples of the Quakers and Shakers. These were highly pacifistic people whose actions had apparently commanded the esteem of the vicious and operated as ''a shield from insult and abuse.''[13] Later in his speech, Whipper alluded to the power of pacifism demonstrated by ''modern abolitionists'' who had been beaten, stoned, and mobbed as they traveled from city to city. Yet they never retaliated with physical militance.

Giving more practicality to the argument, he contended that abolitionists would have been snuffed out by their overpowering opposition if they had not used merely the ''weapons of reason and moral truth'' to make persuasive inroads for their cause. Whipper asserted that if the abolitionists had started their mission with the patriotic cry of ''liberty or death,'' they would long since have been dead ''or a civil war would have ensued; thus would have dyed the American soil with human blood.'' What would have happened to freemen and slaves if the abolitionists had used violence? ''If the abolitionists had started on the principle that 'resistance to tyrants is obedience to God'—what would have been our condition. . . . ? Why we should have perished with the sword.''

Analogously, Whipper urged, "let us, like them, obliterate from our minds the idea of revenge."[14]

The predominant theme of the nonresistance plea was that the nation was awakening to the evils of blacks' treatment and with "patience we shall finally triumph over our enemies." Blacks should not take matters physically into their hands but should instead remember God's saying "Vengeance is mine, and I will repay it."

Whipper's precepts for nonviolence were generally accepted by Northern freemen during the period. His arguments were acceptable in theory, but the idea of nonresistance to slavehunters had some practical objectors. For instance, the matter of nonviolence was seriously considered by a mass meeting of blacks at New York City in 1837, where a resolution on the subject was voted on three times before the chairman finally declared that it was closely rejected. It said, "we cannot recommend non-resistance to persons who are denied the protection of equitable law, and when their liberty is invaded and their lives endangered by avaricious kidnappers."[15]

Whether the resolution gave license only to fugitives who were denied justice or also included those free Negroes who helped them was not entirely clear. Common sense would suggest that a free Negro would not stand idly by while a fugitive was struggling with "kidnappers." Opposing the resolution were Rev. Theodore S. Wright, Rev. Charles B. Ray, W.P. Johnson, Jacob Matthews, and others who said it was inconsistent with the principles of religion and peace advocated by members of the Anti-Slavery Society. Defending the resolution was the articulate David Ruggles, a black New York City businessman and active agent of the underground railroad. Ruggles argued that the resolution was consistent with "liberty, humanity, and justice" and he knew that not a gentleman in the house could "from his conscience recommend submission under such appalling circumstances, when our houses are invaded and we are carried off one by one by avaricious kidnappers.''[16] The argument was complicated by the fact that the so-called kidnappers were not above accepting money to turn free blacks over to slavery as fugitives. Instead of giving reasons why resistance to slavecatchers was justified, the advocates assumed the proposition was self-evident.

GARNET AND VIOLENCE OF THE FORTIES

Although there had been some isolated pleas for physical violence in the 1830s, particularly for resistance to slavehunters, David Walker's *Appeal* went unequalled in intensity of black advocacy of violence and insurrection until 1843. At that time a plea for violence was written and delivered that ranked alongside Walker's; it was Rev. Henry Highland Garnet's ''An Address to the Slaves of the United States of America.'' Garnet's rhetorical appeal was more appropriate to the times than Walker's had been, despite its almost unanimous rejection by white abolitionists.

By the forties there was a younger generation of black leaders, many of them escaped slaves, who gave a new tone of urgency to Negro arguments. Garnet, for instance, had escaped slavery with his parents in 1824 and had spent the period to 1840 acquiring an education. While finishing studies in 1840 at Oneida Institute in New York, Garnet was relatively nonviolent, as indicated in the rhetoric in this poem by him:

> Avenge thy plundered poor, oh Lord!
> But not with fire, but not with sword;
> Avenge our wrongs, our chains our sighs,
> The misery in our children's eyes;
> But not with sword,—no, not with fire,
> Chastise our country's locustry,
> Nor let them feel thine heavier ire,
> Chastise them not in poverty;
> Though cold in soul and coffined dust,

Their hearts are tearless, dead and dry,
Let them in outraged mercy trust,
And find that mercy they deny.[17]

After graduation from Oneida, Garnet had gone to Troy, where he taught school and studied theology for two years. Then he became a Presbyterian minister and a generally recognized black leader. He was a delegate to the 1843 National Negro Convention at Buffalo, the first official National Convention since 1835. From 1840 to 1843, Garnet's militance intensified to the point that he was ready to advocate fire and sword to avenge the plundered poor. At the Buffalo Convention, Garnet presented his "Address," reflecting a new unwillingness to patiently wait for the final triumph over injustice. Garnet's "Address" embodied the basic arguments used by black militants of the forties and was similar in form and substance to Walker's *Appeal*, only this time more blacks were ready to agree with it. It is probable that few slaves ever heard of the speech, but it was undoubtedly read closely by white southerners and both white and black northerners.

Garnet's first argument was that blacks had waited patiently long enough for freedom that was not even in sight. Negroes had been "contented in sitting still and mourning" over their sorrows and waiting for the bright and auspicious day when liberty would come. Yet, he complained, "we have hoped in vain. Years have rolled on, and tens of thousands have been borne on streams of blood and tears, to the shores of eternity."[18]

Second, the "Address" argued, as did Walker's *Appeal*, that slaves were religiously obligated to attempt escape. In addition, Garnet contended that the rules of Christianity made it sinful for slaves not to rebel physically. He told them that "TO SUCH DEGRADATION IT IS SINFUL FOR YOU TO MAKE VOLUNTARY SUBMISSION." As further reason to rebel, he told them they were "duty bound" to revere and obey the divine commandments, and if they did not obey them by rebelling they would "surely meet with the displeasure of the Almighty." God required all to love Him supremely, love their neighbors as themselves, honor the sabbath, search the scriptures, raise their children to respect His laws, and worship no other God but Him. Yet slavery allegedly defied all that; consequently, Garnet said:

> The forlorn condition in which you are placed does not destroy your moral obligation to God. . . . The diabolical injustice by which your liberties are cloven down, NEITHER GOD, NOR ANGELS, OR JUST MEN, COMMAND YOU TO SUFFER FOR A SINGLE MOMENT. THEREFORE IT IS YOUR SOLEMN AND IMPERATIVE DUTY TO USE EVERY MEANS, BOTH MORAL, INTELLECTUAL, AND PHYSICAL THAT PROMISES SUCCESS.[19]

As stinging as this argument was, it might not have painted a clear picture. Slaveholders tried to make religion work positively for their cause. Slaves were allowed to respect the sabbath, but on the sabbath they were taught the slaveholder's interpretation of religion, i.e., that "an 'all-wise Creator' had designed the Negro for labor in the South."[20]

The last of Garnet's main arguments for physical violence was the same one Walker had used. He contended that the slave condition was so bad that it was better to die, if necessary, than continue the *status quo*. He said:

> You had better all die—*die immediately*, than live slaves and entail your wretchedness upon your posterity. . . . If you receive good treatment [after rebellion], it is what you could hardly expect; if you meet with pain, sorrow, and even death, these are the common lot of slaves. . . .
>
> Brethren, arise, arise! Strike for your lives and liberties. Now is the day and the hour. Let every slave throughout the

land do this, and the days of slavery are numbered. You cannot suffer greater cruelties than you have already. *Rather die freemen than live to be slaves*. Remember that you are THREE MILLIONS.[21]

Garnet's arguments for violence were directed completely to the slave and did not directly affect actions of free blacks. When the Convention's vote was taken on whether or not to endorse the "Address," it was rejected with a small balloting of nineteen votes "against" and eighteen votes "for." Among those in favor of the "Address" was, surprisingly enough, Rev. Theodore S. Wright, who had opposed a New York City black "physical resistance" resolution in the previous decade. Along with Wright's, all but four "yes" votes were from New York delegates; three were from Michigan, and one from Ohio. The next year at Cortland Village, New York, Jermain W. Loguen echoed Garnet's impatient cry for violence because blacks had waited long enough. Loguen's incitement, however, was for freemen as well as slaves:

If our rights are withheld any longer, then come war—let blood flow without measure—until our rights are acknowledged or we perished from the earth. White men fight—all men fight for their freedom, and we are men and will fight for ours. Nothing can stop the current of blood but justice to our people.[22]

At the 1847 National Negro Convention held at Garnet's hometown of Troy, New York, there was just one resolution suggesting violence, and it was rejected. It stated, "Resolved, That the Convention recommend to our people the propriety of instructing their sons in the art of war."[23] No mention of violence was made at the only other National Convention of the decade in 1848, but Garnet did have his and Walker's pleas for violence published and distributed that year. Then, the 1849 Ohio State Colored Convention gave more life to Garnet's rhetoric when they resolved:

> That we still adhere to the doctrine of urging the slave to leave immediately with his hoe on his shoulder, for a land of liberty, and would accordingly recommend that five hundred copies of Walker's *Appeal* and Henry H. Garnet's *Address to the Slaves*, be obtained in the name of the Convention, and gratuitously circulated.[24]

By 1849 even Frederick Douglass joined the impatient blacks by saying of slaveholders that "if the slave should put every one of them to the sword tomorrow, who dare say that the criminals deserved less than death at the hands of their long-abused chattels?"[25] Douglass was not urging slaves to revolt but was merely asserting that they deserved to do so. Such appeals could only increase hostility of slaveholders and add to their defensiveness.

Those opposing violence, either by freemen or slaves, were Garrisonians and such political abolitionists as Amos G. Beman who put faith in other means for achieving justice. In speaking against Garnet's address at the 1843 Convention, Beman "opposed it principally upon moral grounds." It had "too much of the physical and not enough of the moral weapon about it." The remarks of Beman were reportedly "of great force, and produced effect upon the audience." Charles L. Remond, Charles B. Ray, and Frederick Douglass also spoke against the address. Douglass thought "there was too much physical force" and was for "trying the moral means a little longer."[26]

A more thorough case against physical violence was advanced at the 1847 National Negro Convention by the Committee on Abolition. The Committee was composed of Alexander Crummell, Thomas Van Renslear, and John Lyle, all of New York

State, and Frederick Douglass of Massachusetts. Its overall recommendation was, "We should . . . wholly discountenance any attempt to lead our people to confide in brute force as a reformatory instrumentality. All argument put forth in favor of insurrection and bloodshed, however well intended, is either the result of impatience or an atheistic want of faith in the power of truth as a means of . . . reforming the world."[27]

The tone of the Report was not so completely religious as the appeals from the AMRS. Instead, it more strongly emphasized practical aspects of combating slavery. It said that the "voices of God and common sense, equally" point to a better way. Perhaps the most sensible argument against violence, particularly an all-out slave insurrection, was that it was a suicidal action. Whereas at the 1843 Convention Douglass had passingly alluded to the "catastrophe" that would result from insurrection, the 1847 Report laid the odds out statistically. The oppressed were three million while their oppressors numbered seventeen million. Slaves lacked arms, means of organization, and government, while slaveholders had all three. With those odds, the Committee opposed resorting to bloodshed. It concluded, "With the facts of our condition before us, it is impossible for us to contemplate any appeal to the slave to take vengeance on his guilty master, but with the utmost reprobation. Your committee regard any counsel of this sort as the perfection of folly, suicidal in the extreme, and abominally wicked."[28]

It was necessary, however, for the opponents of violence to instill some hope in the slaves and in free blacks who were so vitally concerned with them. Walker and Garnet had made it clear that the slave was so degraded that he had nothing to lose even if he died in attempting to gain liberty. The promoters of violence had capitalized on the "liberty or death" theme and used that theme to counter the argument that insurrection was suicidal. Douglass and his colleagues argued that nonviolent methods such as moral suasion would gain freedom for the slave. They submitted that "the human voice must supersede the roar of the cannon. Truth alone is the legitimate antidote of falsehood—Free speech, free discussion, [and] peaceful agitation . . . under God, will subvert this giant crime."[29] Slavery existed only because it was popular, and if the sins of slaveholding were kept before the public, the peculiar institution would die. The job of blacks in the North was to speed liberty for slaves by showing the slaveholder to be disreputable and causing him to be regarded as a "moral leper —shunned as a loathsome wretch—outlawed from Christian communication, and from social respectability—an enemy of God and man." They were confident that if the sins of slavery were kept before the public, the bonded would be freed. As an alternative to advocacy or use of physical insurrection, the Committee saw hope of redemption through agitation. They resolved that "in all the language of inspired wisdom, there shall be no peace to the wicked, and this guilty nation shall have no peace, and we will do all that we can to *agitate*! AGITATE! ! AGITATE! ! !"[30]

The new breed of black leaders vowed to help God with their own action—rhetorical perseverance. However, their confidence in nonviolence would be put to an even greater test during the "fitful fifties."

MILITANT BLACK REACTIONS OF THE FIFTIES

Rhetoric that urged slaves to rebel, such as Garnet's "Address," was primarily theoretical and designed to agitate white slaveholders of the South. Rhetoric of a more tangible realistic nature continued to concern the subject of physical action to be used against fugitive slave hunters, especially during the first half of the 1850s. When the Fugitive Slave Law of 1850 was passed, federal officers were offered fees as inducements for capturing fugitives. As a consequence, more widespread radical endorsement of bloodshed was advocated by black leaders than had been seen previously. This served to threaten potential "slave hunters" into thinking that the money was not worth the consequences. Furthermore, the publicity given the meetings could draw more public attention to the problem and probably help the Negro in the long run. It was not pleasant to visualize a person who risks his life for freedom being turned back to slavery. The meetings served as reminders to white society that fugitives were human beings struggling for their liberty. Under those circumstances, the use of violence could be made to appear even more justifiable. In light of America's revolutionary background, it was hard not to respect and sympathize with a man who showed that his liberty was worth fighting for.

Within a month after the 1850 law was passed, protest meetings were held at Brooklyn, Philadelphia, Providence, Boston, and numerous other cities at which delegates vowed to use violence in defying the Law.[31] Samuel R. Ward's short-lived newspaper, the *Impartial Citizen*, referred to some five cities in which black meetings were almost immediately held to protest passage of the Fugitive Slave Law. Blacks at those meetings had sworn to imperil their lives rather than "submit to being enslaved by the hyenas which this law creates and encourages." He concluded, "So let all the black men of America say, and we shall teach the Southern slavocrats, and Northern doughfaces, that to perpetuate the Union, they must beware how they expose *us* to slavery, and themselves to death and destruction, present and future, temporal and eternal."[32]

Soon after the Bill was passed, there was a meeting of fugitive slaves at Cazenovia, New York. In their "Address to the American Slaves," the fugitives claimed that "the colored American for the sake of relieving his colored brethren, would no more hesitate to shoot an American slaveholder, than would his white brother hesitate to shoot an Algerine slaveholder. The State motto of Virginia, 'Death to Tyrants,' is as well the black man's as the white man's motto."[33]

In Boston, a mass meeting of "Colored Citizens" organized the

League of Freedom, composed of blacks who were "ready to resist the law, rescue and protect the slave at every hazard."[34] At Providence, Rhode Island, black delegates to a mass meeting resolved to "sacrifice our lives and all upon the altar to our wives, our children, and our fellow sufferers in common with us."[35] The frustrated delegates to the National Emigration Convention at Cleveland in 1854 proclaimed that liberty could only be obtained at the price which others had paid for it, and they were *"willing to pay that price, let the cost be what it may."*[36]

Those asserting that blacks should use physical violence in response to slavehunters used four basic arguments. The first one alleged that fugitives were as justified in using violence to secure and protect their freedom as the American revolutionaries had been in securing theirs. This argument, like so many used by blacks in the movement, was based on an *a priori* value judgment and could be accepted or rejected at face value. Naturally, there were many people who were willing to accept the argument, particularly if Negroes stressed the comparison between the infringement on colonists' rights by George III and the infringement on slaves' rights by their so-called owners. In their "Address" at Cazenovia, the fugitives declared, "If the American revolutionaries had excuse for shedding one drop of blood, then have the American slaves for making blood to flow 'even unto the horsebridles'."[37]

A second argument was that physical violence is justified in self-defense. A meeting of Negroes from Brooklyn, Williamsburg, and New York City concluded that all history teaches "that every people should be prepared to defend themselves by the knowledge and use of offensive weapons." They therefore resolved to urge their young men to "organize military companies."[38] Although the argument for self-defense continued to be pressed, the plan for the formation of military companies was abandoned. The *Bristol Examiner*, which had published the proceedings of the above meeting, was "happy" that the resolution for military companies was ultimately abandoned and that the convention seemed to "place more confidence in moral force than in the bloody arbitration of the sword."[39]

The self-defense argument was also used by Frederick Douglass in an 1854 editorial in his paper entitled "Is it Right and Wise to Kill a Kidnapper?" The editorial was in response to the editor of the *Rochester Daily American*, who had criticized black advocacy of violence in situations calling for self-defense. Douglass asked Mr. Mann what he would do if someone "should lay his horney paws upon his own dignified shoulders, with a view to reduce him to bondage" and asked if he would hold as a murderer any friend of his "who, to save him from such a fate, shot down the brute?" Douglass concluded by saying "there is not a citizen of Rochester worthy of the name who would not shoot down any man in defence of his own liberty."[40]

Of the four main arguments supporting physical violence, the one most often and most strongly presented was that physical violence was the only alternative for a suspected fugitive since laws did not protect his rights. A brief review of the Fugitive Slave Law gives a more thorough understanding of the argument. The Law provided that any claimant who could establish affidavit proof of ownership before a special federal commissioner could take possession of a Negro. Captives had no recourse to ordinary legal protections such as a jury trial or judicial hearing. Furthermore, the new law gave ten dollars to the commissioner if he ordered the captive's return to slavery but only five dollars if he ordered the captive's release. This fee differential was justified by the comparative costs of paperwork involved in the two kinds of cases.

At a Negro convention at Portland, Maine, the delegates resolved that the Fugitive Slave Bill passed a few days earlier threatened them and their children with immediate hopeless bondage. It did so by depriving them of the "inestimable trial by jury, in a free State." After considering the legal penalties to be inflicted on those who resisted enforcement through their assistance, they concluded, "There is no remedy left us but to solemnly warn our fellow citizens that, being left without legal and governmental protection for our liberties, we shall as God may help us, protect our own right to freedom at whatever cost or risk."[41]

Just after passage of the Law, an "Anti-Webster" meeting was held at Fanueil Hall in Boston. Samuel R. Ward of New York addressed the meeting and argued that the Law gave blacks no legal alternative to resorting to violence. He explained that a fugitive traced to New York State would have the law of "Almighty God" to protect him, the law which says, "Thou shalt not return to the master the servant that is escaped unto thee." Thus, Ward suggested that being obedient to God in such situations left blacks strictly to "the right of Revolution, and if need be, that right we will, at whatever cost, most sacredly maintain."[42] Ward's argument was slightly different from the others' in that he was not only saying there was no legal defense for the alleged fugitive but was adding that the Fugitive Slave Law contradicted God's law, thus giving a further reason for defying it. That same argument was given at a New York City "Meeting of Colored Citizens," of which John Thompson was President, and James McCune Smith, Samuel E. Cornish, and John T. Raymond were Vice Presidents. The New York meeting swore that the Fugitive Slave Law was "at varience [sic] with the laws of nature and of God." They further argued that with the provisions of the Law "leaving no other alternative, we must adopt the motto . . . [that] 'Resistance to Tyrants is obedience to God'."[43]

Justification of physical violence as the last alternative against their disfranchisement was later used by Ohio blacks. In their 1853 Convention, they argued that whites of their state could effect reform peacefully through the ballot box "but we, by the organic law of the State, are prevented from defending those precious rights by any other than violent means."[44]

Regardless of the persuasive advantage or disadvantage of their arguments, it is evident that possibly out of desperation, more Negroes were advocating the use of physical violence during the first part of the 1850s.

In opposition to the increasing number of blacks who advocated violence, especially in defying the Fugitive Slave Law, there existed a persistent and dedicated majority expounding essentially the same position that Whipperites had made popular nearly twenty years earlier. They argued that violence should be avoided at nearly all costs because religion was against violence. In addition, they tried to develop a stronger case showing that comparatively greater progress could be made with nonviolent weapons.

Among the fugitives themselves meeting at Cazenovia, there was a minority report on the "Address" by those who had "discarded the use of [violent] weapons" and recommended the scriptural advice to "love your neighbors; do good to them which hate you; bless them that curse you; and pray for them which despitefully use you."[45]

At the aforementioned violence-advocating meeting in New York, of which John T. Raymond was one of the vice presidents, Raymond expressed a minority viewpoint. Believing in political abolitionism, he explained that instead of bowie knives his "armour is prayer, and I think that will be sufficient, and that no other man or woman will be carried into bonds."[46] Yet even Raymond, either to keep his audience with him or to admit doubts about the efficacy of prayer alone as a weapon in every case, said that violent resistance might be necessary as a last resort. He explained that "we are a peace-loving people, law abiding, and we are not assembled here for the purpose of striking down our fellow men." However, he continued, "if we are compelled to defend our liberties, even with our lives, we shall do so. (loud cheering)."[47]

Appeal to religion was strengthened with the appeal that "united moral action" of blacks would be comparably better than violence. The "Call" for the 1853 National Convention emphasized that regardless of how frustrated or desperate some blacks might become, there were much better means for jointly fighting injustices than violence. The forty-four persons issuing the "Call" were convinced that only a small number among them "so far miscalculate and undervalue the importance of united and intelligent moral action, as to regard it as useless," so they did not feel called upon "to give an argument" in favor of their proposed peaceful efforts.[48] They proclaimed that their "warfare is not one where force can be employed." Instead, they were meeting to enforce anew their nonviolent appeals. Among the "Call's" undersigners were names of some who believed in resistance against slavehunters even though they were basically supporting nonviolence as a necessity; these included David Ruggles of Massachusetts, Jermain W. Loguen and James McCune Smith of New York, and William H. Day of Ohio. Among those signers who were apparently for nonviolence under any circumstances were J. W.C. Pennington and Charles B. Ray of New York and Amos G. Beman and Jehiel C. Beman of Connecticut. All proponents of the "Call" realized the futility of violence as a weapon in their struggle.

AGITATION FOR VIOLENCE

Events occurring from 1857 to 1861 so sharpened sectional division as to make unity less and less possible. The Dred Scott decision in 1857, John Brown's raid on Harper's Ferry in 1859, and Lincoln's election in 1860 amid threats from Southern states that they would secede if he became President brought the country closer to the war that broke out in April of 1861.

The attitudes of black leaders were changing during this period. Submissive actions more widely supported during previous years had brought little appreciable progress. Moral suasion through deeds and words had not achieved its purpose. Political aspirations were now in the hands of the Republican party, which was against slavery but had some policies which were less than encouraging for blacks in general. A review of the frustrated leaning toward violence was given by Frederick Douglass just a month before Lincoln's election:

> If speech alone could have abolished slavery, the work would have been done long ago. What we want is anti-slavery government, in harmony with our anti-slavery speech, one which will give effect to our words, and translate them into acts. For this, the ballot is needed, and if this will not be heard or heeded, then the bullet. We have had cant enough, and are sick of it.[49]

A common strategy at this time was to threaten whites, particularly slaveholders, with the possibility of physical violence. Slaves and free blacks stood no chance of surviving when being ultimately faced with organized and armed local forces as well as federal ones. Nevertheless, the slaveholder or Negro oppressor could be killed just as easily at the outbreak of black violence with the entire nation pledged to support his oppression militarily as he could without that support. Thus he was faced with a nearly uncontrollable threat which black spokesmen could aggravate.

The threat of insurrection was given by Charles Lenox Remond at the Massachusetts State Negro Convention at Bedford in August 1858. Remond proposed a resolution to procure appointment of a committee to "publish an address to the slaves of the South on the subject of the right and duty of insurrection."[50] This move had shades of the Garnet appeal but more blacks were now thinking in this direction. Even Rev. Amos G. Beman of Connecticut, who had spoken against Garnet's *Address* on moral grounds just after it was delivered, said in 1859 of Walker's *Appeal*, "Its pages thunder—its paragraphs blaze. Let everyone procure a copy, and get the edition published a few years since by Rev. Henry Highland Garnet, which contains his address to the slaves of the country."[51] In Tremont Temple at Boston in December 1860,

Frederick Douglass endorsed "John Brown's way of accomplishing our object." He threateningly explained that "the only way to make the Fugitive Slave Law a dead letter is to make a few dead slavecatchers. (laughter and applause)"[52]

Many blacks who were opposed to insurrection and to using the threat of violence took a new approach. They sympathized with advocates of violence and some even implied that it should be used whenever practical but rejected urging mass slave insurrection; perhaps they feared that much needless death and suffering would result from inciting unprepared slaves to rebel. At the 1858 Massachusetts Convention a response was given to Remond's rebellious proposal by Josiah Henson, the prototype for Uncle Tom in Harriet Beecher Stowe's novel *Uncle Tom's Cabin*. Father Henson completely avoided religious objections and instead made the practical suggestion that he did not want to see "three or four thousand men hung before their time." If Remond's proposition were carried out, everything would be lost. Henson alleged that the "address" urging rebellion could not be circulated among blacks in the South. "Catch the masters permitting that and you catch a weasel asleep." Besides, slaves had "nothing to fight with at the South—no weapons, no education." Henson's auditors were left, however, with the threatening reminder that "when I fight, I want to whip somebody."[53]

Henson further suggested that Remond might talk and then run away but "what would become of those poor fellows that must stand?" Another opponent of the resolution, Henry Johnson, opined that those who made the loudest professions, such as Remond, were the first to run. On the whole, the discussion showed more serious consideration of violence under some circumstances, but Remond's proposal was rejected.

By arguing the impracticality of rebellion, blacks could give the impression that they might fight in a situation where they could win. Therefore, they were able to convey a subtle threat while at the same time opposing mass insurrection on grounds of practicality. That position was assumed by Frederick Douglass just after John Brown's raid at Harper's Ferry. Douglass was rumored to have promised to accompany Brown but to have been frightened away at the last minute. To set the record straight, Douglass wrote the Rochester *Democrat American*, "I am ever ready to write, speak, publish, organize, combine and even conspire against slavery, when there is reasonable hope for success." He had not involved himself in Brown's raid because he regarded it impractical. Douglass assured readers that his "field of labor for the abolition of slavery has not extended to an attack upon the United States arsenal."[54] Nevertheless, Douglass was leaving open the possibility of violence wherever he thought it might work.

The October 16, 1859 raid on Harper's Ferry was a symbolically important event in black rhetoric of violence. There was now recognition of the prospective use of whites on a broad scale in securing liberty for slaves. A vocal minority of blacks began advocating disunion but carried it a step further than white moral suasionists and pledged an ultimate bloody showdown, if necessary, for the liberty of their people.

At the time of John Brown's trial and execution, there were sympathy meetings of blacks throughout the country expressing understanding and gratitude for the Captain's futile attempt.[55] Admittedly there was some skepticism about the fighting involved, but this did not block their overall perspective. For instance, in a meeting of "Colored Citizens" in Providence, Rhode Island, it was resolved that "notwithstanding our abhorrence to bloodshed and civil war, we fully sympathize with our friend Captain John Brown, and we believe him to be a hero, philanthropist, and unflinching champion of liberty."[56] A New Haven, Connecticut meeting chaired by Amos G. Beman on the day before John Brown was hanged predicted that Brown's execution would "raise a beacon in Virginia that would be seen throughout the world."[57]

The more militant black leaders at sympathy meetings, such as

Charles H. Langston of Ohio, did not "abhor" any of the
bloodshed. Instead, they saw John Brown's action as being in
perfect harmony with and resulting from the teachings of the
Bible, of our revolutionary fathers, and of "every true and faithful
anti-slavery man in the country and the world." Langston repeated
Bible passages calling for putting manstealers to death and concluded, "Did not Captain Brown act in consonance with these
Biblical principles and injunctions?" Langston then repeated the
revolutionary doctrines of the founding fathers about abolishing a
government that is destructive of the ends of liberty, justice, and
happiness. He concluded by asking, "Did not Captain Brown act
in accordance with the foregoing revolutionary principles?"[58]

Just a few weeks prior to Brown's raid, Charles Lenox Remond
was a precursor to the new black agitation for violent disunion. At
the New England Anti-Slavery Society Convention in 1859, Remond combined that Society's doctrine of disunion with his own
belief in the violence that would probably accompany it. After
calling for agitation against the Union, Remond said, "if the result
of that speaking must be bloodshed, be it so . . . if it must be
dissolution of the Union, be it so." With a more widespread type
of physical violence in mind, Remond avowed, "I believe American slavery will go down in blood. I am not only prepared to see it,
but I long for the time to come, for I believe it will be a retribution
that the American people deserve, and it will be a lesson by which
those who come after them will not fail to profit."[59]

On the day of John Brown's execution, Henry H. Garnet predicted violent national bloodshed as the inevitable result of the
Negro question. At a New York black meeting, he said:

> I am not a man of blood. I hold human life to be sacred, and
> would spare even a man-stealer, if he stood not in the
> bondman's path of freedom. . . . In the signs of the times, I
> see the dreadful truth, written as by the finger of
> Jehovah—"*For the sins of this nation, there is no atonement*

without the shedding of blood.'' If it must come, Oh God! prepare us to meet it.[60]

Blacks were beginning to have little hope for achieving freedom for the slaves by peaceful means. The South had experienced many years of peaceful slaveholding and slaveholders were firmly entrenched in national political positions. Consequently, some blacks thought slaveholders were beyond the reach of moral or human appeals. In June 1860, Frederick Douglass wrote a letter to James Redpath of Massachusetts stating his lack of faith in non-violent measures:

> The only penetrable point of a tyrant is the *fear of death*. The outcry that they make, as to the danger of having their *throats* cut is because they deserve to have them *cut*. The efforts of John Brown and his brave associates, though apparently unavailing, have done more to upset the logic and shake the security of slavery, than all other efforts in that direction for twenty years.[61]

Lincoln's election brought new strategic considerations for black spokesmen. Some northerners may have favored Negro rights, but to what length would they go in alienating Southern slaveholders? The Southern states were distressed by Lincoln's election and they made northerners realize that secession might be a reality. Northerners recognized that separation of the sections of the country would upset not only the political system but the economy of the country as well.

Meanwhile, the abolitionists were worried that the Republican party might appease the Southern states with some form of compromise. Election of a Republican President did not serve to calm or satisfy black leadership, but those blacks who remained vocal were spurred on to agitate greater conflict between the sections. Perhaps the most vocal and influential black, Frederick Douglass, wanted secession so there would be no possibility of appeasement. It was advantageous to blacks when Southern states seceded after Lincoln's election because the Republican party was still committed to enforce slavery in states belonging to the Union; Douglass thus felt obligated to agitate for disunion. In his paper issued just a month after the 1860 election, Douglass gave his strategy. He declared:

> A dissolution of the Union would be highly beneficial to the cause of liberty—the South would be a Sicily, and the North a Sardinia. Mr. Lincoln would then be entirely absolved from his slave-hunting, slave-catching and slave-killing pledges . . . In truth, we really wish those brave, fire-eating, cotton growing States would just now go outside the Union and set up for themselves, where they could be got at without disturbing other people.[62]

At precisely that point, Douglass' rhetoric struck the note it had sounded during the 1840s when he was advocating disunion; now, however, he appeared to know that physical violence would necessarily follow secession, and he was now ready to accept war. His speeches were now directed not so much at either Negroes or Northern whites, as many of his earlier persuasive pleas had been. Instead, his appeals were designed for whites of the South in an attempt to provoke them into secession. "Radicalism" was essential in the new appeals as he did not aim simply to prevent the extension of slavery but "to abolish the system altogether."[63]

As agitation increased among abolitionists, some Northern whites felt compelled to repress "disunion agitators" in the wake of increasing secession threats from the South. The result was that advocates of disunion were subjected to violence of white mobs. On December 3, 1860, a meeting was held at Tremont Temple in Boston in commemoration of the anniversary of John Brown's execution. Those attending believed in John Brown's method of combating slavery. The meeting was to hear featured speeches from Frederick Douglass and Wendell Phillips, but the crowd was set upon by a mob. One reporter of the incident wrote that "Mr. Douglass fought like a trained pugilist; and, although a score opposed him, he cleared his way through the crowd to the rostrum, which he clutched with an air that indicated his determination to hold his place."[64] His friends, however, were "less combative" and so he was left to fend for himself, and several policemen dragged him away and "threw him down the staircase to the floor of the hall."

They dispersed and reassembled at a Negro Baptist Church on Joy Street. The minister of the church, J. Sella Martin, had been one of the persons seated on the platform when the riot occurred. After the meeting at the Negro church ended, the mob waiting outside attacked the participants with clubs and stones and proceeded through the Negro section of town smashing the windows of several houses.

On the following Monday, the Boston abolitionists met at Boston's Music Hall to hear Frederick Douglass denounce the mob action, make a plea for free speech, and justify the agitative action that was taking place. To the objection that the December 3 meeting was ill-timed and the parties to it unwise, he said, "Why, what is the matter with us? Are we going to palliate and excuse a palpable and flagrant outrage on the right of free speech, by implying that only a particular description of persons should exercise that right?"[65] This was hardly an oldtime demonstration of turning the other cheek; it was a bold insistence upon the right to agitate. Mob action against abolitionism only served to intensify the attack on the South.

South Carolina seceded from the Union on December 20, 1860, a step which encouraged abolitionists, for they knew there was an even greater chance for provoking other states to join South

Carolina in seceding before compromise or appeasement could be extended. Abolitionist agitation continued almost without a break until the firing on Fort Sumter.

Mob violence against abolitionists was seen by Douglass as another advantage for abolitionism. An article in the January 1861, issue of his paper gave Douglass' reasoning behind that belief. It said that mob action over a quarter of a century had brought on the "irrepressible conflict," overthrown political parties, remodeled public opinion, made slavehunting unpopular, and made South Carolina "almost mad to get out of the Union."[66]

In light of Southern threats of secession, agitation also motivated mobs to break up abolition meetings around Buffalo and other cities in New York State during the early part of 1861.[67] Mob action was a visible way for members of Northern society to show their disapproval of abolition action and their genuine desire for the South to remain in the Union. In February 1861, Douglass was still worried about potential appeasement halting the secession movement of the South. He thought the only hope was in the "unreasonableness of the South in rejecting all conciliation and concessions. The headstrong policy of the seceding States, which may involve the destruction of slavery, may at the same time save the Northern conscience from a new demoralization, and Northern self respect from a new humiliation."[68]

The agitation promoted by blacks during the Winter of 1861 did not stem merely from strong philosophical convictions. They were talking about an unwillingness to appease Southern states with the flesh of their racial brethren. They attempted to make the North feel "above" giving up their self-respect through concessions to the slavepower. At the same time, they wanted to agitate the South to the point where they were too proud to do anything but secede. In short, the main strategy of black spokesmen was to increase the polarization or divisiveness between sections. There had to be destruction of any effort to maintain the Union by "new concessions to slaveholders." If the Union had to be "held together by a new drain on the Negro's blood'' and continued elimination of rights, then ''will every right minded man and woman in the land say, let the Union perish.''[69]

Fear of compromise loomed large in abolition circles. Garrisonian Negroes continued their work for disunion but they made it patently clear that violence was acceptable to them in the achievement of or the event of disunion. On January 24, 1861, the Massachusetts Anti-Slavery Society held its Annual Convention in Boston. Prominent black leaders in attendance were William Wells Brown, Dr. John S. Rock, J. Sella Martin, and Charles Lenox Remond; Remond was elected vice president for the following year.[70] Among the speakers were Rock, Remond, Martin and Brown. Martin made a speech extolling the virtues of violence used by slaves. He said it was a very great mistake to suppose that the slaves in the South were quiet and submissive; a dozen insurrections occurred yearly. Martin had spent eleven years in Georgia and affirmed that the violent attempts were ''carefully and systematically kept out of the papers.'' To show the black man's approval of violence and enhance the agitative effect of his speech, Martin asserted the belief that John Brown had ''more disciples than any other man in the land.''[71]

Many extant transcripts of black rhetoric at the time are by Frederick Douglass, the recognized leader of his people. In order to encourage Lincoln not to compromise with the South, Douglass reminded all Republicans that Lincoln had promised the people of the country that slavery would be on the road to ultimate extinction under his administration. Thus, compromising with the Southern states would mean to ''put the razor to the throat of his party, write himself down a coward, and make political platforms worse than a mockery.''[72] A compromise was not worked out during that crucial winter after the 1860 election. Within six weeks after South Carolina seceded, she was joined by Mississippi, Florida, Alabama, Louisiana and Texas.

The secession of Southern states had been applauded by Douglass and the blacks whose views were published in the period from the secession of South Carolina to the Civil War. In the April issue of his newspaper, Douglass asserted, "The fire is kindled, and cannot be extinguished. The 'irrepresible conflict' can never cease on the continent. It will change its methods and manifestations, but it will be none the less real for all that."[73]

Fort Sumter was attacked on April 12, 1861. Prior to that time, there had only been hope that such a provocation would take place. As long as the secessionists merely issued threats to the North and displayed their palmetto and rattlesnake flags, they influenced the public mind, but with the firing on Fort Sumter, Northern sympathy was lost.

The attitudes of black spokesmen toward violence varied throughout the movement, yet they retained a strong thread of commonality in the form of religion. The staunchest black advocates of violence attempted to find religious justification for it. At the same time, those who opposed violence did so because they thought it was contrary to their religious principles. While a majority of blacks opposed violence for reasons of religion or practicality of numbers, it is true that more blacks supported physical action than did their white counterparts. The white moral suasionists strongly objected to violence, yet a prominent black moral suasionist, Charles Lenox Remond, became impatient at times and advocated slave insurrection. Moreover, the white politically-oriented abolitionists denounced violence. Yet one of the first black Liberty party members, Henry Highland Garnet, also became impatient in the early 1840s and advocated bloody slave revolt.

After passage of the Fugitive Slave Law of 1850, the blacks held numerous meetings to advocate physical resistance to slavecatchers. Some whites sympathized with the tendency of a minority of blacks toward violence, but they denounced its use as a reformatory instrument. Only in rare instances, such as John Brown's 1859 raid, did white antislavery men find recourse in violence.

Blacks who had personal friends and relatives in slavery were more inclined to suggest violence. Their suggestions at least contained "threat" value which made slaveholders and slavecatchers more cautious in their treatment of blacks.

Finally, as the Civil War neared, several black and white abolitionists agitated for secession and disunion. These blacks knew violence and bloodshed would probably follow, but they were willing to endure that for the cause. They welcomed the Civil War.

NOTES

[1] *Walker's Appeal, With a Brief Sketch of his Life by Henry Highland Garnet. And Also Garnet's Address to the Slaves of the United States of America*, p. 20.

[2] Ibid., p. 37.

[3] Ibid., p. 56.

[4] Ibid., p. 12.

[5] A summary of reactions to the violence advocated in the *Appeal* is in Clement Eaton, "A Dangerous Pamphlet in the Old South," *Journal of Southern History* (August 1936), p. 323-34.

[6] A chapter each is devoted to violent protestors Nat Turner, David Walker, Henry Garnet, and the white John Brown, in Lerone Bennett, Jr., *Pioneers in Protest* (Chicago: Johnson Publishing Company, Inc., 1968).

[7] *Liberator*, August 20, 1831, p. 133.

[8] *Fourth Annual Convention for the Improvement of the Free People of Colour, New York, 1834*, p. 58.

[9] *First Annual Meeting of the American Moral Reform Society, Philadelphia, 1837*, p. 21.

[10] *Colored American*, September 9, 1837, p. 1.

[11] Ibid., September 16, 1837, p. 1.

[12] Ibid., p. 1.

[13] Ibid., September 23, p. 1.

[14] Ibid., September 30, 1837, p. 4.

[15]Ibid., December 9, 1837, p. 4.

[16]Ibid., p. 4.

[17]*National Anti-Slavery Standard*, May 22, 1840, p. 82.

[18]*Walker's Appeal and Garnet's Address*, p. 90.

[19]Ibid., p. 93.

[20]Kenneth M. Stampp, *The Peculiar Institution* (New York: Vintage Press, 1956), p. 11.

[21]*Walker's Appeal and Garnet's Address*, p. 96.

[22]Jermain W. Loguen, *The Rev. J. W. Loguen, as a Slave and as a Freeman* (Syracuse, N.Y.: J.G.K. Truair and Co., 1859), p. 379.

[23]*National Convention of Colored People and Their Friends, Troy, 1847*, p. 17.

[24]*State Convention of Colored Citizens of Ohio, Columbus, 1849* (Oberlin: J. M. Fitch's Power Press, 1849), p. 18.

[25]*North Star*, February 9, 1849, p. 9.

[26]*National Convention of Colored Citizens, Buffalo, 1843*, p. 23.

[27]Ibid., p. 13.

[28]*National Convention of Colored People and Their Friends*, Troy, 1847, p. 31-32. Also in *North Star*, January 14, 1848, p. 4.

[29]Ibid., p. 32.

[30]Ibid., p. 32.

[31]See *Liberator*, October 11, 1850, p. 162, and *National Anti-Slavery Standard*, October 10, 1850, p. 78.

[32]*Impartial Citizen* cited in *Liberator*, October 11, 1850, p. 162.

[33]*National Anti-Slavery Standard*, September 5, 1850, p. 58.

[34]*Liberator*, October 11, 1850, p. 162.

[35]*National Anti-Slavery Standard*, December 5, 1850, p. 110.

[36]*National Emigration Convention of the Colored People, Cleveland, 1854*, p. 26.

[37]*National Anti-Slavery Standard*, September 5, 1850, p. 58. For resolutions containing the same argument, see ibid., October 10, 1850, p. 78.

[38]*Bristol Examiner* cited in *Liberator*, May 9, 1851, p. 74.

[39]Ibid., p. 74.

[40]*Frederick Douglass' Paper*, June 2, 1854, p. 2.

[41]*Liberator*, September 20, 1850, p. 150.

[42]Ibid., April 5, 1850, p. 1. Also in Carter G. Woodson (ed.), *Negro Orators and Their Orations* (Washington, D.C.: The Association for the Study of Negro Life and History, 1925), p. 196.

[43]*National Anti-Slavery Standard*, October 10, 1850, p. 78.

[44]*Ohio State Convention of Colored Freemen, Columbus, 1853* (Cleveland: Printed by W. H. Day, Aliened American Office, 1853), p. 5.

[45]*National Anti-Slavery Standard*, September 5, 1850, p. 58.

[46]Ibid., October 10, 1850, p. 79.

[47]Ibid., p. 79.

[48]*Colored National Convention, Rochester, 1853*, p. 4.

[49]*Douglass' Monthly*, October 1859, p. 149.

[50]*Liberator*, August 13, 1858, p. 132.

[51]*Weekly Anglo-African*, October 29, 1859, p. 1.

[52]*Douglass' Monthly*, January 1861, p. 1.

[53]*Liberator*, August 13, 1858, p. 132.

[54]*Democrat and American*, cited in Foner (ed.), *Life and Writings of Frederick Douglass*, II, p. 461-62.

[55]See *Weekly Anglo-African*, November 19 and 26, and December 3, 10, and 17, 1859.

[56]Ibid., December 17, 1859, p. 2.

[57]Ibid., p. 2.

[58]Ibid., December 3, 1859, p. 1.

[59]*National Anti-Slavery Standard*, June 4, 1859, p. 2.

[60]*Weekly Anglo-African*, December 10, 1859, p. 2.

[61]*Liberator*, July 27, 1860, p. 1.

[62]*Douglass' Monthly*, December 1860, p. 370.

[63]Ibid., p. 370.

[64]*National Anti-Slavery Standard*, December 8, 1860, p. 2.

[65]*Liberator*, December 14, 1860, p. 1.

[66]*Douglass' Monthly*, January 1861, p. 386.

[67]Mobs broke up antislavery meetings at Buffalo. *National Anti-Slavery Standard*, January 12, 1861, p. 3; Rochester, ibid., January 19, 1861, p. 3; and Syracuse, ibid., February 16, 1861, p. 1.

[68]*Douglass' Monthly*, February 1861, p. 403.
[69]Ibid., January 1861, p. 388.
[70]*National Anti-Slavery Standard*, February 4, 1861, p. 3.
[71]Ibid., p. 3.
[72]*Douglass' Monthly*, January 1861, p. 436.
[73]Ibid., April 1861, p. 436.

Robert Purvis—Nonexclusivist

5

Black Exclusivism

During the early 1830s there was considerable controversy within the predominantly white antislavery organizations concerning the nature and extent of their inclusion of or integration with blacks. A similar controversy soon took place among blacks over the degree to which they should seek separate distinction from whites in American society. Some blacks advocated complete racial separation from whites in some activities as an advantageous departure from the policy of most blacks of the time who wanted varying degrees of integration or assimilation into the white economic, civil, and social system. Black leaders in that period debated whether to work exclusively for the betterment of their own race or to ignore lines of racial separation and distinction in their struggle.

ORGANIZATIONAL EXCLUSIVISM

From 1830 through 1835, the National Negro Conventions were conducted under the auspices of an exclusive Negro organization called the "American Society of Free Persons of Colour." The constitution of that society was published along with the minutes and proceedings of the pioneer Negro convention at Philadelphia in 1830. As the organizational title implied and Article I of their constitution confirmed, the membership of the organization was limited to "Persons of Colour as shall pay not less than *twenty five cents* on entering, and thereafter quarterly, *eighteen and three quarter cents*."[1] There were some white guests invited, such as at the 1832 convention when R. R. Gurley of the American Colonization Society and William Lloyd Garrison of the New England Anti-Slavery Society debated the merits of colonizing Negroes. However, conditions appeared sufficiently oppressive and discriminatory against blacks for them to believe an exclusive organization was appropriate and necessary.

The prevailing view among blacks at the time was presented at the 1834 National Negro Convention by William Hamilton of New York City, the President of the Conventional Board. Hamilton told the delegates that "under the present circumstances it is highly necessary that free people of colour should combine and closely attend to their own particular interest. All kinds of jealousy should be swept away from among them, and their whole eye fixed, intently fixed, on their own peculiar welfare."[2]

At the 1834 National Negro Convention, another viewpoint was emerging as the skeleton of a new organization was being formed; the name of the new group was to be the American Moral Reform Society. This group was responsible for initiating some issues concerning racial exclusivism. The philosophy behind the new group was to eliminate lines of racial distinction. Two of the founders of the AMRS, William Whipper and Robert Purvis, gave a preview of the new organization's philosophical emphasis when they respectively proposed and seconded the following motion at the 1835 National Negro Convention: "Resolved, That we recommend as far as possible, to our people to abandon the use of the word 'Colored,' when either speaking or writing concerning themselves: and especially to remove the title African from their institutions, the marbles of churches &c." After an "animated and interesting discussion," Whipper's resolution was "unanimously adopted."[3]

At that same 1835 Convention, William Whipper of Philadelphia, Alfred Niger of Providence, and Augustus Price of Washington, D.C. were assigned "to prepare an address to the people of the United States, giving an exposition of the principles of our society, and the wants of our people." The address appeared in the Minutes of the 1835 convention and contained the newer nonexclusive tone that was to be representative of the AMRS. It read, "We have buried in the bosom of Christian benevolence all those national distinctions, complexional variations, geographical lines, and sectional bounds that have hitherto marked the history, character, and operations of men; and now boldly plead for the Christian and moral elevation of the human race."[4]

The 1835 convention was the last one held by the "Free People of Colour" until 1843. In the meantime, some national structure existed in the form of the AMRS. The first annual meeting of the AMRS was in August 1837 in Philadelphia, with most delegates being from Pennsylvania; there were only a handful of representatives from New Jersey and New York added to the local list.

The "Address to the American People" from the 1835 convention, stressing noncomplexional distinction, also appeared in the minutes of the new organization's first independent meeting in 1837. This was about the only evident continuity between the two groups. Unlike the specialized activities for Negro elevation that had characterized the earlier National Negro Conventions, such as opposition to colonizing Negroes or promotion of Negro schools, the AMRS wanted a Garrison-like expansion to include such nonracial subjects as temperance, economy, and liberty for all Americans. Membership was open to any person who would "pledge himself to practise and sustain the general principles of Moral Reform as advocated by our country."[5]

Whipper rapidly became the major influence in the society and became editor of its official paper, the *National Reformer*. Whipper and Purvis performed the chief administrative work of the organization. In addition to the Philadelphia headquarters, perhaps the strongest auxiliary group was established in Pittsburgh under the leadership of John B. Vashon and Lewis Woodson, both of whom remained supporters of the Garrisonian branch of abolitionism.

Regardless of its actual accomplishments, however, the AMRS can be credited with initiating some "exclusivism" controversies. The AMRS wanted to help people avoid racial distinctions; to them, any exclusive action by or for Negroes would only draw attention to the line of racial demarcation and thus perpetuate the problem. While they were devising plans for the betterment of the "human family," opposition to their activities was emerging within the race. Some blacks assumed that they should take specific action by and for themselves rather than deal with the abstract idea of bettering humanity.

One argument was that specific projects should be promoted so blacks would not get bogged down by vagueness and indefiniteness. This was propounded by Samuel Cornish, who had attended the first AMRS meeting as a New York delegate. Cornish wrote back to the *Colored American*, of which he was editor at the time, telling of the confusion which apparently resulted from the new philosophy: "We found a Purvis, a Whipper, and others (of whose Christian benevolence and cultured intellect, we have so many and such strong evidences) vague, wild, indefinite, and confused in their view. They created shadows, fought the wind, and bayed the moon for three days."[6]

Another argument for specific action and opposed to AMRS action was based on the fact that history showed successful precedents of specific groups having taken action to right specific wrongs. That particular argument was stressed by David Ruggles, a New York black abolitionist who was active in promoting the underground railroad. Ruggles founded a "Vigilance Committee" in 1835 for assisting fugitives in their efforts to obtain freedom. In 1840, Ruggles wrote an open letter to Whipper and Purvis giving the historical justification for independent action:

What would have been the condition of American liberty, "the great principle of man's equality," as taught by the Revolutionary Fathers of our country in the Declaration of Independence, had they hesitated to convene as oppressed Americans to consider and act in reference to the burden under which they groaned? . . .

It is to be found in history containing the rise and progress of nations from the earliest ages of the world to the present . . . that a people who have felt "the scorpion's lash and the viper's sting," . . . always extricated themselves from the tyrant's yoke, . . . [by] considering their own exclusive, their every condition and employing . . . action in the cause of reform and equal rights.[7]

An additional argument for concentration on specific problems of the Negro was that the narrowed effort could more likely produce tangible results. In 1838, the editors of the *Colored American* contended that results of specific projects would be more discernible and that the whole nation could profit from a concentration on exclusive goals. Thus they turned the tables on the AMRS, saying that the "human family" in this nation stood a better chance of being helped by exclusivism. The editors said:

Shall the colored people of the free states form a great national society for the improvement of the whole nation, or one confined to themselves? Certainly, one definitely for themselves. This is the only way that they can do anything *for themselves*, and the most likely way to benefit the nation. It is time our efforts were combined and concentrated, that all our moral and mental means may tell upon a point.[8]

As a confirmation of the fact that Negro efforts could be spread too thin and thus lose their effectiveness, Charles B. Ray, a black who was associated with the editorial staff of the *Colored American*, visited the Boston area and wrote back concerning the AMRS Auxiliary's efforts there:

> In their zeal . . . other subjects of a kindred character such as peace, and women's rights begin very much to engross their attention. . . . Such a course, I am persuaded, if persisted in, must have a tendency to alienate friends, now engaged together for the good of the slave; of this I have much testimony and personal observation.[9]

Somewhat related to the above issue was the question: Should blacks use exclusive terms such as "colored," "Negro," or "Afro" in their titles and symbols? As their unanimously passed resolution at the 1834 Convention indicated, Whipper and Purvis favored the abolition of all distinctly racial designations. Even the title, American Moral Reform Society, was to set the new trend of placing all people above complexional considerations.

On the other side of the question, a rapidly increasing number of blacks were supporting a proposition that Negroes should retain their "color badge" because such terms as "colored" or "Negro" gave them a symbol of identity around which to rally and about which they could develop pride. That argument was given by Junius Morel, a black abolitionist from Philadelphia, in a letter endorsed by fellow Philadelphian Frederick A. Hinton: "When the pages of *our* history shall be complete, when the tale of our sufferings is told, and we are delivered from the house of bondage, then and not until then—can I consent to drop the distinguishing term COLORED MAN."[10]

The attempt to inspire pride in race was also made by Cornish in an attack on black Philadelphians' pledge to eliminate the use of the term "colored": "To us, and we think to anyone of good sense, laboring under such persecutions as the colored citizens of Philadelphia are, to be called Colored Americans would be like a ray of *Heavenly Light*, shining amid the blackness of darkness.''[11] Cornish was also strongly defending the name of his newspaper.

In the same editorial, Cornish argued that it would be foolish to ignore a title applied to them almost universally by whites: ''But what caps the climax is that while these sages are frightened half to death, at the idea of being called COLORED, their FRIENDS and their FOES, in the convention, in the assembly and in the Senate; through the pulpit and the press, call them nothing else but NE- GROES, NEGROES, THE NEGROES of Pennsylvania.''[12]

Unlike the lingering question over how to employ independent action in relation to whites, the question over racial terms died much more quickly. Most blacks favored retaining their racial identity and they cared little whether some or all the terms ''col- ored,'' ''Negro,'' ''Afro'' and the like were used in referring to them; they had more important matters to deal with than quibbles over terms.

The question was put clearly into perspective by Henry H. Garnet in a discourse he delivered in 1848 to the Female Benevol- ent Association of Troy, New York. Garnet said, ''How unprofit- able it is for us to spend our golden moments in long and solemn debate upon the questions whether we shall be called '*Africans*,' '*Colored Americans*,' or '*Africo-Americans*,' or '*Blacks*.' The question should be, my friends, *shall we arise and act like men, and cast off this terrible yoke?*''[13]

Eventually, even the most conflicting members of the black race simply placed the matter of racial ''terms'' to one side. At their national convention, the emigrationists gave the conclusion that could just as easily have been made by about any other black spokesman after 1840 regardless of philosophy on substantive issues. They said that ''the relative terms Negro, African, Black, Colored, and Mulatto, when applied to us, shall ever be held with the same respect and pride; and synonimous [*sic*] with the terms Caucasion, white, Anglo-Saxon, and European, when applied to that class of people.''[14]

Although the controversy over terms appears relatively unimportant in retrospect, at the time it seemed closely intertwined with other issues brought forth by the AMRS, such as ones concerning independent action in organizations by and for blacks; those latter issues remained important for some time to come. Furthermore, as will be seen, the same questions were equally applicable to the subjects of churches and schools.

Independent Action

The controversy about the advisability of Negroes' acting independently either for or by themselves was still being waged in the 1840s after the American Moral Reform Society had its early decease as an active force among blacks. Regardless of his views on moral suasion, political activity, or any of a number of internal issues among abolitionists, the question of independent action was a significant and unique one for the Negro. Should Negroes continue the trend of losing themselves in those organizations which were "inevitably" controlled by whites?

By 1840, there were many individuals in the race who were presenting a case for reactivating such independently initiated Negro activities as the national conventions which had disbanded in 1835. A handful of blacks under the leadership of William Whipper and Robert Purvis still objected to such proposed reactivations. In addition, some whites thought black independent organizational activity was unwise. For example, the white editors of the *National Anti-Slavery Standard*, the official organ of the American Anti-Slavery Society, reacted negatively to proposed Negro conventions:

Now, our friends may be compelled to act separately in schools and churches and benevolent associations, or do worse.

. . . Then, why should our friends seek to put themselves in a position, to say the least, that looks like an admission of the rightfulness of demarcation? Out upon it, brethren. A man is a MAN.[15]

Still, many Negroes argued for independent action. They did not reject white help; instead, they tended to praise the integrated work done in organizations that were confessedly directed or dominated by whites. Yet they asserted that blacks needed to initiate some supplementary activities which they themselves could direct. The main argument by most black spokesmen was that Negroes were obligated to form and dominate some activities in their behalf since it was their problem. That argument was needed to show that Negroes truly felt the responsibility for caring for themselves, and it could also demonstrate that blacks were capable of tackling their own problems with manful ingenuity. This argument was presented at a Negro convention in Hartford, Connecticut in May 1840. In attendance were such well known Negroes as Rev. J.W.C. Pennington, Rev. Amos G. Beman, and the guest speaker for the occasion, David Ruggles of New York. A report that included the recommendation for a national convention was unanimously adopted and distributed to various papers. It stated:

We are the party concerned. We are the party suffering. We are the party that are bound to act in the use of all those legitimate means which God has ordained in the hands of every people. Therefore—we recommend a National Convention. . . .
Our indiscriminate connection with abolitionists *never has and does not now* affect the necessity of this measure. . . . We cannot delegate the protection of our rights to others in any such sense as to relieve us of the measure.[16]

Even Charles Lenox Remond, who adhered strongly to much of

the Garrisonian American Anti-Slavery Society doctrine, believed that blacks needed to initiate some independent organized activity despite their grateful participation in integrated white antislavery societies. At a Boston meeting of colored citizens in 1840 under the direction of such renowned Negro citizens as Remond and William C. Nell, resolutions were passed calling for independent action:

> Resolved, That the unwearied interest manifested by our friends the abolitionists for the emancipation of the "oppressed" in this country, calls for our everlasting gratitude, inasmuch as they have done their duty, by endeavoring to restore us those rights their fathers and themselves have robbed us of.
>
> Resolved, That while we fully approve of the course pursued by our friends, we nevertheless feel it a duty incumbent upon us to labor unceasingly for ourselves.[17]

The above is not to be construed to mean that the Negroes wanted to completely exclude whites from their activities, but it does mean that Negroes wanted to initiate and take a leading role in at least some activities designed for their own benefit.

On July 20, a month before the national convention convened at Buffalo in 1843, the Boston Negroes conducted a meeting to consider the wisdom of having an exclusive meeting as proposed. They finally voted to endorse the convention despite its proposed exclusiveness because they recognized their obligation to unite with other blacks in combating racial problems.[18] Similarly, a public meeting was held by blacks of a non-Whipper philosophy in Philadelphia on August 23, 1841 in which they supported the proposal for a National Negro Convention in Buffalo so they could unite behind the cause, but the 1841 Convention did not materialize. Among the blacks attending that Philadelphia meeting were James McCrummell and Frederick A. Hinton. Those names are especially significant in that the founding meeting of the American Anti-Slavery Society was held in the home of Frederick A. Hinton; moreover, the original Declaration of Intention for the American Anti-Slavery Society bore the signatures of both Frederick Hinton and James McCrummell. Yet despite their close association with the white abolitionists from the very beginning, they defiantly urged some independent action.

Another argument for an exclusive black convention was that such an organization would prove to white doubters that Negroes could think for themselves; otherwise blacks might be regarded as mere puppets of white abolitionists. That argument was given by Philip A. Bell, a black journalist from New York City, in a letter to the *National Anti-Slavery Standard*. Bell said, "If we act with our white friends . . . the words we utter will be considered theirs, or their echo. That will be the general impression, the voice of the majority will be heard; theirs only will be considered. That such is always the case under all circumstances, even Mr. Whipper acknowledges."[19]

As long as Negroes were uniquely oppressed, they could meet, said David Ruggles of New York, without being considered "exclusivists." In the early 1840s, David Ruggles was a sponsor of an organization called "The American Reform Board of Disfranchised Commissioners." This was a New York organization designed to work for the removal of the specifically discriminatory $250 property requirement for Negroes to vote in that state. In the aforementioned open letter that Ruggles wrote to Whipper and Purvis, he said "as we are disfranchised, we can assemble as oppressed Americans without disfranchising the human family, or doing violence to that great principle of human liberty."[20]

As Corresponding Secretary for the Reform Board, Ruggles issued a call for an 1841 convention in which he reiterated the words of Lord Byron in asserting the need for specifically oppressed people to hold an exclusive convention:

—Know ye not who would be free,
Themselves must strike the blow![21]

Whipper and Purvis were not the only ones to oppose exclusive action, however. In the 1840s there were black leaders who thought that exclusive Negro organizational activity was more harmful than beneficial. For instance, when most Negroes approved a call for an exclusive New York State Convention in 1841, James McCune Smith, a black New York physician, stated his objection to its exclusiveness in a letter to James G. Birney. Smith said the views of the convention were too narrow and were based upon "*a violation of the same principle* to enforce which it assembled. In other words, it called a 'caste convention' in order to abolish caste."[22] The New York Convention soon ceased excluding whites. The State Central Committee, chaired by Henry H. Garnet, stressed their nonexclusive position in their 1842 convention call. They said, "we invite every town in the state . . . to send delegates WITHOUT RESPECT TO COMPLECTION [*sic*] OR PARTY."[23]

Furthermore, though a Boston group of black spokesmen gave tacit approval of the proposed 1843 national convention, a meeting at New Bedford, Massachusetts under the chairmanship of John Bailey completely objected to the segregated nature of the meeting. It was argued that because the proposed convention "is exclusive in its character, calling only on colored men," it was undesirable. The New Bedford blacks were convinced that measures already being proposed by abolitionists, "if properly encouraged by the colored people, in common with the white people, will ultimately do away with the necessity of calling conventions, either by or for the especial benefit of the colored people."[24]

To build upon their antiexclusivism argument, some blacks thought they should encourage all oppressed to unite regardless of color. This would give them greater numbers as well as keep the convention from assuming a black-against-white appearance.

Such was the argument presented at the Boston meeting which had reluctantly endorsed the 1843 convention proposal. At that meeting, William C. Nell and other Bostonians had suggested that although the convention would "result in much good," it should have more noncomplexional objectives. They considered that such a proposed convention should be one of "the people, and not exclusively for any particular class," for they thought the time had arrived when all distinction except that of "common humanity" should be abolished. That way they could concentrate on uniting their energies in "warfare against oppression and injustice."[25]

Meanwhile, Whipper, Purvis, and J. J. G. Bias were pleading the same case in Pennsylvania. They had effected removal of a clause in the constitution of the Eastern Pennsylvania Anti-Slavery Society that pledged to "elevate people of color." In its place, they inserted a clause that aimed to "abolish all distinctions of CIVIL RIGHTS or religious privileges founded on complexion."[26]

As the 1840s drew to a close, however, there was a general agreement arrived at by almost all Negro leaders. Negroes would try to initiate and direct some activities for themselves whenever they were the party specifically oppressed by statutes and other policies, yet they would not preclude whites from attending or participating. A sign of this new attitude was the title of the call and subsequent minutes of the 1847 convention: *Proceedings of the National Convention of Coloured People and Their Friends*. This pragmatic black position was articulated by Frederick Douglass in his newly established *North Star* in December 1847:

> The man who has *suffered the wrong* is the man to demand redress,—. . . the man STRUCK is the man to CRY OUT —and . . . he who has endured the *cruel pangs of slavery* is the man to *advocate liberty*. It is evident we must be our own representatives and advocates, not exclusively, but peculiarly—not distinct from, but in connection with our

white friends. In the grand struggle for liberty and equality now waging, it is meet, right, and essential that there should arise in our own ranks authors and editors, as well as orators, for it is in these capacities that the most good can be rendered to our cause.[27]

More specific advice for blacks to act "not exclusively but peculiarly" was presented in the 1848 National Convention's "Address to the Colored People of the United States" composed by a committee which included Frederick Douglass of New York, Henry Bibb of Michigan, William H. Day of Ohio, and Abner Francis of New York. They advised:

Attend Anti-Slavery meetings, show that you are interested in the subject, that you hate Slavery, and love those who are laboring for its overthrow. Act with white Abolition Societies wherever you can, and where you cannot, get up Societies among yourselves, but without exclusiveness. It will be a long time before we gain all our rights; and although it may seem to conflict with our views of human brotherhood, we shall for many years be compelled to have institutions of a complexional character, in order to attain the very idea of human brotherhood. We would, however, advise our brethren to occupy membership and stations among white persons, and in white institutions just so fast as our rights are secured to us.[28]

Thus, the 1848 Convention Address was implying an ultimate goal of complete integration, but it saw plenty of opportunity for blacks to act independently in cases where they were forced to segregate. There was no apparent need for deliberately exclusive activities to gain the recognition that Philip Bell had feared would be denied blacks unless they had exclusive organizations. The 1848 Convention Address went on to advise blacks,

Never refuse to act with a white society because it is white, or a black one, because it is black; but act with all men without distinction of color. By so acting, we shall find many opportunities for removing prejudices and establishing the rights of all men.—We say, avail yourselves of *white* institutions, not because they are white, but because they afford a more convenient means of improvement.[29]

Admittedly, the black spokesmen were only hoping they would get the "recognition" as leaders and thinkers to which Bell had referred; but the chief concern of most black leaders at the time was with *action*. Rightly or wrongly, they felt there was little advantage in avoiding organizations just out of fear that blacks would not be fully credited with whatever accomplishment was made. If racial elevation could be effected, then reaching that goal was what they thought most important. This pragmatic approach to organizational activity and affiliation remained predominant among most black leaders throughout their freedom crusade.

INSTITUTIONAL EXCLUSIVISM—CHURCHES

Black membership in predominantly white antislavery societies became a common phenomenon during the thirties as those white societies eliminated their barriers to complete integration. Yet the internal segregation policies of churches remained strong during the period, so Negroes were faced with a choice: either fight within white churches to eliminate their segregation policies or withdraw and form churches of their own. Many blacks had chosen the latter alternative, as indicated by the number of black churches that had provided meeting facilities at the beginning of the movement and by the number of black ministers who gave leadership and direction.

Many white churches of the period had affiliated with slaveholding. Some had supported colonization and had refused to take a stand on slavery. They featured special pews for Negro members and often placed them at a distant location, such as a balcony. George W. Williams described the frustration blacks encountered when trying to gain recognition and assistance from the churches. He said that after courts, companies, and the like had refused to accord the Negro the rights that were his due as a man, he carried his case to the "highest earthly court," the church. The Negro felt sure of sympathy and succor from this source "but alas! the church shrank from the Negro as if he had been a reptile . . . And . . . when it was popular to plead the cause of the slave and demand the rights of the free Negro, the church was the last organization in the country to take a position on the question; and even then, her 'moderation was known to all men.' "[30] Perhaps Williams made too much of a blanket indictment in that some church people such as the Quakers and Unitarians were assisting the slave from the very beginning; yet the policies of many churches during the period were highly discriminatory.

In 1836, Rev. Theodore Wright expressed deep concern that prejudice in churches "drives the colored man away from religion. I have often heard brethren say they would have nothing to do with such a religion. They are driven away, and go into infidelity."[31] Rather than go into "infidelity," of course, many blacks became members of separate exclusively Negro churches, wherever they were available, or raised funds in order to build black churches. For example, J. C. Beman of Connecticut, travelled and helped organize fundraising projects for building black churches where none existed. In a letter to the *Colored American*, Rev. Beman explained a typical problem of internal segregation that he observed in Providence, R.I.: "Why is it that the colored brother must have a separate table in the church as well as in the steamboat?" He explained that the world was looking to the church for an example of humaneness, yet "she colonizes her colored members, and they must wait for the crumbs after the white brethren have partaken, even at the LORD'S TABLE!"[32]

It was exceptionally difficult for the black to be treated as less than an equal member of God's family in the very house of God. In 1839, Jeremiah Asher protested against the "Negro Pew" at a large Baptist Church he attended in Hartford, Connecticut. He told the whites in charge of policy that "if men will disfranchise me from the rest of my Father's children, they shall do it at their own expense, not mine. I cannot prevent it, but . . . I will lift up my voice against it."[33] In this case, exceptional though it was, the church conceded to Asher's demands for eliminating internal segregation. However, even Asher broke away from the white church at Hartford as he became a minister at the Shiloh (Coloured) Baptist Church in Philadelphia.

In the thirties, many blacks focused on organizing separate exclusive Negro churches and on criticizing the white churches for their failure to treat blacks justly and take a stand against slavery. After the murder of white abolitionist Elijah P. Lovejoy in 1837, the editors of the *Colored American* asserted that "the pulpit, also standing aloof from the contest . . . is guilty. Upon it is the blood of the murdered Lovejoy, and before the gathering wrath of a just God it will stand condemned as recreant to its trust."[34]

Rather than make a blanket indictment of all churches for a lack of involvement in the problem, blacks often qualified their criticisms with such remarks as, "With few noble and splendid exceptions, the Pulpit. . . ."[35]

Just after he escaped from slavery, Frederick Douglass also delivered some stinging indictments about prejudicial treatment he received in some Massachusetts churches. In a speech at a meeting of the Plymouth Church Anti-Slavery Society in 1841, Douglass described the treatment he had been given at a Methodist Church in which all the white persons had partaken of communion first. The minister "Took a long breath, and looking out toward the door exclaimed 'Come up, colored friends, come up! for you know God is no respecter of persons!'' Douglass assured his listeners "I haven't been there to see the sacraments since.''[36]

The key issue concerning exclusivism in churches was whether there was a greater advantage to disassociating from white churches and forming black ones or remaining with white churches and trying to reform them internally. A significant debate took place at the 1843 National Negro Convention over a resolution that "the great mass of American sects, falsely called churches, which apologize for slavery and prejudice, or practice slaveholding, are in truth no churches, but Synagogues of Satan.''[37] This resolution passed.

Among those supporting the resolution were Frederick Douglass and Charles Lenox Remond, then both of Massachusetts. The chief opposition spokesman was Theodore S. Wright of New York. Those supporting the resolution argued that the existing churches in this country were corrupt. In their opinion, "the passage of anti-slavery resolutions, as indicated on the face of them, was no evidence of their not being pro-slavery, while they keep what is called the negro pew, and make a distinction at the communion table on the ground of color; this with them was slavery in another form, its very spirit.'' They further claimed of white churches that in their judgment, there was "no hope of reforming them, they were so wedded to public opinion, so popularity-seeking, that they were past reforming.''[38] Thus the black man could not be consistent with his principles if he remained in fellowship with members of the white churches. The majority of delegates further passed a resolution stating that it was "the bounden duty of every person to come out from among those religious organizations in which they are not permitted to enjoy equality.''

The negative case was briefly summarized in the convention's minutes. Wright and others thought internal reform was possible if black members stayed in white churches and felt this was a positive move toward integration and greater racial understanding:

The brethren on the other side of the question took the old ground that if they withdrew church fellowship, they would cut off all the influence they had with which to reform. Some of them did little more than define their position as members of churches in affiliation with the great ecclesiastical bodies; they referred to acts of these bodies, to show an improvement in anti-slavery action, and which to them was great ground of hope; they thought, should they withdraw from them, they would have withdrawn from a body which soon would be as much anti-slavery as could be desired, and that they felt called upon to remain and help bring about that end. This was the ground taken, especially by Mr. Wright of New York.[39]

More intraracial argument was to take place about the role of blacks in churches, but these were the basic positions assumed during much of the forties. This period witnessed a firming of lines between separate black and white churches. Many Negro leaders harshly criticized the ''proslavery'' sects and warned black members of such churches to withdraw or the ''blood of perishing millions will be upon their heads.''[40]

The 1847 National Negro Convention passed a resolution opposing internally segregated white churches in almost the same words they had used in 1843. They said ''that those sects (falsely called Christian Churches) who tolerate caste, and practice Slave holding, are nothing more than Synagogues of Satan.''[41] In this period near the end of the decade, however, there was a greater change in opinion concerning the encouragement of exclusive churches.

Frederick Douglass was going through judgment changes on several subjects during the late forties; notably, he changed his opinion concerning the wisdom of separate churches. Douglass still thought that the motive the Negro church founders had in separating from white churches was ''in every respect commendable.'' Yet the establishment of those exclusive institutions was, he now thought, "unwise" and "injudicious." In March 1848, Douglass expressed concern over the situation:

> We raise this question, (and are prepared to discuss it with Dr. [James McCune] Smith, Alexander Crummell, or any other advocate of separate religious organizations,) to wit: Are churches especially assigned to the use of colored persons in this country, consistent with the true idea of human brotherhood, the spirit and precepts of Christian religion, and the best means of improving the moral and religious condition of the colored people? We recommend this question to the consideration of debating societies, as well as to our entire fellow countrymen.[42]

The arguments against separate churches were mounting. One of the most worrisome had to do with the precedent that establishing separate churches would set for the establishment of exclusive institutions of other kinds, especially schools. Would it not appear that if separate churches were necessary and appropriate then separate schools would also be mandatory? In the *North Star*, Douglass contended that "if there be any good reason for a colored church, the same will be held good in regard to a colored school, and indeed to every other institution founded on complexion." Of course, the black advocates for separate schools, who will be discussed in the next section, would not find the "precedent" argument such a problem, but to Douglass, "one of the greatest evils resulting from separate religious organizations for the exclusive use of colored persons, is the countenance and support which they give to exclusive colored schools."[43]

Another argument against separate churches was that the number of qualified black ministers at that time was smaller than the trend demanded. Douglass proceeded, "Another reason against colored churches originates in the character and qualifications of the men almost universally employed as their teachers and pastors. With a few exceptions, colored ministers have not the mental qualifications to instruct and improve their congregations."[44] Thus it was argued, even if separate institutions were justifiable, the manpower problem made them impracticable.

Finally, there was a problem in the cost of maintaining them. Douglass balked at the "expensiveness" and said that "colored people are scattered over the country in small numbers, and are generally poor." As an alternative to building separate churches, Douglass suggested that Negroes should go to white churches on the very next sabbath and "take seats, without regard to their complexion, and allow themselves to be dragged out by the ministers, elders, and deacons. Such a course would very soon settle the question, and in the right way."[45]

At this point, those black ministers defending separate churches added to their old list of arguments one on the basis of practical business. Leonard Collins, a black from Springfield, Massachusetts, stated the problem in the form of a comparison between churches and Douglass' publishing agency, the North Star Office: "Shall we have Mr. Douglass set the first example, by dismissing his colored coadjutors in his printing establishment, and knocking loudly at the door of the 'white' printer, demanding to be admitted 'equal' editorship?"[46]

It is questionable whether one can make as valid an analogy between a church with a business as easily as between a church and a school as was done earlier, but Collins' argument implies that his investment of time and effort in his black church was not to be relinquished easily. In addition, Collins objected to the idea of joining "corrupt" white churches. Although the 1848 National Negro Convention passed a resolution stating that internally segregated and proslavery churches merited their "severest reprobation," the delegates did not pass any resolutions demanding that blacks withdraw from them.

By the 1850s, there were changes taking place in the abolition movement and in the white churches themselves that demanded

less severe denunciation of the pulpit. Generally, the black arguments for separate black churches were not extensive in the fifties.
The schism between the Northern and Southern branches of the
churches during the latter half of the 1840s was making a different
kind of institution of the former. Northern churches showed what
blacks were willing to regard as more positive signs of antislavery
involvement. For instance, instead of ignoring the slavery question, there were more denunciations of the Southern institution by
Northern white ministers. The abolition newspapers of the time,
for instance, made special note of the efforts of the clergy in
submitting antislavery petitions to Congress. In protest against the
Fugitive Slave Law, there was a petition sent to Congress that
contained the names of over one hundred Methodist clergymen.
Likewise, when the Kansas-Nebraska Bill was passed, there were
petitions sent by clergymen of all faiths. One petition in New
England contained the names of well over a hundred clergymen
with the names of their churches. The same was true elsewhere, as
exemplified by a petition from New York containing 151 names of
ministers from the Episcopal, Presbyterian, Reformed Dutch,
Congregationalist, Baptist, Methodist, Lutheran, and Unitarian
Churches.[47]

With all the potential and existing antislavery support from the
churches, there appeared to be justification for the Negroes to
soften their attacks on white churches. As Foner put it: "the
schism between northern and southern churches showed clearly
that the former were not as reprobate as the Garrisonians had
charged. New tactics consequently had to be devised to gain
support of these churches. But the Garrisonians continued to battle
the churches as if nothing had happened, alienating many people
who should have been allies."[48]

Many Negroes in a tone more moderate than Garrison's, refrained from making blanket denunciations. The majority viewpoint of blacks was expressed in the National Convention Address
of 1853. They expected only fair treatment from the clergy.

Instead of attacking white churches, the "Address" aimed at encouraging the good ones to disassociate themselves from the less considerate. To accomplish the goals of the blacks, the Address said, "We shall invoke the aid of the pulpit and press to gain them. We shall appeal to the church and to the government to gain them."[49]

For the remainder of the crusade there were still *some* scathing attacks on churches, but the new approach was one of emphasizing the good exceptions among churches in terms of their treatment of blacks. Thus there was less advice for blacks to form exclusive churches.

INSTITUTIONAL EXCLUSIVISM—SCHOOLS

For a number of reasons, the black spokesmen did not have great occasion in the 1830s to debate the merits of exclusive schools for their people. In fact, they fully devoted their time to providing whatever educational opportunities they could for blacks. This was often done through literary societies rather than the more formal educational institutions, and they were inevitably designed for the people who needed them—the blacks. An outstanding example of the effort by blacks to provide an education for their youth, regardless of the school's being for blacks only, was the attempt by three white abolitionists to erect a "manual labor" college for Negroes in New Haven, Connecticut. Rev. S.S. Jocelyn of New Haven, Arthur Tappen of New York, and William Lloyd Garrison of Boston spoke at the 1831 National Negro Convention, on the subject of building such a school. Rev. Samuel E. Cornish was elected General Agent to raise funds and assist with the planning of it. The delegates were delighted at the prospects of a "College for the Instruction of Young Men of Colour."[50]

However, the specific plan for founding a manual labor college in New Haven was soon stifled by the mayor, alderman, and

common council of that city. Those "city fathers" felt that the
founding of colleges for educating colored people was "unwar-
rantable and dangerous." The effort by blacks continued, though,
as the delegates at the 1832 convention found the proceedings of
the New Haven citizens to be a "disgrace" that would "cast a
stigma on the reputed fame of New England and the country."
They also continued to insist on the development of "Colleges and
high schools on the Manual Labor System. . . . If we ever expect to
see the influence of prejudice decrease, and ourselves respected, it
must be by the blessings of an enlightened education."[51]

The following years of the thirties brought even more widespread philanthropic efforts from whites in the establishment of
exclusive schools for blacks, especially on the manual labor system. One was founded in New York and another in Pennsylvania,
where the deceased Richard Humphrey had willed $10,000 for that
purpose; more were founded in the northeastern states, where the
New England Anti-Slavery Society opened subscriptions for construction of them in that area.[52]

Other philanthropically endowed schools built for the especial
benefit of black students met with considerable consternation from
the local white citizenry. For instance, Noyes Academy of Canaan, New Hampshire, at which Henry Highland Garnet, Alexander Crummell, and Thomas S. Sidney had been students, was
dragged to a swamp by some one-hundred oxen amid the approv-
ing yells of 300 local citizens. Prudence Crandall established a
school for "Negro girls only" at Canterbury, Connecticut in April
of 1833 and was thereafter subjected to multiple abuses, including
having all the windows broken and the building set afire. Although
she was convicted of "harboring, boarding, and instructing colored persons who were not inhabitants of Connecticut," the case
against Crandall was eventually set aside on technical grounds by a
higher court. Because of harrassment and intimidation, however,
Crandall closed her school down.[53]

In light of the violence and public attitudes, there was a general understanding in the 1830s that if blacks received an education, it would be in separate schools from whites. Even the AMRS emphasized establishing a "Manual Labor School," and although they said it would be for "instruction of youth," there was no reason to believe that such a school would not be virtually all-Negro.

The controversy among blacks over exclusivism in schools began in the forties. The 1847 convention had a Committee on Education, chaired by Alexander Crummell, which reported the need to establish a college for "colored young men." After some debate, the committee's report was adopted in a close vote. The debate preceding the vote contained the main issues on exclusivism as they applied to Negroes at all academic levels. Those favoring the exclusive school included Alexander Crummell and James McCune Smith, and those opposing it included William C. Nell, Henry H. Garnet, and Frederick Douglass.

Alexander Crummell argued that black students needed the opportunity of admission to a higher educational institution and that the proposed college would afford that opportunity. Crummell also argued that the exclusive college was needed so black students would not get depressed or discouraged as they well might in schools with whites. Crummell argued that a "colored youth under care of colored teachers, associating with those of his own complexion and condition, would not feel depressed as [he is] likely to be in other institutions, surrounded by those whom he always regarded as opposed to his equality." Therefore, he thought a Negro college was most favorable to the black student's "mental growth." Furthermore, Crummell's committee had fear of "colored children sinking under the prejudice of white institutions."[54]

Some delegate support for the report may have arisen more out of respect for the committee members involved than out of other considerations. The person reporting the Convention proceedings for the *North Star* wrote:

The Committee on Education reported, by Alexander Crummell, the expediency of the establishment of a college for colored young men. In this report was embodied a fund of argument illustrated with all that beauty of diction for which its talented author has long enjoyed a distinguished reputation. It was ably supported by James McCune Smith, who brought in aid of his extensive learning and tact in statistical expression. Their views were concurred in by a large party in the delegation, but especially by the New York delegation.[55]

Despite the strong case for the college, the convention's decision to build it was never carried out. On the negative side were the arguments that the Negro College was neither needed nor practicable. In submitting that Negro colleges were not needed, Henry Garnet just stated that he was "in favor of Colored Academies, but did not see the necessity of Colored Colleges, because there were those to which colored youth could be admitted."[56]

A more extensive opposing argument was designed to counter the contention that Negro youth had a psychological need for separate schools. William C. Nell, a black leader from Boston, argued that Negro youth should be challenged by study in white schools. Furthermore, their participation in white schools would help gain respect and elevation for the race. Nell said that:

the colored youth should be stimulated to establish such a character, in those seats of learning, by his energy in study, and deportment towards teachers and pupils as to disarm opposition, show himself an equal, and, despite of cold looks and repulsive treatment hew out a path to eminence and respect, and, like the gem which shines brighter by attrition, become himself among good scholars the very best.[57]

Finally, Nell referred to the attempt many years earlier to establish a colored college that failed because the measure was then considered extravagant and "uncalled for." He considered it "too late in the day for colored people themselves to found any exclusive institutions; there are, now, colleges and academies where they can be admitted on equal terms with white students."[58]

Since Nell was from Massachusetts and under the strong influence of William Lloyd Garrison, he may have perceived of integrated schools as a greater possibility than did blacks in other parts of the country. He preferred to have black youths struggle with the challenge of integrated schools rather than separate from them. Two years later, a committee representing the Colored Citizens of Boston, chaired by John T. Hilton, drafted a statement opposing Boston's Smith School-house, which operated for black students only. The committee wrote that "as citizens, we ask *our rights* in the promises. It is our desire that this 'exclusive school' be abolished and *free access* to schools for the education of the young, be the privilege of *all*."[59] At a follow-up meeting of the Colored Citizens of Boston, William C. Nell headed the committee drafting resolutions, one of which resolved that "we again renew our pledge to each other never to countenance for one moment an exclusive school, and that although we have often so decided, we are not weary in our efforts in so just a cause."[60] With this dedication, the Boston Negro spokesmen carried their battle against segregation into the 1850s.

There was a desire by many black leaders during the last decade of the movement to achieve integration of public schools, yet they willingly requested adequate construction and maintenance of segregated public schools rather than have "no schools at all." In New York, for instance, the Negroes had a Society for the Promotion of Education Among Colored Children. When Charles B. Ray was elected President of the organization, his appeals to the New York Board of Education were for integration of public schools, but he recommended adequate segregated schools in case "in the judgment of your honorable body common schools are not thus common to all."[61]

The Pennsylvania Negroes continued to make efforts on their own to improve schooling facilities for their race and were eventually given public support for segregated schools. Massachusetts had started integrating long before the 1850s, but Boston, Nell's home, did not succeed in desegregating until 1855. In the Midwest, public educational opportunities for blacks were nearly nonexistent, as legislators in those states wanted to discourage black immigration in every way possible.

While much work concerning schooling was done at the local level, the National Negro Conventions of the 1850s argued the issues of exclusivism, particularly as they applied to industrial education or manual labor schools for blacks. At the 1853 Convention, a Committee on Manual Labor School consisting of Charles L. Reason (New York), George B. Vashon (Pennsylvania), and Charles H. Langston (Ohio) submitted a report recommending a manual labor school. A case for the establishment of a black manual labor school was also given at the convention in a letter which was included in the Convention Minutes. The letter was from Frederick Douglass to Harriet Beecher Stowe; Mrs. Stowe had asked Douglass what he thought would elevate the Negroes most, and he responded with a proposal for a manual labor school. The controversy over manual labor schools and/or industrial schools continued in the movement, and this intraracial conflict brought out the basic black exclusivism issues as they applied to schools.

The nearly unanimous position of Negroes in this final phase of the movement was that black children should go to integrated schools if possible but exclusive ones if necessary because of social attitudes or specific needs that blacks had. They felt black children should have the best training possible whether it best be found in a white school or one adapted to their specific needs.

One argument for the manual labor school was that such training for blacks was a necessary transition between their degraded condition and the status to which whites had advanced because of their superior opportunities. Frederick Douglass included that argument in his letter to Harriet Beecher Stowe, saying:

> Accustomed as we have been, to the rougher and harder modes of living, and of gaining a livelihood, we cannot, and we ought not hope that, in a single leap from our low condition, we can reach that of *Ministers, Lawyers, Doctors, Editors, Merchants*, etc. This will, doubtless be attained by us; but this will only be, when we have patiently and laboriously, and I may add successfully, mastered and passed through the intermediate gradations of agriculture and the mechanic arts.[62]

The same argument was given at the 1853 convention in the Report of the Committee on Social Relations and Polity, composed of William J. Wilson, William Whipper, and Charles B. Ray. While calling for integrated public schools in their own respective localities, Whipper and Ray recognized the unique needs of black youth and apparently placed that uniqueness above the desire for integration. The Report said:

> Colored youth is to be educated so as to catch up in the great race he is running; hence schools must be adapted so as to train him; not that he himself is so widely different from the white youth, but different. The training, therefore, necessary to propel him, so that he can gain up with the whites . . . is to be obtained only in schools adapted to his wants. . . .
>
> We are more than persuaded . . . that . . . it should be our special aim to direct . . . the whole process of education to meet entirely our particular exigencies, continuing so long, only, as such exigencies exist.[63]

At both the 1853 and 1855 conventions, it was evident that a strong majority of delegates placed greater value on meeting the special educational needs of Negro children than on integrating for the sake of integrating. The special needs for a manual labor college were particularly compounded in that local businesses and shops would not admit black apprentices. The 1853 convention's Committee on Manual Labor School explained:

> We know that we cannot form an equal useful part of any people without the ability to contribute our full share to the wealth, activity, social comforts, and progress of such people. If, then, the necessary education to fit us to share in these responsibilities, cannot be generally had, by reason of the prejudices of the country, where best they can be taught, namely in the work-shops and the counting-houses and other varied establishments of the land . . . we must need to consider the importance of making our Literary Institutions contribute by a change of form to filling up the want in our midst. [64]

If the "Literary Institutions" adapted their curricula or if private enterprises admitted Negro apprentices, a manual labor school would no longer be necessary. However, under the circumstances blacks had no alternative.

Pure integration was excellent in theory or principle, but the facts of American life made exclusive schools more realistic in meeting blacks' needs. In his letter to Mrs. Stowe, Frederick Douglass explained that his arguments during the preceding dozen years had depended too much on admitted principles rather than a "presentation of facts." He argued that "now, firmly believing as I do, that there are skill, invention, power, industry, and real mechanical genius among the colored people . . . which only need the means to develop them, I am decidedly in favor of . . . such a college." [65]

At the 1855 convention, the special needs of blacks were pleaded for in the proposal of numerous local "Industrial Associations," since a manual training college might preclude opportunities for youth because of its cost and distance from many black youths. The proponent of the Industrial Associations was James McCune Smith, and he recommended that localities set up Industrial Associations to work with local businesses and philanthropists in "pursuit of Mechanical or Artistic employment," each with its own autonomous rules and regulations.[66] The associations were to be open to youth of all complexions, but it was probably assumed that they would be frequented almost completely by Negroes.

During the 1850s there were still some blacks opposed to manual labor schools or industrial associations. Opponents were led by Robert Purvis of Pennsylvania. On the basis of practicality, Purvis argued that there was not enough money for blacks to provide the variety of equipment and training or to make it close enough to black students' homes to fill their needs. Besides, Purvis objected in particular to the manual labor school because of its exclusiveness:

We have institutions of learning of the first stamp open to us, where the rising generation can draw from the fountains of knowledge side by side with the most favored of the land, and at the same time by their contact and influence help materially to do away with that deep-rooted prejudice of which we so bitterly complain. The Industrial School being necessarily (if not in theory, yet in fact) a complexional institution, must foster distinctions, and help draw more definitely (so far as educational privileges are involved) those lines of demarkation [sic] under which we have labored and still are endeavoring to eradicate.[67]

In opposition to Purvis, the majority of blacks conceded that lines of distinction needed to be erased in schools, but were willing to keep those lines drawn just as long as necessary to meet the special educational needs of their people. As was the case with other subjects, they chose a pragmatic route and integrated wherever possible just as soon as it was advantageous in terms of educational needs. At the final stages of the movement, their specific educational needs were of greater importance than the "temporary" problems of exclusivism in schools.

During the crusade, several priorities and values of the blacks were brought out as they confronted issues of exclusivism and nonexclusivism. Most blacks preferred integrating into America's economic, civil, and to some extent, social system whenever possible. Yet there were some considerations that took precedence over integration. In organizations such as antislavery societies, blacks wanted to integrate, yet they felt obligated to organize as a race and initiate and run some activities. Thus, although blacks began their movement with mostly exclusively black organizations, they finally developed a tacit policy of initiating and conducting some organizational activities—"not exclusively, but peculiarly."

Blacks began their movement having exclusive churches for many of their people. This was mainly because blacks strongly objected to the internal segregation policies such as "Negro pews" in many predominantly white churches. Some black spokesmen began to doubt the wisdom of separate churches as the movement progressed, especially because they implied that blacks recognized and encouraged the rightfulness of segregated institutions in general.

Black attitudes toward exclusivism in schools also showed a general change during the movement. While at first a main consideration appeared to be integration of schools whenever possible, that philosophy was soon replaced by a new one—one of meeting the specific educational needs of black people first and secondarily considering how or where schools should be integrated.

Generally, while it remained important for most blacks to work for integration during the period, they became more willing to subordinate questions of exclusivism and nonexclusivism to the objective of meeting their own specific needs as a people.

NOTES

[1]*Constitution of the American Society of Free Persons of Colour*, p. 5.

[2]*Fourth Annual Convention for the Improvement of the Free People of Colour, New York, 1834*, p. 4.

[3]*Fifth Annual Convention of the Free People of Colour, Philadelphia, 1835*, p. 14-15.

[4]Ibid., p. 26-7.

[5]*First Annual Meeting of the American Moral Reform Society*, p. 13. A review of details concerning the organization's activities is in Bell, "A Survey of the Negro Convention Movement: 1830-1861," p. 44-60.

[6]*Colored American*, August 26, 1837, p. 2.

[7]*National Anti-Slavery Standard*, October 1, 1840, p. 66.

[8]*Colored American*, March 3, 1838, p. 26.

[9]Ibid., July 7, 1838, p. 78.

[10]Ibid., November 11, 1837, p. 2.

[11]Ibid., March 15, 1838, p. 31.

[12]Ibid., p. 31. Other comments for the proud employment of the term "Colored" are in *Colored American*, August 26, September 2, and September 9, 1837.

[13]Henry Highland Garnet, *The Past and Present Condition of the Colored Race: A Discourse Delivered at the Fifteenth Anniversary of the Female Benevolent Society of Troy, New York, February 14, 1848* (Troy, N.Y.: Steam Press of J. C. Kneeland and Co., 1848), p. 19.

[14]*National Emigration Convention of Colored People, Cleveland, 1854*, p. 27.

[15]*National Anti-Slavery Standard*, June 18, 1840, p. 6.

[16]*Liberator*, June 19, 1840, p. 98.

[17]Ibid., p. 98.

[18]*National Anti-Slavery Standard*, August 10, 1843, p. 38.

[19]Ibid., July 16, 1840, p. 23.

[20]Ibid., October 1, 1840, p. 66.

[21]*Liberator*, August 13, 1841, p. 1. Also in Carter G. Woodson (ed.), *The Mind of the Negro as Reflected in Letters Written During the Crisis* (Washington, D.C.: The Association for the Study of Negro Life and History, Inc., 1926), p. 25.

[22]"James McCune Smith to Birney, New York, New York, February 8, 1841," *Birney Letters*, II, p. 624.

[23]*Emancipator and Free American*, July 7, 1842, p. 40.

[24]*National Anti-Slavery Standard*, September 7, 1843, p. 1.

[25]Ibid., August 10, 1843, p. 38.

[26]Ibid., August 21, 1845, p. 46.

[27]*North Star*, December 3, 1847, p. 2.

[28]*National Colored Convention, Cleveland, 1848*, p. 19.

[29]Ibid., p. 19.

[30]George W. Williams, *History of the Negro Race in America*, II (New York: G. P. Putnam's Sons, 1883), p. 132.

[31]*Liberator*, July 2, 1836, p. 108.

[32]*Colored American*, September 23, 1837, p. 2.

[33]"Fighting the Negro Pew, 1839," in Herbert Aptheker (ed.), *A Documentary History of the Negro People in the United States* (New York: The Citadel Press, 1951), p. 191.

[34]*Colored American*, November 18, 1837, p. 4.

[35]Aptheker (ed.), *Documentary History*, p. 175.

[36]*National Anti-Slavery Standard*, December 23, 1841, p. 114.

[37]*National Convention of Colored Citizens, Buffalo, 1843*, p. 15.

[38]Ibid., p. 11.

[39]Ibid., p. 11.

[40]*North Star*, December 3, 1847, p. 1.

[41]*National Convention of Colored People and Their Friends, Troy, 1847*, p. 16.

[42]*North Star*, March 3, 1848, p. 2.

[43]Ibid., March 10, 1848, p. 2.

[44]Ibid., p. 2.

[45]Ibid., p. 2.

[46]Ibid., March 24, 1848, p. 2.

[47]*Liberator*, May 30, 1851, p. 1, and *National Anti-Slavery Standard*, March 18, 1854, p. 170.

[48]Foner, *Frederick Douglass*, p. 149.

[49]*Colored National Convention, Rochester, 1853*, p. 10.

[50]*First Annual Convention of the People of Colour, Philadelphia, 1831*, p. 14.

[51]*Second Annual Convention for the Improvement of the Free People of Colour, Philadelphia, 1832*, p. 34.

[52]*Third Annual Convention for the Improvement of the Free People of Colour, Philadelphia, 1833*, p. 34.

[53]A book on the Prudence Crandall case, presenting its issues and significance for the antislavery crusade, is: Edmund Fuller, *Prudence Crandall: An Incident of Racism in Nineteenth-Century Connecticut* (Middletown, Conn.: Wesleyan University Press, 1971).

[54]*North Star*, December 3, 1841, p. 1.

[55]Ibid., p. 1.

[56]*National Convention of Colored People and Their Friends, Troy, 1847*, p. 9.

[57]*North Star*, December 3, 1847, p. 1.

[58]Ibid., p. 1.

[59]*Liberator*, August 10, 1849, p. 127.

[60]Ibid., September 7, 1849, p. 143.

[61]*Anglo-African Magazine*, I, July, 1859, p. 223.

[62]*Colored National Convention, Rochester, 1853*, p. 34.

[63]Ibid., p. 22-3.

[64]Ibid., p. 31.

[65]Ibid., p. 38.

[66]*Colored National Convention, Philadelphia, 1855*, p. 26.

[67]Ibid., p. 11.

Charles Lenox Remond—Moral Suasionist

6

Antislavery Labors

Many efforts by free blacks to elevate themselves during antebellum times were in effect antislavery. In his autobiography, Samuel R. Ward defined antislavery labor as "the refutation of all miserable nonsense and heresy," for he regarded slavery as both. The refutation was performed by more than lecturing, holding antislavery conventions, distributing antislavery tracts, maintaining antislavery societies, editing antislavery journals, or "making a trade of these, for certain especial pets and favourites to profit by and live in luxury." In conjunction with these labors, which are "right and necessary when properly pursued," antislavery labors involved the "cultivation of all the upward tendencies of the coloured man."[1] The hardworking black in any business or profession was, to Ward, an antislavery laborer. Blacks in the antislavery movement were models on display and they sometimes served to remind white co-workers that antislavery involved more than a unidirectional attack against the institution in the South.

CIVIL EQUALITY IN ABOLITION RANKS

Since prejudice against blacks existed in much of Northern white society, an issue arose over the extent of equality to be demanded by abolitionists for blacks; should they plead for civil equality, social equality, or both? During the early part of the 1830s, white abolitionists varied somewhat in their attitudes concerning the best appeal to make. The American Anti-Salvery Society had pledged "to elevate the free people of color by intellectual and moral improvement." However, the meaning behind that "elevation" was not specific. The white abolitionist, James G. Birney of New York, wrote a letter to Theodore Dwight Weld of Ohio concerning the problem. He thought the white abolition demands would be misunderstood as favoring a "forced or factitious elevation" that would do much harm to the cause. About the subject of social equality, Birney asked, "May not urging it now be throwing too much in our way the prejudice against it, and defeat the elevation of the colored people to *civil* privileges?"[2] There was caution among some abolitionists in New York about trying to mix the races indiscriminately. Some refrained from demonstrating any visible signs of social equality in public situations. In Ohio, Theodore Weld explained the feeling that he possessed during these early years of the movement. He responded to a white abolitionist, Lewis Tappen of New York, regarding whether or not he would walk "arm in arm with a colored lady at mid-day down the main street in Cincinnati": "Answer *No*. Why?! Because to do it would bring down a storm of vengeance upon the defenceless people of Color, throw them out of employ, drive them out homeless, and surrender them up victims to popular fury."[3]

By 1836 the American Anti-Slavery Society completely renounced the reluctance of abolitionists to associate with blacks on a socially open and equal basis in public. The Society avowed that if color or public opinion alone explained the abolitionist's reluctance, then "he wrongs the cause in which he is engaged."[4]

Even though Negroes were active in antislavery organizations during these early years of the abolition movement, there is no indication that they advocated the objective of social equality for Negroes. Their rhetoric reveals that they were not unaware of the ire they might arouse by stressing complete social equality. Negro convention activities were directed to their "speedy elevation" as men. Blacks apparently thought their social rights would be slow in coming and therefore emphasized reaching the "summit of civil and religious improvement." In reminiscing about the 1830s, the composers of the "Address" at the 1848 National Negro Convention explained that many blacks of the earlier time had worried that white abolitionists were hurting the cause by demanding too much. The "Address" said that ten or twelve years ago:

> many of us uttered complaints against the faithful abolitionists, for the broad assertion of our rights; thought they went too far, and were only making our condition worse. This sentiment has nearly ceased to reign in the dark abodes of our hearts; we begin to see our wrongs as clearly, and comprehend our rights as fully, and as well as our white countrymen.[5]

In light of the social context when the Society was founded in 1833, the 1855 accusation of James McCune Smith, black abolitionist from New York, does not seem fully justified. He said in a letter to Gerrit Smith, the white political abolitionist of New York, that, "It is a strange omission in the Constitution of the American Anti-Slavery Society that no mention is made of social equality, of either the slave or Free Blacks, as the aim of that Society."[6] While some blacks were even cautious about asserting what they meant by "elevation," which they were working for during the early thirties, Samuel Cornish made it definite in 1838 that civil equality was the minimal goal: "When we speak of elevation, we mean a perfect equality with the whites, in moral and mental character—in rights and immunities—in usefulness and in honors. Nothing short of this will meet our approbation, or bound our ambitions. Anything short of it is ungodlike and ignoble."[7]

ATTACKING PREJUDICE

During the latter half of the 1830s, when the blacks began using words to point up their hard work, black spokesmen used racially mixed antislavery societies as forums at which to give speeches against the refusal of whites to grant civil rights. Black speakers demanded equal civil privileges and job opportunities for free blacks. It emphasized the inconsistency of opposing slavery in the South when so few opportunities were afforded blacks in the North. Black advocates fulfilled the responsibility of (1) reminding white abolitionists that the problem of prejudice existed in their own ranks in the North, (2) arguing that this prejudice was nullifying any antislavery attitudes that the societies wanted to create, and (3) contending that antislavery societies were not doing their share to fight prejudice. In conjunction with this, they proposed policies to be pursued by white abolitionists in fighting Northern prejudice against Negroes.

First, the blacks had to draw the attention of whites to the problem, and the white antislavery societies were the reasonable source for getting friendly white sympathizers to help with the problem. The Negro's concern with the problem of prejudice is indicated in a speech presented by Theodore S. Wright at a meeting of the New England Anti-Slavery Society in 1836:

Why, sir, prejudice is slavery. No man can really understand this prejudice unless he feels it crushing him to the dust because it is a matter of feeling. It has bolts, scourges and bars, wherever the colored man goes. It has bolts in all the schools and colleges. The colored parent, with the same soul as a white parent, sends his child to the seats of learning, and he finds the door bolted, and he sits to weep beside his boy. . . . Does the child of a colored man show a talent for mechanics? The heart of the parent beats with hope. He sees the children of a white man engaged in employment, and he trusts that here is a door open to his boy, to get an honest living and become a useful member of society. But, when he comes to the workshop with his child, he finds other bars. He can't work. Let him be ever so skilled as a mechanic, up starts prejudice, and says, "I won't work in a shop if you do."

. . . But, it is asked, "What do you colored people want us to do?" We do not ask you to break any of the rules of society. Treat us just according to our moral worth and nothing more.

. . . Try us fairly and see if the colored race cannot improve and elevate themselves in the scale of moral being.[8]

A reporter who saw the speech said, "a profound silence and attention commenced with his speaking, and continued to the close. Some of the time the eyes of the whole audience were suffused with tears; and the effect was evidently great. The speech must have been effectual in removing the prevailing prejudices as to the capacity of the colored people."[9] The report points up another aspect of black protest speaking of the times—the speakers demonstrated the intellectual ability of blacks through their presentations to white audiences.

On a more local level, Charles Lenox Remond, who was regarded by many as the foremost black abolition orator in America before Frederick Douglass, also made use of the antislavery society to remind whites that prejudice in the North was a major problem in the overall racial struggle. To the Rhode Island Anti-Slavery Society, he said: "To every individual present, the fact must be familiar that no situation in counting rooms, . . . the mechanic arts, or any other employment at all lucrative in its prospects or results, is accessible by the young man of color, be his qualifications, merits, or circumstances what they may."[10]

The argument even more directly appropriate to antislavery societies was that antislavery attacks on the South were futile as long as prejudice denied the black man's rights in the North. In 1838, James McCune Smith, a black delegate to an American

Anti-Slavery Society convention, stressed the need for granting opportunities to northern Negroes. Being more conservative than in his later criticism about the Society not stressing social equality from its beginning, Smith said, "Let us begin at home. Let us purify our own soil, and then we call upon the South to follow the example." He submitted that the North could not fight slavery in the South while slavery still existed in the North, "for semi-emancipation is slavery still." In his opinion, the most telling argument for abolition of slavery would be "the sight of free colored men, elevated in these northern white communities to the dignities and privileges of citizens of the republic."[11]

A breach between moral suasionists and political abolitionists did not halt the effort by black spokesmen to urge white colleagues that the fight against race prejudice must supplement attacks on slavery. In the latter part of 1838, Samuel Cornish, editor of the *Colored American*, appealed to all white abolitionists to fight prejudice as an integral part of the antislavery crusade. He was anxious that abolitionists, "whether of the old school or the new, should turn their attention and devote their means, to the most practical measures of colored men." He asked white abolitionists to give advice and money to the cause of encouraging husbandry, manufactures, and mechanics among Negroes. Like Smith, Cornish warned antislavery advocates that "in vain will be their efforts . . . if these things are neglected."[12] In the same vein, Theodore Wright was saying that "prejudice must be killed or slavery will never be abolished."[13]

As a policy to start antislavery societies toward more positive steps in meeting prejudicial barriers to black elevation, Rev. J. C. Beman submitted and secured passage of a resolution that recommended to the American Anti-Slavery Society that the antislavery society of every town secure the appointment of committees to "investigate the moral and civil condition of the colored people in their vicinity, and to encourage their improvement in those respects, to improve any embarrassment under which they labor."[14]

Antislavery societies were soon to hire black agents and lecturers to travel from town to town in order to help reduce prejudice while speaking out against slavery. A sign that fighting prejudice in the North was becoming recognized as a vital part of abolition's persuasive strategy, with which blacks were needed, was a letter from Theodore Weld to Gerrit Smith in October 1839, saying:

> The attention of abolitionists should be turned far more to the great importance of getting into the lecturing field intelligent colored men. T. S. Wright, J. McCune Smith, Whipper, Gardner, Payne, Raymond, and twenty others ought to be put out as lecturers. Surely twenty five colored men of such talents, character, and address, as would render them mighty in good doing, might be found and got into the field. They would do more in three months to kill prejudice (and our cause moves only as fast as that dies) than all the operations up to now. Besides, a colored man who is eloquent will in all parts of the North draw larger audiences than if white, in most places far larger . . . W. G. Allen has gone on to you . . .—suppose he is now at Oneida . . . Young Crummel who was bastioned out of the Episcopal Orders the other day is about leaving the country to get under a monarchy what the despotism of a republic denies him.[15]

BLACK ANTISLAVERY LECTURERS

Long before Theodore Weld began his search for black abolitionist lecturers, there were numerous blacks speaking against the peculiar institution at various antislavery society meetings throughout the country. Their very presence served to reduce prejudices of white observers and instill doubts and hostilities toward holding blacks in bondage. While both blacks and whites could philosophize and theorize about Negro equality, only blacks could demonstrate it in the flesh. From the founding of antislavery societies, many blacks served as agents and officers wherever possible, in addition to assuming their regular duties as business-men, ministers, doctors, and in other jobs ranging to the most menial positions available.

In *The Negro Vanguard*, Richard Bardolph discusses some thirty-nine black leaders of the period from 1831 through 1865. Of these, he notes some thirty who are "remembered chiefly for contributions to the Negro protest and race-advance effort."[16] The influx of black speakers was so great that J. Saunders Redding has said that in the 1840s, "every antislavery society in the North had a Negro, usually a fugitive slave, as a featured speaker."[17] Of this extremely diverse group of Negro antislavery speakers, some were escaped slaves who told narratives describing their lives and experiences in slavery; others gave more refined, analytical lectures on the subject. Of the latter group, some began as narrators but developed more reasoned lectures as they acquired more knowledge and experience.

This section is devoted to recognizing some of the more noteworthy itinerant black antislavery lecturers, and the next section will consider some of those speakers who remained as narrators of their experiences in slavery and their escapes therefrom. Among the outstanding itinerant black lecturers were Charles Lenox Remond, Frederick Douglass, William Wells Brown, Samuel Ringgold Ward, Henry Bibb, and Sojourner Truth.

Charles Lenox Remond. In the year 1838, the Executive Committee of the American Anti-Slavery Society, under Theodore Weld's direction, made a dedicated effort to recruit black lecturers. Soon after listening to Daniel A. Payne lecture in New York City in behalf of the slave, Weld and Lewis Tappan offered Payne a commission as itinerant lecturer. Payne's commitments as a Presbyterian minister made it impossible for him to accept.[18] However, in that same year, the person reputed to be the first traveling black antislavery lecturer was commissioned under the auspices of the American Anti-Slavery Society. This was Charles Lenox Remond.

Remond was born and schooled at Salem, Massachusetts. In 1838, at the age of twenty-eight, he spent the first year of his new position traveling throughout Massachusetts, Rhode Island, and Maine in the company of Ichabod Codding, giving speeches against slavery. In 1840, Remond went to England as a delegate to the World Anti-Slavery Convention. He did not take his seat at the convention, however, because Lucretia Mott, a woman delegate also from the United States, had not been allowed admission. In protest against the convention's refusal to seat women delegates, Remond and his two American male companions, William Lloyd Garrison and Nathaniel P. Rogers, joined Mrs. Mott in the convention's gallery, where they remained throughout the meetings. Remond stayed in the British Isles for nearly two years, however, lecturing extensively in Britain and Ireland.[19]

After his return from England in December 1841, Remond remained as a lecturer for various Garrisonian "moral suasion" antislavery societies for the duration of the movement. He was articulate, refined, and excellent proof of the contention that the black was truly a man. After Remond visited Chicago in 1849, a reporter for the *Daily Tribune* stated that, "Everyone who hears him [Remond], or comes in contact with him, is charmed by his singular eloquence, his polish and his suavity. He is a living refutation of the stereotyped falsehood of inferiority." Of one of Remond's speeches at City Hall in Chicago, the reporter said, "It was a masterly vindication of his race, and conclusive in its proofs as to the causes of their inferiority, where any exists. The cause the eloquent lecturer showed to be an unnatural prejudice, alike unreasonable and disreputable to the whites who indulge it."[20]

Remond's antislavery work was confined primarily to the platform, and he wrote little for the press. Although well-practiced, Remond disclaimed any attempt at methodically studying oratory.

In a letter to the *National Anti-Slavery Standard*, Remond described his professed aversion to carefully preparing or practicing speech material:

> Men, women, and children, who never spent the better half of their best days in learning to speak, cannot fail to interest. They speak from the heart, and the natural heart seldom, if ever, when left free, proves traitor to its God, Liberty, or the Truth. I once loved to hang upon the lips of a favorite minister, the popular orator, and the prized student; but my taste, like their eloquence, was empty, heartless, and selfish; and painful experience tells me, it is all a trade with them.[21]

In his book, *The Rising Son*, William Wells Brown described Remond as being "small, of spare make, neat, wiry build, and genteel in his personal appearance. He has a good voice, and is considered one of the best declaimers in New England."[22]

The philosophy behind Remond's speaking remained similar to Garrison's. Remond was essentially opposed to the Constitution although, unlike Garrison, he voted under the Constitution whenever he thought it expedient. He was also essentially non-violent like Garrison, but on occasion during the 1850s he put principle to one side and urged that slaves physically revolt in the South. Remond was relentless in his attacks on "proslavery" churches, just as Garrison was.

It was Remond's belief that, from the beginning of the black convention movement, his people should have been less compromising in dealing with slaveholders. In 1841, Remond surveyed the past and asserted "we need more radicalism among us, before we can speak as becomes a suffering, oppressed, and persecuted people. We have been altogether too fearful of martyrdom—quite too indefinite in our views."[23] Remond saw his mission as agitating and denouncing. At a convention of the New England Anti-Slavery Society in 1854, Remond explained his self-perceived role as an antislavery lecturer in noting that he was not a "peacemaker." Instead, he was "irritable, excitable, quarrelsome—I confess it, Sir, and my prayer to God is that I may never cease to be excitable, that I may never cease to be quarrelsome, until the last slave shall be made free in our country, and the colored man's manhood acknowledged (loud applause)."[24]

Although Remond's speaking was highly literate and stylistically impressive, an honest evaluation would shed some doubt on the profundity of his material. Perhaps William Wells Brown was correct in asserting, "Mr. Remond's abilities have been very much overrated. His speeches when in print, attracted little or no attention, and he was never able to speak upon any subject except slavery, upon which he was never deep."[25]

Nevertheless, Remond served as a living refutation of the common stereotypes of Negroes. From the speakers platform, Charles Lenox Remond was a significant weapon in the battle against slavery and race prejudice.

Frederick Douglass. Remond was soon to be overshadowed by the eloquent Frederick Douglass, who had escaped slavery in 1838 when he was twenty-one years old. Three years later, Douglass became a traveling agent for the Massachusetts Anti-Slavery Society. He had learned to read while in slavery, and with the first fifty cents he earned from blacking boots at age thirteen he purchased *The Columbian Orator*, a popular school book of the time. In that book, he read and admired speeches of Chatham, Pitt, Fox, and Sheridan. Such reading broadened Douglass' vocabulary, stimulated his thinking, and exposed him to "powerful denunciation of oppression and a most brilliant vindication of the rights of man."[26]

The career of Frederick Douglass is replete with antislavery lecturing, from just a few months after he began speaking with a narrative presentation at an antislavery meeting in Nantucket in 1841 until long after the Civil War. His start was a reluctant one, as exemplified in his much-later reflection on that first speech:

My speech on this occasion is the only one I ever made, of which I do not remember a single connected sentence. It was with the utmost difficulty that I could stand erect, or that I could command and articulate two words without hesitation and stammering. I trembled in every limb. I am not sure that my embarrassment was not the most effective part of my speech, if speech it could be called.[27]

After that meeting he became an agent, and for the first three to four months his speeches "were almost exclusively made up of narrations of my own personal experience as a slave"; for about ten years after that, he, like Remond, developed speeches based on the Garrisonian philosophy of abolition. As he started thinking more thoroughly for himself, Douglass grew tired of merely giving narratives of his life in slavery. In 1855, he looked back upon his early days of speechmaking, when his white fellow lecturers would say, "Give us the facts. . . , we will take care of the philosophy." In Douglass' case, it was frustrating to recite the same old narrative month after month and to try to maintain his interest in it; to repeat his story constantly was "a task altogether too mechanical" for his nature. Douglass explained how his then reverend friend William Lloyd Garrison would whisper "tell your story, Frederick" just as he stepped to the platform. Frederick could "not always obey, for I was now reading and thinking."[28]

Probably the most extensive antislavery lecture tour of Douglass' career was a series of 100 conventions he helped conduct for the New England Anti-Slavery Society in 1843 under the auspices of William Lloyd Garrison and his friends. The territory of the conventions included New Hampshire, Vermont, New York, Ohio, Indiana, and Pennsylvania. Among the seven speakers for the series were both Douglass and Charles Lenox Remond. The tour lasted for nearly six months, and the speakers all preached the doctrine of moral suasion. Douglass thought that "all the American people needed . . . was light."[29]

The moral suasionists staunchly opposed any political action, interpreted the Constitution as proslavery, were nonviolent, made relentless attacks on the churches, and opposed establishment of separate schools or other institutions for or by Negroes. Being a hired lecturer during his ten years of pure moral suasionism, Douglass probably traveled more and had more exposure to the white public than black leaders who guided majority decisions during that time.

In 1845, Douglass' *Narrative of the Life of Frederick Douglass* appeared and became a fast seller. This narrative included detailed information about his old master as well as his experiences under slavery. Soon after the narrative was released, Douglass left the country for England, where he continued lecturing.

After his return in 1847, Douglass established the *North Star* in Rochester, New York and edited this newspaper with few intermittent interruptions under different titles for the remainder of the movement. He simultaneously resumed his career as a platform antislavery lecturer, although editing responsibilities somewhat inhibited the extent and regularity of his travel.

In describing Douglass' speaking, William Wells Brown wrote:

There is a kind of eloquence issuing from the depth of the soul as from a spring, rolling along its copious floods, sweeping all before it, overwhelming by its force, carrying, upsetting, ingulfing its adversaries, and more dazzling and more thundering than the bolt which leaps from crag to crag. This is the eloquence of Frederick Douglass. . . .

As a speaker, Frederick Douglass has had more imitators than almost any other American, save, perhaps, Wendell Phillips.[30]

Douglas, like Remond, was impatient with being required to *prove* what he regarded as obvious or self-evident. In most situations, his rhetorical strategy was to presume that slavery was sinful and to enhance what he hoped were existing attitudes. At Corinthian Hall in Rochester, Douglass delivered an Independence Day oration to a white abolition audience on July 5, 1852. He asked his white audience if he had to argue that man is entitled to his liberty or argue the wrongfulness of slavery. This seemed an "unlikely question for republicans":

> Is it to be settled by rules of logic and argumentation, as a matter beset with great difficulty, involving a doubtful application of the principle of justice, hard to be understood? How should I look to-day, in the presence of Americans dividing and subdividing a discourse, to show that men have a natural right to freedom? speaking of relatively and positively, negatively and affirmatively. To do so, would be to make myself ridiculous, and to offer an insult to your understanding. There is not a man beneath the canopy of heaven that does not know that slavery is wrong *for him*.[31]

To Douglass, the "harsh language" which had been used by abolitionists was justifiable. In fact, he felt that language probably did not exist that was "sufficiently stern and denunciatory" to characterize the proslavery advocates. In a lecture on slavery at Corinthian Hall in 1851, Douglass compared the denunciatory language of abolitionists to Christ's words to the Scribes and Pharisees: "Woe unto you, Scribes, Pharisees, hypocrites. . . . Ye blind guides, which strain at a knat and swallow a camel. . . . Ye serpents! ye generation of vipers, how can ye escape the *damnation of hell*?"[32]

Many black spokesmen of the time were not as denunciatory as Frederick Douglass, especially when Douglass was lecturing on slavery. Nevertheless, from the early 1850s until the end of the movement, Douglass reflected the philosophies of the majority of his race. Probably more than any other black of that later period, he was truly the spokesman for his people.

William Wells Brown. Soon after the emergence of Frederick Douglass, another uncompromising, Garrisonian, black antislavery lecturer appeared in the person of William Wells Brown. Brown, whose mother was a slave and whose white paternal lineage was allegedly traceable back to Daniel Boone as grandfather, escaped from slavery into Ohio from Missouri at the age of eighteen in 1834. He was given refuge by a Quaker, Wells Brown, and he later assumed his benefactor's name. Soon he took a position as a steward on a steamer on Lake Erie; Brown remained on Lake Erie during the sailing seasons and made Buffalo his home during the winters. A contemporary, Alonzo D. Moore, wrote that Brown gave free passage across the lake to sixty-five fugitives in one year alone while working on the steamer.[33]

In the autumn of 1843, he was invited by the officers of the New York Anti-Slavery Society to accept a commission as lecturer in behalf of his enslaved countrymen. For the next six years Brown traveled and lectured under the auspices of antislavery societies in New York and Massachusetts, much of his time being spent in western New York. During that period, he wrote his *Narrative of William W. Brown, A Fugitive Slave*, which was released in 1847. In the preface to Brown's narrative, J. C. Hathaway, a traveling and lecturing companion of Brown's in western New York, stated the motivation behind Brown's extensive lecturing campaigns:

During the past three years, the author has devoted his entire energies to the anti-slavery cause. Laboring under all the disabilities and disadvantages growing out of his education in slavery—he went forth, impelled to the work by a love of liberty—stimulated by the remembrance of his own sufferings—urged on by the consideration that a mother, brothers, and sister, were still grinding in the prison-house of bondage, sustained by an unfaltering faith in the omnipotence of truth, and the final triumph of justice—to plead the cause of the slave, and by the eloquence of earnestness carried conviction to many minds, and enlisted the sympathy and secured the co-operation of many to the cause.

His labors have been chiefly confined to Western New York, where he has secured many warm friends, by his untiring zeal, persevering, continued fidelity, and universal kindness.[34]

Brown lectured on slavery in the British Isles from 1849 through 1854, after which he returned to the United States and resumed his career as a lecturer. In addition, he wrote plays and expository treatises on the history of the black man.

Throughout his career, William Wells Brown was a strong moral suasionist. For instance, at the 1847 National Negro Convention, Brown urged that Moral Suasion was needed in order to "convince and convert the white people here in favor of abolishing Slavery."[35] He assumed that whites could be persuaded to peaceably dissolve the Union and thus allow for the dismantlement of the slave system. As Brown reported during his early lecture tours in western New York, "I sounded the tocsin of Disunion into the ears of that vast assemblage. Not a hiss or groan was heard, but all was calm as death."[36] In contrast to his philosophical idol William Lloyd Garrison, Brown opposed the Constitution but was also known to have presided at meetings seeking the franchise for blacks so they could vote under the very Constitution he opposed.

While in Europe, Brown's lectures prompted the *Scotch Independent* of Glasgow to write in 1852 that he was "one of the best arguments against the institution of slavery in America." The paper made note of the natural genius displayed in Brown's lecturing. He was lauded for being a "vigorous expositor of the evils and atrocities of that system whose chains he has shaken off so triumphantly and forever."[37]

Brown's antislavery appeals were bitingly denunciatory as he advocated disunion, yet they were also designed to elicit sympathy for the plight of the slave and oppressed free black. For instance, his appeal to the sympathies of his audience is demonstrated in the introduction to a lecture Brown delivered before the Female Anti-Slavery Society of Salem, Massachusetts. He explained that he did not go there for the purpose of "making a grammatical speech, nor for the purpose of making a speech that shall receive the applause of my hearers." Instead, said Brown:

> I accepted the invitation because I felt that I owed a duty to the cause of humanity. I felt that I owed a duty to three millions of my brethren and sisters, with some of whom I am identified by the dearest ties of nature, and with most of whom I am identified by the scars which I carry upon my back. This, and this alone, induced me to accept the invitation to lecture here.[38]

Yet Brown's greatest strength did not lay in his oratorical or lecturing abilities. The aforementioned Glasgow newspaper rightfully observed that "it is not on the platform that this gentleman makes his best show of talent. It is as a writer that he creates the most profound sensation."[39] The talented young black girl Charlotte Forten wrote in her diary after observing one of Brown's speeches in 1854 that she thought "he spoke much better than he usually does. His manner was more animated. But . . . I do not think he is a very good lecturer. As a writer he is very highly spoken of by some of the leading English journals."[40] His communicative power was apparently more in the written than the spoken word.

As Brown's career progressed, some audiences preferred that he read from his written dramatic works rather than deliver lectures. Fortunately, he was able to comply in providing that additional antislavery instrument. During a tour in Ohio, Brown wrote Marius Robinson, editor of the *Anti-Slavery Bugle* in Salem, Ohio, that, "You appear not to comprehend my meaning about the Drama. There are some places when it would take better than a lecture. People will pay to hear the Drama that would not give a cent in an anti-slavery meeting. . . . [However] I had rather give two lectures than to give one Reading."[41] His original dramatic readings also dwelt on the antislavery theme.

William Wells Brown was a living refutation of proslavery charges of Negro inferiority. He and Remond continued espousing the Garrisonian doctrine, whereas Douglass continued lecturing on a different philosophical basis.

Samuel Ringgold Ward. While Remond, Douglass, and Brown were among the representative black antislavery lecturers who spent some or all of their careers advocating Garrisonianism, there were also black traveling lecturers of a non-Garrisonian type from the beginning of the black antislavery crusade, and one of the foremost among these was Samuel Ringgold Ward. Ward's parents had escaped slavery with him in 1817, when he was only three years old. They fled from Maryland to New Jersey, and Samuel's education was obtained at schools in New York.

In the latter part of 1839, Ward was appointed as an agent for the American Anti-Slavery Society to "travel and lecture for them." His commission was signed by James G. Birney, then a Secretary for the Society, who soon broke away and helped form a politically-oriented branch of abolitionists. The new branch believed in working within the system to overcome slavery, especially in interpreting the Constitution as an antislavery instrument. Samuel Ward was of the same philosophy as Birney. Although Ward was in sympathy with their good intentions, he asserted "I never belonged to the Garrison branch of abolitionists." There was little animosity in this connection because in December 1839, just one month after he made his "debut" as an antislavery lecturer, Ward was "transferred to the service of the New York State [Anti-Slavery] Society," thus "avoiding official connection with the quarrels which divided the Anti-Slavery Society in 1840, and the subsequent dissensions among them."[42]

In early 1841, Ward assumed the pastorate of a white church

congregation in the township of Butler in the county of Wayne, New York. For the following ten years, Ward divided responsibilities between being a traveling antislavery lecturer and being a minister. William Wells Brown said that between 1840 and 1850, Ward "either preached or lectured in every church, hall, or school house in Western and Central New York."[43] Ward also spoke in numerous areas of Pennsylvania, Ohio, Illinois, Wisconsin, Michigan, Indiana, Connecticut, Rhode Island, Massachusetts, and New Hampshire, especially during the last two years of his residence in the country. In September of 1851, Ward and his wife, who were living in Syracuse, decided he should quit abolition labor in the United States and move to Canada. From that date on, he worked outside the United States for elevation of his people. The frustrations caused by the Fugitive Slave Law of 1850 weighed heavily in his decision. Financial uncertainty was also a factor, as he noted that "the anti-slavery cause does not, cannot find bread and education for one's children."[44]

Ward was an unadulterated black whose father was allegedly an African prince. He ultimately gained the reputation of being "the black Daniel Webster." Standing above six feet in height, "possessing a strong voice, and energetic in his gestures, Mr. Ward always impressed his . . . speeches upon his hearers. No detractor of the negro's abilities ever attributed his talents to his having Anglo-Saxon blood in his veins."[45]

As a speaker, Ward's continuity of thought and tightness of organization were not as strong, for instance, as Henry Garnet's. In 1852, a black professor of belles lettres at New York Central College, William G. Allen, made comparative evaluations of the speaking of Ward, Garnet, and Frederick Douglass:

Garnet, as an orator, is more polished than Ward, as well as more elaborate. He has more application as [a] student—is more consecutive in his thoughts, and employs more method in their arrangement. He would, consequently, be more pleasing to a select audience, while a more promiscuous one would be swayed by Ward.

Douglass is not only great in oratory, tongue-wise, but considering his circumstances in early life, still marvelous in composition penwise. He has no fear of man; is no abstractionist; he has a first rate philosophy of reform.[46]

In attempting to justify his lack of more careful attention to the continuity of his speech materials, Ward stated his attitude in an address to the American and Foreign Anti-Slavery Society in 1849: "Eloquent addresses, rounding periods, with all the grace and flourish of attractive rhetoric, when something [is] to be said about nothing, might do, but in grappling with the horrors, and wickedness, and disastrous consequences of Slavery, [we] want no set speeches; the set speeches had better be reserved for hallelujah times (applause and laughter)."[47]

William J. Wilson, himself an effective black teacher and speaker of the time from New York, most aptly described Ward's strengths as a speaker when he wrote:

Ideas are the basis of all Mr. Ward utters. If words and ideas are not inseparable, then, as mortar is to the stones that compose the building, so are his words to his ideas. In this, I judge, lies Mr. Ward's greatest strength. Concise without abruptness; without extraordinary stress, always clear and forcible; if sparing of ornament, never inelegant,—in all, there appears to be a consciousness of strength, developed by close study and deep reflection, and only put forth because the occasion demands it. His appeals are directed rather to the understanding than the imagination; but so forcibly do they take possession of it, that the heart unhesitatingly yields.[48]

Two specific characteristics also distinguished Ward's speaking. One was that he, unlike some other black antislavery speakers, stayed away from emotional appeals to sympathy or, as Ward put it, appeals to pity. Said Ward:

> In pleading the cause of the blacks before the whites . . . I never stooped to ask pity. . . . Wronged, outraged, "scattered, peeled, killed all the day long," as they are, I never so compromised my own self-respect . . . as to condescend to ask pity for them at the hands of their oppressor. I cast no reflections upon, and certainly utter no censures àgainst, those who do; but I never did.

Secondly, like Frederick Douglass, Ward asserted, "Nor could I degrade myself by arguing the equality of the Negro with the white."[49] To Ward, this was self-evident, as Negroes had produced their "full quota of doctors, lawyers, divines, editors, orators, and poets." With those facts before them, Ward could not see how others could not concede the obvious. Philosophically, Ward's views were very similar to those of the three white abolitionists he admired most: Gerrit Smith, Beriah Green, and William Goodell, the acquaintance with whom he regarded a "priceless privilege."

Until his departure from America, Ward was for political action through the formation of a pure third party. At the same time, there was a need for blacks to speak and lecture to whites who were increasingly anxious to give them an audience. At the time he wrote his autobiography, Ward said, "Now no man is so eagerly, so tearfully, so rapturously listened to in America, on this subject [slavery] as the coloured man."[50]

Henry Bibb. When he addressed a Women's Rights Convention in 1850, William Lloyd Garrison reviewed the antislavery efforts and impressed his listeners with the progress movements could make when the people who are directly affected take the field. Garrison emphasized the great change in the antislavery movement during the preceding ten years by asking, "Who are among our ablest speakers? Who are the best qualified to address the public mind on the subject of slavery? Your fugitive slaves—your Douglasses, Browns and Bibbs—who are astonishing all with the cogency of their words and the power of their reasoning.''[51] At that time, both Douglass and Brown were still moral suasionists, but Bibb was an advocate of the very political action to which Garrison was strongly opposed. Yet by 1850, Henry Bibb had gained such popularity as an antislavery lecturer that he could hardly go unrecognized by any abolitionist, regardless of philosophy.

Henry Bibb was born a Kentucky slave in 1815 and vowed at an early age to escape slavery; at age ten he escaped but was quickly captured and resold. He successfully escaped in 1837, but went back to the southern states within the year to free his wife. Again he was captured and sold as a slave to a Cherokee Indian in the Red River country. Upon the Indian's death after a brief illness in 1841, Bibb again escaped. After spending some time as a laborer in Perrysburg, Ohio, Bibb went to Detroit in 1842, where he had the only official schooling in his life, "about two weeks," under the tutelage of W. C. Monroe, a black.

Finally, in May 1844, Bibb gave his first speech to a public audience. It was "a narrative of [his] own sufferings and adventures, connected with slavery."[52] From that time until 1850, Bibb was a lecturer traveling throughout Michigan, Ohio, New York, and New England. In 1849, Bibb's *Narrative of the Life and Adventures of Henry Bibb* was released. The next year, Bibb went to Canada after the passage of the Fugitive Slave Law. He settled in Sandwich, where he edited the *Voice of the Fugitive*, and continued lecturing on the promotion of black education and Canadian colonization.

As a speaker, Bibb spent much time giving narratives. Unlike Ward and some other black speakers, Bibb appealed to the sympathy and pity of his white auditors. For Bibb, the sadness of his narrative was something of a device to gain the support of potentially hostile audiences. He described the effect it had on an audience at Steubenville, Ohio during a lecture tour with Amos Dresser and Samuel Brooks in 1844:

After Mr. Dresser was through, I was called to take the stand. Just at this moment there was no small stir in rushing forward; so much indeed, that I thought they were coming to mob me. I should think that in less than fifteen minutes there were about one thousand persons standing around, listening. I saw many of them shedding tears while I related the sad story of my wrongs.[53]

Bibb's tours were all endorsed by Liberty party men, the party he supported. In 1845, Bibb lectured for Liberty party antislavery men after they promised to restore his enslaved wife and child to him if indeed they were still alive. A circular from the *Signal of Liberty* was distributed in April 1845 which stressed Bibb's emotional power and appeal:

His narrative always excites deep sympathy for himself and favorable bias for the cause, which seeks to abolish the evils he so powerfully portrays. Friends and foes attest his efficacy.
Mr. Bibb has labored much in lecturing, yet has collected but a bare pittance.[54]

The pathetic appeal of Bibb's narrative was no doubt more effective for some than a regular lecture or discourse. As the *Chronotype* was quoted in Bibb's *Narrative*, "Argument provokes argument, reason is met by sophistry. But narratives of slaves go right to the heart of men."[55] To satisfactorily complement his emotional substance, Bibb reportedly possessed a "musical voice and a wonderful power of delivery. . . . His natural eloquence and his songs enchained an audience as long as the speaker wanted them."[56] To vary his appeal to emotions, Bibb sometimes sang songs, such as "The Mother's Lament," a sad ballad about slaves who were being sold away from loved ones.

However, like Frederick Douglass, Henry Bibb did not satisfy himself with telling his story or otherwise appealing to the emotions of his audience. He was a Liberty party man, and he began speaking more and more in behalf of the party in extensive travels in New York and New England in 1846 and 1847. From Rhode Island in April 1847, Bibb wrote Joshua Leavitt, a white Liberty party man, of the substantive principles of his thinking:

> The great cry has been everywhere, can you not come and give us a lecture? We want to hear something from actual experience on this subject. . . .
>
> The people are grossly deceived and misled by the leaders of this [Whig] party. They went so far as to print *Liberty* with law and order over some of their tickets, and telling colored people that they were the true Liberty party. I know that the name of law and order sounds well in the ear of a *colored* man. For we as a people are fond of both law and order. But nothing sounds so well in my ear, as the sound of LIBERTY and JUSTICE, which are the fundamental principles and objects of the *Liberty party*![57]

Bibb was active in promoting his political beliefs at the 1848 National Negro Convention, serving on several committees including the one to draft the convention's "Address to the Colored People of the United States." Bibb also spoke "at length" at the convention in support of a preamble and subsequent resolutions supporting the "Buffalo Convention" and the newly formed Free Soil party; Frederick Douglass opposed the preamble. Although the resolutions were defeated, the preamble was sustained and attached to another resolution endorsing the "Free Soil movement.'' The preamble asserted that American slavery was both ''politically and morally evil.''[58]

The substance and delivery of Bibb's antislavery lectures were more emotional than those of most black itinerant lecturers of the time. William Wells Brown observed that ''there are few characters more worthy of study and imitation than that of Henry Bibb.''[59]

Sojourner Truth. The ranks of black antislavery lecturers were not devoid of women. The most unique female itinerant black lecturer was Sojourner Truth. Whereas the male lecturers heretofore discussed were agents for specific antislavery societies, Sojourner Truth was not commissioned as a lecturer by any society. As Harriet Beecher Stowe indicated in an 1863 article about Sojourner Truth in the *Atlantic Monthly*, ''Many years ago, the few readers of radical abolitionist papers must often have seen the singular name of Sojourner Truth, announced as a frequent speaker at anti-slavery meetings, and as traveling on a sort of self-appointed agency through the country.''[60]

Sojourner Truth, whose name originally was Isabella, was born a slave in New York around 1797. After being sold several times, she obtained her freedom from New York's emancipation act in 1829. During her enslavement, Isabella often would retreat to a small island by a stream and have prayers or ''talks with God.'' When she finally left the house of bondage, the Lord gave her the name of Sojourner because she was ''to travel up an' down the land, showin' the people their sins, an' bein' a sign unto them.'' The Lord gave her a second name of Truth because she was ''to declare the truth to the people.'' She lived in New York City working as a maid until 1843, when the ''Spirit called'' her and she began a pilgrimage that finally took her to Northampton, Massachusetts.

After that time she gained a reputation as a ''preacher-prophet,''

Sojourner Truth—Itinerant Antislavery Lecturer

a somewhat phenomenal occurrence in that she did not know how to read or write. Yet she developed a coherent philosophy of the world and regularly had the Bible read to her. She sang and spoke at camp meetings, with her text often being "WHEN I FOUND JESUS." The 128-page first edition of the *Narrative of Sojourner Truth*, written by a friend, Olive Gilbert, was published in 1850. It eventually became Part I of a 320-page, two-part edition published in 1878.

In 1851, she left her home in Northampton, Massachusetts and conducted her first antislavery lecture tour in western New York with several distinguished abolitionists including George Thompson of England. For the next twenty-five years she "traveled thousands of miles [and] lectured in many states."[61] After spending several months in western New York with Rochester as her headquarters, Sojourner spent two years traveling around Ohio lecturing on both antislavery and women's rights. While in Ohio she went "from town to town, attending conventions, and holding meetings of her own."[62] A friend and co-laborer of Sojourner's in her Ohio antislavery activities was Marius Robinson of Salem, Ohio, editor of the *Anti-Slavery Bugle*. Sojourner next moved from Ohio to Battle Creek, Michigan, which remained her home base from which to travel and lecture until well after the Civil War.

It is significant that Sojourner Truth did her antislavery speaking after 1850, during a period so threatening that such renowned lecturers as Samuel R. Ward and Henry Bibb left the country. It was written of her New York tour in Part II of Sojourner's *Narrative* that "to advocate the cause of the enslaved at this period was both unpopular and unsafe. Their meetings were frequently disturbed or broken up by the proslavery mob, and their lives imperiled. At such times, Sojourner fearlessly maintained her ground, and by her dignified manner and opportune remarks would disperse the rabble and restore order." During one of Sojourner's later lecture tours, the *Detroit Post* described the characteristics of the tall, gaunt, dark black speaker's lecturing:

Her lecture will be highly entertaining and impressive. She is a woman of strong religious nature, with an entirely original eloquence and humor, possessed of a weird imagination, of most grotesque, but strong, clear mind, and one who, without the aid of reading or writing, is strangely susceptible to all that in thought and action is now current in the world. At the antislavery and women's rights meetings she has been one of the chief attractions, and her shrewd good sense, mixed with oddities of speech and whimsical illustrations, never fail of producing a sympathetic interest as well as exciting the curiosity of the audience.[63]

Sojourner Truth had a charisma that prompted Harriet Beecher Stowe to remark that she never knew anyone who possessed so much "subtle, controlling personal power" as Sojourner Truth. Even Wendell Phillips, one of the most renowned orators of the period, said of Sojourner that he had known "a few words from her to electrify an audience and affect them as he never saw persons affected by another party."[64]

Sojourner's emotion, like that of Henry Bibb, was uninhibited, and her having been once a personal victim of slavery made her more effective. This was a person who probably was strongest at adapting to the immediacy of occasions with appropriate emotional observations. One reporter saw Sojourner in such a moving situation at an Iowa meeting:

I was present at a large religious convention. Love in the family had been portrayed in a manner to touch the better nature of the auditory. Just as the meeting was about to close, Sojourner stood up. Tears were coursing down her furrowed cheeks. She said: "We has heerd a great deal about love at home in de family. Now, children, I was a slave, and my husband and my children was sold from me." The pathos with which she uttered those words made a deep impression on the meeting. Pausing a moment, she added: "No, husband and children is *all* gone, and what has *'come* of de affection I had for dem? *Dat is de question before de house!*" The people smiled amidst a baptism of tears.[65]

In contrast with the sad emotion was the humor that evolved from Sojourner's "weird imagination." Her Garrison-like attitude toward the Constitution was expressed in a humorous figurative analogy:

"This morning I was walking out, and I got over the fence. I saw the wheat a-holding up its head, looking very big. I go up and take holt of it. You b'lieve it, there was *no* wheat there. I say, 'God, what is the matter with this wheat?' And He says to me 'Sojourner, there is a little weasel [weevil] in it!' Now I hear talkin' about the Constitution and the rights of man. I come up and I take hold of this Constitution. It looks mighty big, and I feel for my rights, but there ain't any there. Then I say 'God what ails this Constitution?' He says to me, 'Sojourner, there is a little weasel in it.' "[66]

Sojourner's peculiar humor was also demonstrated in the introduction of a speech at Florence, Massachusetts just after she arrived from a tiring trip. Being unprepared, Sojourner began by saying: "Children, I have come here tonight like the rest of you to hear what I have to say."[67]

Although Sojourner Truth was a dramatic speaker, with philosophical materials that carried her beyond simple narration of her personal story, she never rose to a position of acknowledged "leadership" among her people. Her illiteracy made that impossible. Yet perhaps her very lack of education, accompanied by an abundance of common sense, made Sojourner the strong lecturer she was.

Other traveling lecturers of the time included Lunsford Lane, alternately of Oberlin and Boston, and Jermain W. Loguen of the Syracuse area. In addition to Sojourner, women sometimes traveling as lecturers included Sarah Remond, who occasionally traveled and spoke with her brother Charles, and Frances Ellen Watkins Harper, a poetess and teacher from Philadelphia.

Henrietta Buckmaster tells us that in the 1850s

> Negro lecturers were submitting to indignities and personal dangers. There was no extraneous drama here. Mrs. Frances Harper, the genteel and soft-voiced teacher, and Sojourner Truth, the great, gaunt sibyl who seemed the very soul of Africa were pleading for the race with profound effectiveness . . . Douglass and James McCune Smith [a New York black doctor] were writing and lecturing at top speed.[68]

Thus, the full-time lecturers ranked alongside other black leaders in effectiveness. Probably the best affirmation of their effectiveness was given by John Mercer Langston, a black attorney from Ohio. Langston, who was himself regarded by William Wells Brown as representing the "highest idea of the orator," made a survey in 1858 of the great living orators produced by the antislavery movement. He alluded to speakers who wielded "resistless eloquence" by their "incomparable rhetoric." Of the ten orators praised by Langston, two were black and both were itinerant lecturers—Frederick Douglass and Charles Lenox Remond.[69]

NARRATIVES

Autobiographical stories of former slaves which revealed their qualities as feeling, thinking human beings while depicting their experiences in the slave system were important weapons in the antislavery arsenal. Some narratives appeared in written form while others were delivered haltingly and pathetically from the antislavery platform. As mentioned earlier, while some narrators rose from delivering their personal stories to become lecturers with antislavery philosophies and analyses, others remained as storytellers and were used extensively by abolitionists to draw curious prospective converts to their antislavery meetings.

WRITTEN NARRATIVES

Before discussing the storytellers, however, recognition should be made of written narratives. Several former slaves added written narratives to the antislavery propaganda operation. Some narratives were written by the fugitives themselves and varied considerably in quality according to the background and ability of each writer. Reference has already been made to the narratives of Frederick Douglass, William Wells Brown, Samuel R. Ward, and Henry Bibb, all of which were autobiographical. Among other important self-written narratives were those by James W. C. Pennington,[70] and Jermain W. Loguen.[71] Still more narratives were either ghostwritten or written in the third person by whites. Some of the more prominent ones of this type were about Sojourner Truth, Lunsford Lane,[72] and Henry Box Brown.[73]

All narratives served a special antislavery purpose. Proslavery advocates had thoroughly developed apologies or rationales for the slave system, alleging that slaves were contented with the system and were inherently incapable of caring for themselves. In response, the narratives of ex-slaves could provide first-hand refutation of the assumption that people can truly be contented in slavery, being deprived of freedom or opportunity.

Naturally, slave narratives were not free from falsehoods and exaggerations. Many fugitives understandably bore considerable hatred and resentment, especially if they had been ''sold away'' from loved ones or treated inhumanely. Objectivity was also hampered by problems of memory and judgment. Yet there was an attempt by antislavery society officials to carefully examine the validity of stories and verify factual information through letters to other parties close to the scene in question. The narratives frequently contained letters and other documents to help prove their authenticity. A further problem arose, however, when white abolitionists wrote the narratives and let their crusading zeal transcend the black narrators' reports. Regardless, narratives gave the readers of those popular materials a better understanding of the humanity of blacks.

Spoken Narratives. Reading a written narrative may have had great propaganda value for abolitionists, but a bigger impact could possibly have been obtained by having doubters listen to a black tell his story directly. It is little wonder that so many antislavery societies tried to feature a black narrator as a "stage prop" or drawing card.

Even in the 1830s, antislavery societies in the Northeast were using black narrators to gain sympathy for their cause. At a New England Anti-Slavery Society Convention in 1836, it was mentioned that a black was in the audience who, on three different occasions, had earned and paid the amount his master agreed would buy his freedom before he was finally let go. A call was made for the man to "tell his story," and a convention participant gave this report:

> He came to the platform . . . and told his own story. . . . His brother and his children had been taken from him, carried he knew not where, and were now in bondage. One of the audience asked: "can we believe what the man says? for slaveholders say the slaves could not take care of themselves if set at liberty." "Look here," said he, holding up his brawny arms, "these arms were strong enough to take care of my master by day, and to earn my own freedom three times in the night."
> The story was confirmed by a gentleman from Virginia.[74]

The "brawny arms" and the "confirmation by a gentleman

from Virginia'' were far from indisputable evidence in response to the question, but the impact on the audience under those circumstances was probably highly favorable for the black. The doctrine of inferiority of blacks was so common that through exposure to narratives, many white abolitionists themselves had their own doubts erased about whether a slave was a real human being with feelings and intellect.

Frederick Douglass had probably been the most electrifying narrative teller of them all, as he gained much attention and many favorable reactions during the first half of the 1840s. Reference has often been made to exclamations by such famous white abolitionists as William Lloyd Garrison and Wendell Phillips about slaveholders having the nerve to call such narrators as Frederick Douglass pieces of property. For instance, after Douglass' very first spoken narrative, Garrison asked, ''Have we been listening to a thing, a piece of property, or to a man?'' ''A man! A man!'' came from five hundred voices.[75]

Douglass and Brown, by becoming lecturers, joined the ranks of those who traveled with and introduced those narrators who remained in the storytelling ranks. Some of the most widely publicized storytellers escaped from slavery in the late 1840s, including Henry Box Brown and William and Ellen Craft. Brown and the two Crafts became famous primarily for their dramatic escapes in 1848.

Henry Box Brown effected his escape from Richmond to Philadelphia in a box which was only 3'1'' long, 2' wide, and 2'6'' high. At Brown's request, a friend nailed him into the box along with only a bladder of water. Brown curled into the tight area with only three gimlet holes for air and was mailed to William H. Johnson, a member of the Philadelphia Vigilance Committee. His friend was to have accompanied the box, but ''he failed to do so; and contented himself with sending a telegraph to his correspondent in Philadelphia, that such a box was on its way to his care.''[76]

The trip was a dramatic one; Brown was placed on his head for a brief but painful period despite the box's being marked "this side up with care." During that period, Charles Stearns, Brown's narrative ghost-writer, interpreted Brown as saying, "My eyes were almost swollen out of their sockets, and the veins on my temples seemed ready to burst. . . . Death seemed my inevitable fate, and every moment I expected to feel the blood flowing over me, which had burst from my veins."[77] However, the box was turned over in time for him to recover. After a few more reported ordeals, Brown arrived in Philadelphia. He tapped the lid of the box to affirm his live presence, and the vigilance committee opened the box nervously. Up rose Brown who supposedly said, with a Stanley-greeting-Livingston confidence, "How do you do gentlemen." He was weak and "swooned away," but soon recovered. Shortly afterward, Brown was a featured narrator at anti-slavery meetings, giving a first-hand account of the wrongfulness of slavery. Most of Brown's traveling was in the New England area, and it was in Boston that he first related "in public, the story of my suffering, since which time I have repeated my simple tale in different parts of Massachusetts, and in the State of Maine." His appearance was regular and less guarded before passage of the Fugitive Slave Law in 1850.

Brown's written narrative was composed from a statement of his facts, but the ideas conveyed in his semi-literate personal style still had some of their pathetic strength after being transformed by ghostwriting into a more elegant style. There was no attempt by Brown to depict his master as cruel or malicious in the treatment of slaves. In fact, Brown admitted that his master treated him fairly under the circumstances, but he still longed for his freedom. Thus, he served as one piece of refutation to the argument that slaves could be contented without being free. Brown was interpreted as saying, "Heaven save me from kind masters, as well as those called more cruel; for even the master's 'tender mercies are cruel,' and what no freeman could endure for a moment."[78] He explained that his tale would lack "that thrilling interest which is attached to the more than romantic, although perfectly true descriptions of a life in slavery, given by numerous forerunners in the work of sketching a slave's personal experience."[79] Yet Brown's story served a needed refutative purpose, and it probably seemed even less fictionalized when he told it from the platform.

The account of Brown's wife and children being sold and parted from him probably had a more profound effect coming awkwardly and ungrammatically from Brown in person, but the facts as more elegantly related through Stearns were also touching:

The purchaser of my wife was a *Methodist* minister, who was about starting for North Carolina. Pretty soon five waggon-loads of little children passed, and looking at the foremost one, what should I see but a little child, pointing its tiny hand towards me, exclaiming, "There's my father; I knew he would come and bid me good-bye." It was my eldest child! Soon the gang approached in which my wife was chained. I looked, and beheld her familiar face; but O, reader, that glance of agony! may God spare me ever again enduring the excruciating horror of that moment! She passed, and came near where I stood. I seized hold of her hand, *intending* to bid her farewell; but words failed me; the gift of utterance had fled, and I remained speechless. I followed her some distance, with her hand grasped in mine, as if to save her from her fate, but I could not speak, and I was obliged to turn away in silence.

This is not an imaginary scene, reader; it is not a fiction, but an every-day reality at the South; and all I can say more to you, in reference to it is, that if you will not, after being acquainted with these facts, consecrate your all to the slaves' release from bondage, you are utterly unworthy the name of a man.[80]

For his family and brethren in slavery, Brown pledged "never to refuse to advocate their claims to your sympathy, whenever a fitting occasion occurs to speak in their behalf."[81] And speak he did. Like many other fugitives, Brown risked being caught and returned to slavery in order to tell his story to the many listeners who were drawn to antislavery meetings in order to hear and see a fugitive slave.

In December 1848, William and Ellen Craft, a Georgia slave couple, also made a dramatic escape from slavery. Ellen, a quadroon, was so light that she was able to disguise herself as a white man. She muffled some of her face with linen and wore a pair of green glasses. William, her husband, assumed the role of the young white man's slave. They got a "Christmas pass" from their mistress and boldly headed North. Ellen portrayed a young white man with poor eyesight, sprained right arm, and generally poor health. William acted the part of the loyal slave who worked hard to help his master deal with his physical disabilities.

The Crafts stayed in good quality hotels, though neither could read nor write, for the clerks could not expect the young man to sign the register with his disabled hand. People would often try to talk with the "young man," but William was ever ready to explain that his master's poor health was the reason he was unsociable. When the Crafts rode the trains, the servant was refused passage until he explained how greatly his ailing master needed his assistance. William and Ellen were blessed with money, which they had apparently earned by hiring out on odd jobs and with an abundance of luck. After several days of tense nervewracking travel, the two fugitives finally arrived at Philadelphia, where they too were met by the Philadelphia Vigilance Committee.[81]

After a brief rest, in which Ellen could overcome the nervous exhaustion of the trip, William and Ellen began attending antislavery meetings where they "told their story." News soon spread of their dramatic escape, and the Crafts became further examples of the intelligent and human qualities of blacks who were willing to take great risks in order to gain their freedom. They traveled through the United States, Canada, and England telling their narrative to fascinated audiences. Their stories were brief, but their very appearance let audiences see their obvious humanity and sympathize with their great sacrifice for freedom.

During the first half of 1849, William Wells Brown traveled with the Crafts, arranging their speaking schedules and introducing them at antislavery meetings. At the 1849 meeting of the New England Anti-Slavery Society, the delegates had the privilege of seeing five famous fugitives on the platform together. This report was filed in the *Liberator*:

> William W. Brown, himself a fugitive, asked permission to introduce to the audience Henry Brown, the slave who, to effect his escape, came from Richmond, Virginia, to Philadelphia in a box wherein he was confined for a space of twenty-seven hours.
>
> Henry Brown came forward, and gave a brief, simple but very interesting account of his escape, and of the circumstances which led to it.
>
> . . . Frederick Douglass, the eloquent and noble man, himself a slave up to the period of manhood, then took the floor, and with a few remarks introduced William and Ellen Craft, the fugitives from Georgia, to the audience.[82]

The ex-slaves drew much attention and caused considerable excitement in the North and South. In 1850, the passage of the Fugitive Slave Bill was a counterattack which abolitionists, black and white, had to meet. It was an escalation in the battle in which narrators had taken part.

In the final analysis, blacks made some unique contributions to the antislavery movement. While white abolitionists concerned themselves greatly with the subject of slavery in the South during the first phase of the movement, blacks reminded whites that unless the "semi-slave" treatment of Northern Negroes could be recognized and overcome concomitantly, slavery's underlying problem of the inhuman treatment of the black race would continue to haunt the nation.

Black speakers were able to travel to antislavery meetings and demonstrate the humanity of their people through intelligent analysis and articulation of the issues. They were living refutation of arguments of black inferiority promulgated by slavery's apologists. This refutation was enhanced by narratives, both written and spoken, of former slaves. Audiences for written and spoken narratives were able to vicariously experience the wrongness of bondage. Only blacks could prove, in the flesh, the human qualities of slaves that their white counterparts in the antislavery movement were only able to discuss indirectly. Through such means as lectures, orations, newspaper broadsides, and protest meetings, blacks continued agitating against slavery until the very outbreak of the Civil War.

NOTES

[1]Samuel Ringgold Ward, *Autobiography of a Fugitive Negro* (London: John Snow, 1855), p. 42.

[2]"James G. Birney to Weld, July 21, 1834," *Weld-Grimke Letters*, I, p. 163.

[3]"Weld to Lewis Tappen, March 9, 1836," *Weld-Grimke Letters*, I, p. 274.

[4]*Fourth Annual Report of the American Anti-Slavery Society*, cited in Leon F. Litwack, *North of Slavery* (Chicago: University of Chicago Press, 1961), p. 223.

[5]*Colored National Convention, Cleveland, 1848*, p. 18.

[6]James McCune Smith to Gerrit Smith, March 1, 1855," cited in Howard H. Bell, "Survey of the Negro Convention Movement,

1830-1861'' (Ph.D. Dissertation, Northwestern University, 1953), p. 41.

[7]*Colored American*, July 15, 1837, p. 2.

[8]*Liberator*, July 2, 1837, p. 108.

[9]Ibid., p. 108.

[10]*Colored American*, November 18, 1839, p. 4.

[11]*Liberator*, June 1, 1838, p. 142.

[12]*Colored American*, October 27, 1838, p. 142.

[13]"The Progress of the Antislavery Cause," a speech by Theodore S. Wright, cited in Woodson (ed.), *Negro Orators and Their Orations*, p. 90. Also in *Liberator*, October 13, 1837, p. 165.

[14]*Colored American*, May 20, 1837, p. 2.

[15]"Weld to Gerrit Smith, October 23, 1839," *Weld-Grimke Letters*, II, p. 811-12.

[16]Richard Bardolph, *The Negro Vanguard* (Westport, Conn.: Negro Universities Press, 1971), p. 45.

[17]J. Saunders Redding, *They Came in Chains* (New York: J. B. Lippincott Co., 1950), p. 102.

[18]Daniel A. Payne, "Recollections of Seventy Years," in Sterling Brown et al. (eds.), *The Negro Caravan* (New York: The Dryden Press, Inc., 1941), p. 738.

[19]Remond's trip is described by Benjamin Quarles in *Black Abolitionists* (New York: Oxford University Press, 1969) p. 131-3.

[20]*Chicago Daily Tribune*, cited in *Liberator*, August 10, 1849, p. 1.

[21]*National Anti-Slavery Standard*, April 18, 1844, p. 184.

[22]William Wells Brown, *The Rising Son* (Boston: A. G. Brown and Co., Publishers, 1874), p. 459.

[23]*National Anti-Slavery Standard*, May 27, 1841, p. 1.

[24]*Liberator*, June 23, 1854, p. 100. Also in Woodson (ed.), *Negro Orators and Their Orations*, p. 237.

[25]Brown, *The Rising Son*, p. 460.

[26]Douglass, *Life and Times of Frederick Douglass*, p. 85.

[27]Frederick Douglass, *My Bondage and My Freedom* (New York: Miller, Orton and Mulligan, 1855), p. 358.

[28]Ibid., p. 361.

[29]Douglass, *Life and Times of Frederick Douglass*, p. 226.

[30]Brown, *The Rising Son*, p. 438.

[31]*Frederick Douglass' Paper*, July 9, 1852, p. 2.

[32]*North Star*, January 16, 1851, p. 2.

[33]Alonzo D. Moore, "Memoir of the Author," in Brown, *The Rising Son*, p. 10.

[34]J. C. Hathaway, "Preface," *Narrative of William W. Brown, a Fugitive Slave*, Written by Himself (Boston: Published at the Anti-Slavery Office, 1847), p. ix.

[35]*National Convention of Colored People and Their Friends, Troy, 1847*, p. 14.

[36]*National Anti-Slavery Standard*, August 29, 1844, p. 50.

[37]*Scotch Independent*, cited in William Wells Brown, *The Black Man* (New York: Thomas Hamilton, 1863), p. 28.

[38]*A Lecture Delivered Before the Female Anti-Slavery Society of Salem, at Lyceum Hall, November 14, 1847, by Wm. W. Brown, a Fugitive Slave* (Boston: Massachusetts Anti-Slavery Society, 1847), p. 3-4.

[39]*Scotch Independent*, p. 28.

[40]*The Journal of Charlotte L. Forten: A Free Negro in the Slave Era*, edited by Ray Allen Billington (New York: Collier Books, 1961), p. 64.

[41]"William Wells Brown to Marius R. Robinson, November 29, 1859," Letter in Schomburg Collection.

[42]Ward, *Autobiography of a Fugitive Negro*, p. 66.

[43]Brown, *The Black Man*, p. 284.

[44]Ward, *Autobiography of a Fugitive Negro*, p. 117.

[45]Brown, *The Black Man*, pp. 284-5.

[46]*Liberator*, October 28, 1852, p. 176.

[47]*Annual Report of the American and Foreign Anti-Slavery Society, Presented at New York, May 8, 1849, with Resolutions and Addresses*. (New York: Published at the American and Foreign Anti-Slavery Society, 1849), p. 14.

[48]In Brown, *The Black Man*, p. 285.

[49]Ibid., p. 287.

[50]Ward, *Autobiography of a Fugitive Negro*, p. 98.

[51]*Liberator*, June 7, 1850, p. 91.

[52]*Narrative of the Life and Adventures of Henry Bibb, American Slave*,

Written by Himself, 3rd Edition (New York: Published by the Author, 1850), p. 178.

[53]Ibid., p. 180.

[54]Cited in ibid., p. 185.

[55]Cited in ibid., p. 207.

[56]Brown, *The Black Man*, p. 86-7.

[57]*Emancipator*, April 21, 1847, p. 2.

[58]*National Colored Convention, Cleveland, 1848*, p. 8-15.

[59]Brown, *The Black Man*, p. 87.

[60]*Atlantic Monthly*, cited in *Narrative of Sojourner Truth, with a History of Her Labors and Correspondence* (Battle Creek, Mich.: Published for the Author, 1878), p. 151.

[61]Ibid., p. 130.

[62]Ibid., p. 136.

[63]*Detroit Post* cited in ibid., p. 237.

[64]From "A Topeka, Kansas Paper," in ibid., p. 247.

[65]Ibid., p. 150.

[66]Cited in Bennett, *Pioneers in Protest*, p. 123.

[67]*Narrative of Sojourner Truth*, p. 312,

[68]Buckmaster, *Let My People Go*, p. 225-26. The Life of Sojourner Truth is reviewed in Jacqueline Bernard, *Journey Toward Freedom: The Story of Sojourner Truth* (New York: Norton, 1967).

[69]John Mercer Langston, "The World's Anti-Slavery Movement; Its Heroes and Its Triumphs: a lecture delivered at Xenia and Cleveland, Ohio, August 2 and 3, 1858," in John Mercer Langston, *Freedom and Citizenship: Selected Lectures and Addresses* (Washington, D.C.: Rufus H. Darby, 1883), p. 62.

[70]*The Fugitive Blacksmith* (London: Charles Gilpin, 1850).

[71]*The Rev. J. W. Loguen, as a Slave and as a Freeman* (Syracuse, N.Y.: J.G.K. Truair and Co., 1859).

[72]*Narrative of Lunsford Lane* (Boston: J. G. Torrey, Printer, 1842).

[73]*Narrative of Henry Box Brown, Written From a Statement of Facts Made by Himself* (Boston: Published by Brown and Stearns, 1849).

[74]*Liberator*, May 28, 1836, p. 87.

[75]Foner, *Frederick Douglass*, p. 26.

[76]*Narrative of Henry Box Brown*, p. 60.

[77]Ibid., p. 60-1.

[78]Ibid., p. 13.
[79]Ibid., p. 13.
[80]Ibid., p. 55.
[81]Ibid., p. 55-6.
[82]*Liberator*, June 8, 1849, p. 1.

Conclusion

There were different emphases in black protest appeals at distinct phases of the movement. Along with combating colonization schemes until midway in the 1830s, black spokesmen devoted a great portion of time to encouraging their own people to elevate themselves through hard work and the formation of various mutual beneficent and literary societies. They then began supplementing this rhetoric with appeals to white society to recognize, assist, and reward the conscientious deeds of black people. For nearly a decade beginning in 1840, many black leaders gave extensive support to political activity in the third party movement.

The 1850s saw a shift to strong reactions against increasingly oppressive governmental action. After the Fugitive Slave Law of 1850 was passed, blacks held numerous protest meetings in which they threatened violence to those who dared enforce the new statute. As other actions such as the Kansas-Nebraska Bill and the Dred Scott decision took place, desperation and despair became more evident in the efforts by blacks as some promoted emigration to South and Central America. Others began agitating for a dissolution of the union with Southern states. In general, the 1850s saw a less united and more desperate effort by blacks in their struggle for rights in America.

From among the many topics under the general heading of black protest, there were some overriding and insistent threads woven in the fabric of the movement. The appeals of most black spokesmen were based on strong religious, moral, and legal considerations. Since many black leaders were ministers, their arguments were molded by their own religious precepts and those of their followers. Not only did the nonviolent advocates base their arguments on religion, but their opponents tried to justify violence by religion. People such as David Walker and Rev. Henry Highland Garnet both asserted that obedience to God demanded physical insurrection. God's laws were supreme for man to follow.

On the next rung of the ladder were the laws of man. Blacks swore obedience to the principles of the Declaration of Independence and the Preamble of the Constitution and obeyed most federal and state statutes. The major exceptions were those laws sanctioning slavery and returning fugitives to bondage. Those statutes conflicted with God's law and were therefore to be transcended. Moral decisions were also made concerning whether or not it was right to emigrate and leave bonded brethren behind in slavery or leave freemen to face possible further degradation in their absence. Instead of leaving, they thought it only fair to remain in America and demand equal application of the law to all people.

It might be thought that black protest appeals parroted those of white people in parallel movements. However, an overall summary reveals numerous unique positions assumed on issues by blacks. In the very beginning of the movement, in fact, it was blacks who opposed the gradualism embodied in the American Colonization Society. Blacks were given a great boost when William Lloyd Garrison and other whites came over to the cause of immediate abolition. Independent black thinking was further exemplified when most New England blacks continued support for the Constitution and political activities despite the dominant influence of white moral suasionists in that area who had turned against the Constitution and all political activity within the system. Likewise, many New York blacks who strongly respected the pure abolition politics of white colleagues such as Gerrit Smith adapted to the less pure free soilist political activities in that area when they thought it advantageous to do so.

Another area of independent black protest thought was on the subject of organizations. Despite being criticized by some whites for doing so, black spokesmen initiated and dominated many of their own organizations and activities. Later in the movement, whenever they thought Negro educational needs could best be met by special schools for themselves, they urged establishment of those schools despite prospects of their having mostly if not all black enrollees.

A highly contributive aspect of black protest came in the area of antislavery labor. Free educated black speakers served as living refutation of doubts about Negroes' abilities and qualities. White audiences were attracted by the novel prospect of seeing a Negro speak. They would then be caught up in the spellbinding oratory of black abolitionists. Another unique contribution of special impact in the movement was made by black narratives, both written and spoken. Thousands of curiosity seekers, by reading or listening, were exposed to the warm human qualities of former slaves. In short, blacks, especially fugitives, were able to carry the slavery issue from the abstract to the concrete.

In addition, black antislavery speakers reminded white organizations that it was inconsistent and counterproductive to fight slavery in the South while depriving free northern blacks of the opportunity to elevate themselves in the North. "Semislavery" was slavery still. Blacks made white abolitionists aware that degrading treatment of all humans, whether slave or nominally free, was an abhorrence to be fought in all sections of the country.

There were some geographic variations in black protest philosophies. Although Garrison-type moral suasionist blacks were not numerous, particularly after the third party movement began, the large majority of them were located in Garrison's own New England area and around Philadelphia. Many black leaders holding the generally prevailing viewpoints of their people were in

New York State, especially around New York City. Frederick Douglass, who became a widely recognized black opinion leader after the late 1840s, then worked out of Rochester, New York. Those blacks promoting emigration during the 1850s were primarily from Pittsburgh and parts west. For instance, at the 1854 Emigration Convention in Cleveland, the delegates were predominantly from Ohio, Michigan, western Canada, and Allegheny County in Pennsylvania; only two were from New York, one from Rhode Island, and none from Massachusetts.

There were some important interrelationships concerning different schools of black thought on issues affecting them. The blacks who were disunionists were strongly opposed to the Constitution because they thought it legalized slavery and deprived freemen of rights. Likewise, those blacks who advocated emigration did so because they felt the Constitution allowed no possibility for them to gain freedom. The majority of blacks, who believed in working within the American legal and political system, had to refute the position of both opposing minorities. Much argumentation focused on which plan was the most practicable and advantageous: (1) emigration, (2) disunion, or (3) working for reform within the system. As Southern states began seceding, the number of blacks supporting disunion increased considerably but remained a minority.

In the final analysis, although blacks had little direct influence on government during their crusade, the white public was increasingly exposed to black protest appeals. Not only did black spokesmen draw public attention to their people's plight, but they were a strong force in this great battle of the war for Negro rights in America.

Appendix I

Intraracial Issues

These discourses focus on the differing viewpoints that black leaders advanced on some of the significant issues affecting their people. Although nearly all black leaders could agree on ends being sought, there were frequent controversies among them concerning the means to be employed. As Frederick Douglass said in 1849, "until they can prove that sameness of complexion produces harmony of opinion, they will fail to show that colored men have not as good a right to differ from each other as do white men." The following discourses are divided into sets of two conflicting black viewpoints on each issue. Each set of two differing opinions is not necessarily a formal debate, as some are presented in different years under altered circumstances. Yet they provide separate discernible positions taken by black spokesmen.

A. EMIGRATION vs. ANTI-EMIGRATION

*1. Emigration—"Political Destiny of the Colored Race on the American Continent," by Martin R. Delany, et al.**

During the earlier phases of the antebellum protest movement, blacks were nearly unanimous in their opposition to colonization, particularly to Africa. However, by the early 1850s serious consideration was given by a vocal minority of blacks to the idea of voluntary emigration, especially to Central and South America.

Proceedings of the National Emigration Convention of the Colored People, Cleveland, 1854 (Pittsburgh: Printed by A. A. Anderson, 1854), p. 33-70.

245

A chief spokesman for emigration was Martin R. Delany, a black Harvard-trained physician who resided in Pittsburgh. Delany, the grandson of a slave, was proud of his jet black "unadulterated complexion." In 1852, Delany wrote a book entitled *The Condition, Elevation, Emigration, and Destiny of the Colored People of the United States*. The book, one of the first thorough treatises urging black emigration, was not well received by the majority of blacks. Then, in 1854, some 140 delegates from eleven states plus Canada attended a *National Emigration Convention of Colored People* in Cleveland. Delany chaired the Convention's Business Committee, which composed the following "State Paper." On the afternoon of August 25, 1854, Delany read the paper to the Convention, and it was subsequently adopted unanimously.

———————————

FELLOW-COUNTRYMEN!—The duty assigned us is an important one, comprehending all that pertains to our destiny and that of our posterity—present and prospectively. And while it must be admitted, that the subject is one of greatest magnitude, requiring all that talents, prudence and wisdom might adduce, and while it would be folly to pretend to give you the combined result of these three agencies, we shall satisfy ourselves with doing our duty to the best of our ability, and that in the plainest, most simple and comprehensive manner.

Our object, then, shall be to place before you our true position in this country—the United States,—the improbability of realizing our desires, and the sure, practicable and infallible remedy for the evils we now endure.

We have not addressed you as *citizens*—a term desired and ever cherished by us—because such you have never been. We have not addressed you as *freemen*—because such privileges have never been enjoyed by any colored man in the United States. Why then should we flatter your credulity, by inducing you to believe that which neither has now, nor never before had an existence. Our oppressors are ever gratified to our manifest satisfaction, especially when that satisfaction is founded upon false premises; an assumption on our part, of the enjoyment of rights and privileges which never have been conceded, and which, according to the present system of the United States policy, we never can enjoy.

The *political policy* of this country was solely borrowed from, and shaped and modeled after, that of Rome. This was strikingly the case in the establishment of immunities, and the application of terms in their Civil and Legal regulations.

The term Citizen—politically considered—is derived from the Roman definition—which was never applied in any other sense—*Cives Ingenui*; which meant, one exempt from restraint of any kind. . . . All who were deprived of citizenship—that is, the right of enjoying positions of honor and trust—were termed *Hostes* and *Peregrini*; which are public and private *enemies*. . . .

The Romans, from a national pride, to distinguish their inhabitants from those of other countries, termed them all "citizens," but consequently, were under the necessity of specifying four classes of citizens: none but the *Cives Ingenui* being unrestricted in their privileges. . . . They could vote for one of their superiors—the *Cives Ingenui*—but not for themselves.

Such, then, is the condition, precisely, of the black and colored inhabitants of the United States; in some of the States they, answering to the latter class, [have] the privilege of *voting*, to elevate their superiors to positions to which they need never dare aspire, or even hope to attain.

There has, of late years, been a false impression obtained, that the privilege of *voting* constitutes, or necessarily embodies, the *rights of citizenship*. A more radical error never obtained favor among an oppressed people. . . . To have the "right of suffrage," as we rather proudly term it, is simply to have the *privilege*—there is no *right* about it—of giving *approbation* to that which our *rulers may do*, without the privilege, on our part, of doing the same thing. . . .

Much might be adduced on this point to prove the insignificance of the black man, politically considered in this country, but we deem it wholly unnecessary at present, and consequently proceed at once to consider another feature of this important subject.

Let it then be understood, as a great principle of political economy, that no people can be free who themselves do not constitute an essential part of the *ruling element* of the country in which they live. . . . The liberty of no man is secure, who controls not his own political destiny. What is true of an individual, is true of a family; and that which is true of a family, is also true concerning a whole people. To suppose otherwise, is that delusion which at once induces its victim, through a period of long suffering, patiently to submit to every species of wrong; trusting against probability, and hoping against all reasonable grounds of expectation, for the granting of privileges which never will be attained. . . .

A people, to be free, must necessarily be *their own rulers*: that is, *each individual* must, in himself, embody the *essential ingredient*—so to speak—of the *sovereign principle* which composes the *true basis* of his liberty. This principle, when not exercised by himself, may, at his pleasure, be delegated to another—his true representative. . . .

The colored man in the United States, being deprived of the right of inherent sovereignty, cannot *confer* a suffrage, because he possesses none to confer. Therefore, where there is no suffrage, there can neither be *freedom* nor *safety* for the disfranchised. And it is futile hope to suppose that the agent of another's concerns, will take a proper interest in the affairs of those to whom his is under no obligations. Having no favors to ask or expect, he therefore has none to lose. . . .

In the United States, among the whites, their color is made, by law and custom, the mark of distinction and superiority; while the color of blacks is a badge of degradation, acknowledged by statute, organic law, and the common consent of the people. With this view of the case—which we hold to be correct—to elevate to equality the degraded subject of law and custom, it can only be done, as in Europe, by an entire destruction of the identity of the former condition of the applicant. Even were this desirable—which we by no means admit—with the deep seated prejudices engendered by oppression, with which we have to contend, ages incalculable might reasonably be expected to roll around, before this could honorably be accomplished; otherwise we should encourage and at once commence an indiscriminate concubinage and immoral commerce, of our mothers, sisters, wives and daughters, revolting to think of, and a physical curse to humanity.

But we have fully discovered and comprehended the great political disease with which we are affected, the cause of its origin and continuance; and what is now left for us to do, is to discover and apply a sovereign remedy—a healing balm to a sorely diseased body—a wrecked but not entirely shattered system. We propose for this disease a remedy.

That remedy is Emigration. This Emigration should be well advised, and like remedies applied to remove the disease from the physical system of man, skillfully and carefully applied, within the proper time, directed to operate on that part of the system, whose greatest tendency shall be, to benefit the whole. . . .

Our friends in this and other countries, anxious for our elevation, have for years been erroneously urging us to lose our identity as a distinct race. . . . The truth is, we are not identical with the Anglo-Saxon or any other race of the Caucasian or pure white type of the human family, and the sooner we know and acknowledge this truth, the better for ourselves and posterity. . . .

It would be duplicity longer to disguise the fact, that the great issue, sooner or later, upon which must be disputed the world's destiny, will be a question of black and white; and every individual will be called upon for his identity with one or the other. The blacks and colored races are four-sixths of all the population of the world; and these people are fast tending to a common sense with each other. The white races are but one-third of the population of the globe—one of them to two of us—and it cannot much longer continue, that two-thirds will passively submit to the universal domination of this one-third. . . . Our submission does not gain for us an increase of friends nor respectability—as the white race will only respect those who oppose their usurpation, and acknowledge as equals those who will not submit to their rule. This may be no new discovery in political economy, but it certainly is a subject worthy the consideration of the black race. . . .

There is but one question presents itself for our serious consideration, upon which we *must* give a decisive reply—Will we transmit, as an inheritance to our children, the blessings of unrestricted civil liberty, or shall we entail upon them, as our only political legacy, the degradation and oppression left us by our fathers?

Shall we be persuaded that we can live and prosper nowhere but under the authority and power of our North American white oppressors; that this (the United States) is the country most—if not the only one—favorable to our improvement and progress? Are we willing to admit that we are incapable of self-government, establishing for ourselves such political privileges, and making such internal improvements as we delight to enjoy, after American white men have made for themselves.

No! Neither is it true that the United States is the country best adapted to *our* improvement. But that country is the best in which our manhood—morally, mentally, and physically—can best be developed—in which we have an untrammeled right to the enjoyment of civil and religious liberty; and the West Indies, Central and South America, present now such advantages, superiorly preferable to all other countries. . . .

Had we no other claims than those set forth in a foregoing part of this address, they are sufficient to induce every black and colored person to remain on this continent, unshaken and unmoved.

But the West Indians, Central and South Americans, are a noble race of people; generous, sociable and tractible—just the people with whom we desire to unite, who are susceptible of progress, improvement and reform of every kind. They now desire all the improvements of North America, but being justly jealous of their rights, they have no confidence in the whites of the United States, and consequently peremptorily refuse to permit an indiscriminate settlement among them of this class of people; but placing every confidence in the black and colored people of North America. . . .

Should anything occur to prevent a successful emigration to the South—Central, South America and the West Indies—we have no hesitancy, rather than remain in the United States, the merest subordinates and servites of the whites, should the Canadas still continue separate in their political relations from this country, to recommend to the great body of our people, to remove to Canada West, where being politically equal to the whites, physically united with each other by a concentration of strength; when worse comes to worse, we may be found, not as a scattered, weak and impotent people, as we now are separated from each other throughout the Union, but a united and powerful body of freemen, mighty in politics, and terrible in any conflict which might ensue, in the event of an attempt at the disturbance of our political relations, domestic repose, and peaceful firesides.

Now, fellow-countrymen, we have done. Into your ears have we recounted your own sorrows; before your own eyes have we exhibited your wrongs; into your own hands have we committed your own cause. If there should prove a failure to remedy the dreadful evil, to assuage this terrible curse which has come upon us; the fault will be yours and not ours; since we have offered you a healing balm for every sorely aggravated wound.

>Martin R. Delany, Pa.
>William Webb, Pa.
>Augustus R. Green, Ohio
>Edward Butler, Mo.
>H. [F.] Douglass, La.
>A. Dudley, Wis.
>Conaway Barbour, Ky.
>Wm. J. Fuller, R.I.
>Wm. Lambert, Mich.
>J. Theodore Holly, N.Y.
>T. A. White, Ind.
>John A. Warren, Canada

2. Anti-emigration—"The Late Convention," by George B. Vashon*

On November 17, 1854, George B. Vashon published, in *Frederick Douglass' Paper*, a denunciation of the emigration convention in general and the "State Paper" in particular. George B. Vashon was the son of John B. Vashon, a well-known Garrisonian abolitionist from Pittsburgh. The younger Vashon had received a Master of Arts degree from Oberlin College and then studied law privately and was admitted to the bar in 1847. In 1850, he assumed a professorship at New York Central College. He was serving in that capacity when he issued the following refutation of black emigration.

———————

The proceedings of this body have been placed before the public. If they professed to be simply the resolves of individuals who assisted at that gathering, the plain rule which enjoins upon all persons to mind their own business, would require, perhaps, that they should be passed by in

*Frederick Douglass' Paper, November 17, 1854, p. 3.

silence. But, as they are clearly pervaded by the assumption that they embody the determined purpose of a large portion of the colored people of this country,—an assumption which is entirely unwarranted,—a brief notice of the proceedings could scarcely be looked upon as an impertinent interference.

In looking over the pamphlet Report of the Convention, one is particularly struck by the absence of the names of those who usually figure conspicuously at such gatherings of our people's representatives. The grave seems to have suddenly engulfed nearly all the veterans of our warfare; and their places in the ranks appear to be filled by other and, hitherto, entirely unknown combatants. . . . With the exception of a bare half-dozen persons, all the delegates were new men, who apparently rushed upon the arena of public life, *solely* for the purpose of giving *eclat* to the grand exodus which they were planning. There is no doubt, that by means somewhat analogous to the procedure upon the mimic stage, tremendous effect has been frequently produced in the closing act of some wild and startling melo-drama; but it is questionable whether such clap-trap, introduced into actual life, does not seem rather farcical.

Another peculiarity about this convention is that nearly all the delegates were from the same section of the country. Out of about one hundred and forty persons present in that capacity, upwards of eighty were from the city of Pittsburgh and its environs. The fact is, it seems to have been a convention of Pittsburghers. The call for the gathering emanated from that place, it found its most earnest advocates there; and, now, that city having been designated as the theatre of "practical" operations, there reside the acting members of the "National Board of Commissioners," Foreign, Domestic, Financial Committees, and all. Economy might have suggested a happy thought to the last mentioned committee:—to have held the convention at Pittsburgh, also; and thus, to have secured the six or seven hundred dollars which, undoubtedly, found their way into the coffers of the Cleveland and Pittsburgh Railroad Company, as an aid in the outfit of those convoys extraordinary who are soon to set out upon a tour to the Antilles, and to the States of Central and South America.

It is to be greatly feared that the holding of this Convention may yet be productive of much harm. Its Committee on Publication have assumed what may yet prove a fearful responsibility, in introducing the terms "black" and "colored," as distinctive appellations, into the nomenclature of our people; and although the Convention has declared in its platform, that all such terms shall ever be held by us with pride, it is, probably, an easy matter to say where the guilt will lie, if "Quadroon Societies" and prejudice and hatred be hereafter rife among us. The battlefields of Hayti, reeking with fraternal blood from the days of . . . L'Ouverture up to our own times, might have taught them what "a spell there is in those terms to raise the wild devil withal." But, if this fearful result is not to be anticipated, it is evident that the Reports of the Convention, and especially its "State paper," as it is termed, tend to foster the idea that there is a natural distinction between the white and colored races—the very thing which our enemies are racking Science and Revelation to discover, in order to use it as a stable basis for the God contemning system of Slavery.

And again: This Convention has already galvanized the defunct hope of Colonizationists, that they may yet succeed in overcoming our abhorrence to their scheme of expatriation. It was to be expected that this would happen, although the Report of the Committee carefully ignored Africa as a point of emigration. Indeed, it is a difficult matter to see why they should do so. That division of the globe possesses and offers all the inducements which they took into consideration. It is rich in mineral and other natural resources; and fully as healthy as some of the places they proposed. To crown all, the black race is there, not only a "necessary," but the sole "constituent in the ruling element." It is useless to object that by emigrating thither they would not be able to aid the fugitive slave, as they could do were they to go to Mexico. For, it would be an unpardonable modesty in men whose brilliant conceptions have planned the conquest of more than seven million square miles of territory, to be startled at a proposition for substituting, in lieu of the present Underground Railroad, an *Under Sea Line of Steamers* for the assistance of our fleeing brethren. In view of the magnificent empire which they could, without doubt, establish upon the shores of the mother country, this measure would be feasible.

Yet more. This Convention sides again with the enemies of the colored man, in surrendering the only vantage ground which he has hitherto occupied in the conflict for his rights. It takes away his right of citizenship, and coolly *disfranchises* him, even in States where his *suffrage* is allowed! It will not even accord to him that restricted sort of citizenship which, it tells us, existed in the Roman republic—the condition of "the *Jus Quiritium*, or the wailing or *supplicating* citizen." Truly, if the learned Committee do not err in this matter, then, as Dogberry said, "This is most tolerable, and not to be endured." The most admirable feature about these amateur conventionists, is the calm complacency with which they vaunt their own doings, and the cool assurance with which they disparage the efforts of others. They, forsooth, have transacted business "of vastly more importance than any other similar body of colored people ever before assembled in the United States." "They have established the first platform, necessary as a guide for action;" when in fact, this boasted document consists merely of the ordinary resolves passed by Colored Conventions, coupled with others of a decidedly mischievous tendency! They appear ignorant of the fact, that long before they entered into political *life*,—on the first day of September, 1831,—Pittsburghers did announce to the world a platform, upon which, doubtless, the vast majority of colored citizens of that place are still standing; and that it contained, among other things, the following sentiment: "Here (in the United States) we were born—here we will live by the help of the Almighty—and here we will die, and let our bones lie with our fathers." "The Constitution of the National Board of Commissioners, the *first* and only *practically* useful and comprehensively intelligent organization, unselfish in its motives and designs ever established in this country among the black inhabitants of the republic," amounts, in reality, to a part of the Constitution of the National Council established by the Rochester Convention, with the *impracticable* idea of emigration added thereto.

The "State Paper" on *The Political Destiny of the Colored Race on the American Continent* to which special attention of all persons is requested, is, indeed, a very extraordinary document. It, certainly, must have been written in a dream, whilst dormant volition could exercise no control over orative [*sic*] fancy, nor the realities of actual life bound in its vagaries. Had awakening consciousness suggested the propriety of revising this prosaic Palace of Kubla Khan, by a reference to some convenient Encyclopaedia, it might have been as correct in its varied learning as it is gorgeous in conception. As it is, it is false in history, false in philosophy, and, as may readily be imagined, false in its logical conclusions. These are serious charges to bring against a "State Paper," but let him who questions them refer to its numerous historic citations, to its novel classification of Roman citizens, and to its no less novel distinction between the terms *Suffrage* and *Franchise*,—a distinction by which the Convention, in a marginal note, represents Louis Napolean as having been the only person in France possessed of the elective franchise; and which, by a parity of reasoning, would disfranchise Clay and Webster, were they still living. As to the style of this report, it is better, perhaps to say as little as possible. It appears that, at the Convention, John Mercer Langston was called upon; that "he responded in a lengthy and rhetorical speech, replete with classic elegance;" and, that he was replied to by H. F. Douglass, Esq., of Louisiana; in a speech of the most withering sarcasm. If Mr. Langston's short-comings, upon that occasion, were his rhetoric and elegance, then the Committee who prepared this Report need entertain no fears of a lashing at the hands of Mr. Douglass.

If an attempt is ever made to carry into execution the plans proposed in this document, another chapter must be added to the Romance of History, more marvelous even than that which describes those great national Quixotisms, the medieval crusades—In the contemplation of geographical statistics as to population and territory, the Committee seem to have lost sight of the genious and character of the nations possessing the lands of which they propose the invasion—It is to be feared, that they will be greatly disappointed, when they learn from their Foreign Commissioners, that those nations are not standing (as the call for the Convention declares) "with open arms and yearning hearts, importuning us in the name of suffering humanity to come—to make common cause, and share one common fate,"—that, in the midst of the wild deluge of selfishness and revolution, no place could be found whereon the olive branch might be planted—no nest, wherein the wearied dove might nestle;—that our brethren, who here, in times past, sought by emigration, to "make an issue, create an event, and establish for themselves a position," have acquired one which is by no means to be envied, and from which they would give everything short of life, to be rescued.

It would have been a wise thing in the movers of this Convention, if they had respected the feeling which, as they themselves admit, had caused the subject of emigration to be "shunned by all delegated assemblages of our people which have heretofore met;" and it would now be the part of wisdom for them to conclude, with the great majority of their brethren, that, in attempting to give a national character to their scheme, they made a false move; and that the true issue *for us*, as a people, is upon our recognition as men, entitled to all the rights and privileges enjoyed by our white fellow-citizens.—And if instead of dealing with wholesale vituperations of the Anglo-Saxon race, they carefully examine its history and character, they may, perhaps, discover therein a pretty strong sense of justice; or if not that, at least such wisdom in its "work of universal subjugation" as prompts it to respect, and preserve everything that may be serviceable to its own advancement. In view thereof, they may possibly be led to conclude, that it would be better for colored men to take such a course as would render them indispensably "an essential constituent in the ruling element" of their native land, than to be devising gigantic, but impracticable schemes of emigration to other countries.

B. PROSLAVERY vs. ANTISLAVERY INTERPRETATIONS OF THE CONSTITUTION

1. Proslavery Interpretation—"Speech at the Twenty-Fourth Anniversary of the American Anti-Slavery Society," by Robert Purvis.*

On March 6, 1857, the Supreme Court rendered the famous Dred Scott decision, which asserted that blacks were not citizens under the Constitution. This decision had a serious impact on the attitudes of blacks, most of whom had constantly shown loyalty to that document, regarding it as applying equally in principle to them and to the whites of the United States. A minority of blacks had followed the Garrisonian philosophy on the Constitution and had spoken out against it. With the Dred Scott decision, the bitterness toward the Constitution reached a new high among some blacks, who claimed the Constitution both authorized slavery and denied citizenship to blacks.

Robert Purvis, a freeborn Amherst-educated black, was a loyal Garrisonian abolitionist who spent most of his adult life in Philadelphia. In this speech on May 12, 1857, Purvis not only attacked the Constitution as being a proslavery document, but also attacked the character of

**National Anti-Slavery Standard*, May 23, 1857, p. 1.

Frederick Douglass. Douglass had claimed, in a speech on the previous evening, that the Constitution was really an antislavery document.

Mr. Chairman: In allowing my name to be published as one of the speakers for this morning, which I have consented to do, at the earnest request of the Committee, it is due to myself to say that I have acted with great reluctance. Not that I am not deeply interested in this cause, nor that I have not clear convictions and strong feelings on the subject. On the contrary, my interest is too intense for expression, and my convictions and feelings are so vivid and overpowering that I cannot trust myself in attempting to give them utterance. Sir, I envy those who, with cooler blood or more mental self-command, can rise before an audience like this, and deliberately choose their words and speak their thoughts in calm, measured phrase. This is a task, sir, to which I am not adequate. I must either say too much or too little. If I let my heart play freely, and speak out what I think and feel, I am extravagant, as people call it. If I put a curb on my feelings and try to imitate the cool and unimpassioned manner of others, I cannot speak at all. Sir, how can any man with blood in his veins, and a heart pulsating in his bosom, and especially how can any colored man, think of the oppression of this country and of the wrongs of his race, and then express himself with calmness and without passion (applause).

Mr. Chairman, look at the facts—here in a country with a sublimity of impudence that knows no parallel, setting itself up before the world as a *free country*, a *land of liberty*! ''the *land of the free*, and the *home of the brave*,'' the ''*freest country in all the world*''! Gracious God! and yet here are millions of men and women groaning under a bondage the like of which the world has never seen—bought and sold, whipped, manacled, killed all the day long. Yet this is a *free country*! The people have the assurance to talk of their *free institutions*. How can I speak of such a country and use language of moderation? How can I, who every day feel the grinding hoof of this despotism, and who am myself identified with its victims? Sir, let others, who can, speak coolly on the subject: I cannot, and I will not (applause).

Mr. Chairman, that I may make sure of expressing the precise sentiment which I wish to present to this meeting, I will offer a resolution. It is one which I had the honor of presenting at a meeting lately held in the City of Philadelphia, but to which I did not speak as I could have desired, for the reasons already stated. The resolution is as follows:

> "Resolved, That to attempt, as some do, to prove that there is no support given to slavery in the Constitution and essential structure of the American Government is to argue against reason and common sense, to ignore history and shut our eyes against palpable facts; and while it may suit white men, who do not feel the iron heel, to please themselves with such theories, it ill becomes the man of color, whose daily experience refutes the absurdity, to indulge in any such idle fantasies."

Mr. Chairman, this resolution expresses just what I think and feel about this new-fangled doctrine of the anti-slavery character of the American Constitution. Sir, with all due respect to the Hon. Gerrit Smith, who is a noble and good man, and one whom, from my soul, I honor . . .—I say to the noble-minded, large hearted Gerrit Smith, . . . that the doctrine of the anti-slavery character of the American Constitution seems to me one of the most absurd and preposterous that ever was broached. It is so contrary to history and common sense, so opposite to what we and every man, and especially every colored man, feel and know to be the fact, that I have not patience to argue about it. I know it is said that the word "slave" or "slavery" is not to be found in the document. Neither are those words to be found in the Fugitive Slave Law. But will any man pretend, on this account, that that infamous statute is an anti-slavery statute, or that it is not one of the most atrocious and damnable laws that ever disgraced the annals of despotism (applause). I know, sir, that there are some fine phrases in the Preamble about "establishing justice" and "securing to ourselves and our posterity the blessings of liberty." But what does that prove? Does it prove that the Constitution of the United States is an anti-slavery document? Then Mr. Buchanan's late Message was an anti-slavery document, and Mr. Buchanan himself is a great Abolitionist. Then were all the Messages of your contemptible President Pierce anti-slavery documents, and your contemptible President Pierce was not contemptible, but a much misunderstood and misrepresented

Abolitionist. If these fine phrases make the Constitution anti-slavery, then all the Fourth of July orations delivered by pro-slavery doughfaces at the North, and Democratic slave-breeders at the South, all these are anti-slavery documents. Sir, this talk about the Constitution being anti-slavery seems to me so utterly at variance with common sense and what we know to be facts that, as I have already intimated, I have no patience with it. I have no particular objection, Mr. Chairman, to white men, who have little to feel on this subject, to amuse themselves with such theories; but I must say that when I see them imitated by colored men, I am disgusted! Sir, have we no self-respect? Are we to clank the chains that have been made for us, and praise the men who did the deed? Are we to be kicked and scouted, trampled upon and judicially declared to *"have no rights which white men are bound to respect,"* and then turn round and glorify and magnify the laws under which all this is done? Are we such base, soulless, spiritless sycophants as all this? Sir, let others do as they may, I never will stultify or disgrace myself by eulogizing a government which tramples me and all that are dear to me in the dust (applause).

Sir, I treat as an absurdity, an idle fantasy, the idea of the Constitution of this American Union being anti-slavery; on the contrary, I assert that the Constitution is fitting and befitting those who made it—slaveholders and their abettors—and I am free to declare without any fears of successful contradiction, that the Government of the United States, in its formation and essential structure as well as in its practice, is one of the basest, meanest, most atrocious despotisms that ever saw the face of the sun (applause). And, I rejoice, sir, that there is a prospect of this atrocious government being overthrown, and a better one built up in its place. I rejoice in the revolution which is now going on. I honor from the bottom of my soul, I honor this glorious Society for the part, the leading part, it has taken in this noble work. My heart overflows with gratitude to the self-sacrificing men and women of this Society who have been pioneers in this cause—men and women who, from the beginning till this time, in storm and whatever of sunshine they have had, through evil report and good report, have stood by the side of the slave and unfalteringly maintained the rights of free men of color. Sir, I cannot sufficiently express, the English language has not words strong enough to express, my admiration of the Abolitionists of this country, and my gratitude to them for what they have done for the confessedly oppressed colored people in it. And in saying this, I believe I utter the sentiments of all the true colored men in the country. I know, sir, there are colored men, some of them occupying prominent places before the public, who lose no opportunity of traducing and misrepresenting the character and course of the Garrisonian Abolitionists; but, sir, these are men without principle, men who are actuated by the basest selfishness, and in whose hearts there is not a spark of genuine love for the cause of freedom. They value anti-slavery not for what it is in itself, or for what it is doing for the slave, but for what it does or fails to do for themselves personally. Sir, I should be ashamed and mortified to believe that these men represented truly the views and feelings of the people of color of this country. They do not.

But, Mr. Chairman, I am getting away from the subject of the resolution; and, as I have occupied more time than I intended, I will bring my remarks to a close at once, making way for one who, though following after, is greatly preferred before us—one upon whom no higher praise can be pronounced than the simple enunciation of this name—Wendell Phillips (applause).

2. Antislavery Interpretation—Address on the Dred Scott Decision, by Frederick Douglass*

Frederick Douglass, the renowned black orator and editor, had escaped slavery in 1838, and after giving a simple narrative speech at a meeting of the Massachusetts Anti-Slavery Society in 1841, he was offered a position as traveling agent for that society. For about ten years, Douglass assumed the Garrisonian anticonstitution position of his white companions. However, in the early 1850s, he changed to the position of the majority of blacks, i.e., that the Constitution is an antislavery document in principle. The following speech was delivered on the evening of May 11, 1857 at a preliminary meeting of the American Anti-Slavery Society's Twenty Fourth Convention. Douglass' speech was criticized by Garrison and the delegates at the preliminary meeting, who resolved that they would "allow nothing to stand between the slave and his emancipation— . . . neither Constitution nor Union." In his speech,

*Frederick Douglass, *Address on the Dred Scott Decision* (Rochester: Printed at the Office of Frederick Douglass, 1857), p. 1-20.

Douglass upheld the Constitution, and asserted that it was being misinterpreted.

———————

Mr. Chairman, Friends, and Fellow Citizens:

While four millions of our fellow countrymen are in chains—while
men, women, and children are bought and sold on the auction-block with
horses, sheep, and swine—while the remorseless slave-whip draws the
warm blood of our common humanity—it is meet that we assemble as we
have done today, and lift up our hearts and voices in earnest denunciation
of the vile and shocking abomination. It is not for us to be governed by
our hopes or our fears in this great work. . . . It is a fitting time to take an
observation to ascertain where we are, and what our prospects are. . . .

By all the laws of nature, civilization, and of progress, slavery is a
doomed system. Not all the skill of politicians, North and South, not all
the sophistries of judges, not all the fulminations of a corrupt press, not
all the hypocritical prayers, or the hypocritical refusals to pray of a
hollow-hearted priesthood, not all the devices of sin and Satan, can save
the vile thing from extermination. . . .

I base my sense of the certain overthrow of slavery, in part, upon the
nature of the American Government, the Constitution, the tendencies of
the age, and the character of the American people; and this, notwithstanding the important decision of Judge Taney.

I know of no soil better adapted to the growth of reform than American
soil. I know of no country where the conditions for [effecting] great
changes in the settled order of things, for the development of right ideas
of liberty and humanity, are more favorable than here in these United
States.

The very groundwork of this government is a good repository of
Christian civilization. The Constitution, as well as the Declaration of
Independence, and the sentiments of the founders of the Republic, give
us a platform broad enough, and strong enough, to support the most
comprehensive plans for the freedom and elevation of all the people of
this country, without regard to color, class, or clime. . . .

It is clearly not because of the peculiar character of our Constitution
that we have slavery, but the wicked pride, love of power, and selfish

perverseness of the American people. Slavery lives in this country not because of any paper Constitution, but in the moral blindness of the American people, who persuade themselves that they are safe, though the rights of others may be struck down. . . .

But I come now to the great question as to the constitutionality of slavery. The recent slaveholding decision, as well as the teachings of anti-slavery men, make this a fit time to discuss the constitutional pretensions of slavery. . . .

I have a quarrel with those who fling the Supreme Law of this land between the slave and freedom. It is a serious matter to fling the weight of the Constitution against the cause of human liberty, and those who do it, take upon [themselves] a heavy responsibility. Nothing but absolute necessity, shall, or ought to drive me to such a concession to slavery.

When I admit that slavery is constitutional, I must see slavery recognized in the Constitution. I must see that it is there plainly stated that one man of a certain description has a right of property in the body and soul of another man of a certain description. There must be no room for a doubt. In a matter so important as the loss of liberty, everything must be proved beyond all reasonable doubt. . . .

Now let us approach the Constitution from the standpoint thus indicated, and instead of finding in it a warrant for the stupendous system of robbery, comprehended in the term slavery, we shall find it strongly against that system.

"We, the people of the United States, in order to form a more perfect Union, establish justice, insure domestic tranquility, provide for the common defense, promote the general welfare, and secure the blessings of liberty to ourselves and our posterity, do ordain and establish this constitution for the United States of America."

Such are the objects announced by the instrument itself, and they are in harmony with the Declaration of Independence, and the principles of human well-being.

Six objects are here declared, "Union," "defense," "welfare," "tranquility," "justice," and "liberty."

Neither in the Preamble nor in the body of the Constitution is there a single mention of the term *slave* or *slave holder, slave master* or *slave state*, neither is there any reference to the color, or the physical peculiarities of any part of the people of the United States. Neither is there anything in the Constitution standing alone, which would imply the existence of slavery in this country.

"We, the people"—not we, the white people—not we, the citizens, or the legal voters—not we, the privileged class, and excluding all other classes but we the people; not we, the horses and cattle, but we the people—the men and women, the human inhabitants of the United States, do ordain and establish this Constitution, etc.

I ask, then, any man to read the Constitution, and tell me where, if he can, in what particular that instrument affords the slightest sanction of slavery?

Where will he find a guarantee for slavery? Will he find it in the declaration that no person shall be deprived of life, liberty, or property, without due process of law? Will he find it in the declaration that the Constitution was established to secure the blessing of liberty? Will he find it in the right of the people to be secure in their persons and papers, and houses, and effects? Will he find it in the clause prohibiting the enactment by any State of a bill of attainder?

These all strike at the root of slavery, and any one of them, but faithfully carried out, would put an end to slavery in every State in the American Union. . . .

How is the constitutionality of slavery made out or attempted to be made out?

First, . . . by assuming that the written Constitution is to be interpreted in the light of a secret and unwritten understanding of its framers, which understanding is declared to be in favor of slavery. It is in this mean, contemptible, underhand method that the Constitution is pressed into the service of slavery.

They do not point us to the Constitution itself, for the reason that there is nothing sufficiently explicit for their purpose; but they delight in supposed intentions—intentions nowhere expressed in the Constitution, and everywhere contradicted in the Constitution. . . .

The argument here is that the Constitution comes down to us from a slaveholding period and a slaveholding people; and that, therefore, we are bound to suppose that the Constitution recognizes colored persons of African descent, the victims of slavery at that time, as debarred forever from all participation in the benefit of the Constitution and the Declaration of Independence although the plain reading of both includes them in their beneficent range.

As a man, an American, a citizen, a colored man of both Anglo-Saxon and African descent, I denounce this representation as a most scandalous and devilish perversion of the Constitution, and a brazen misstatement of the facts of history.

But I will not content myself with mere denunciation; I invite attention to the facts. . . .

It is a fact, a great historic fact, that at the time of the adoption of the Constitution, the leading religious denominations in this land were anti-slavery, and were laboring for the emancipation of the colored people of African descent.

The church of a country is often a better index of the state of opinion and feeling than is even the government itself. . . .

Washington and Jefferson, and Adams, and Jay, and Franklin, and Rush, and Hamilton, and a host of others, held no such degrading views of the subject of slavery as are imputed by Judge Taney to the Fathers of the Republic.

All, at that time, looked for the gradual but certain abolition of slavery, and shaped the Constitution with a view to this grand result.

George Washington can never be claimed as a fanatic, or as the representative of fanatics. The slaveholders impudently use his name for the base purpose of giving respectability to slavery. Yet, in a letter to Robert Morris, Washington uses this language—language which, at this day, would make him a terror of the slaveholders, and the natural representative of the Republican party.

"There is not a man living, who wishes more sincerely than I do to see some plan adopted for the abolition of slavery; but there is only one proper and effectual mode by which it can be accomplished, and that is by legislative authority; and this, as far as my suffrage will go, shall not be wanting."

Washington only spoke the sentiment of his times. There were, at that time, Abolition societies in the slave states—Abolition societies in Virginia, in North Carolina, in Maryland, in Pennsylvania, and in Georgia—all slaveholding States. Slavery was so weak, and liberty so strong, that free speech could attack the monster to its teeth. Men were not mobbed and driven out of the presence of slavery, merely because they condemned the slave system. The system was then on its knees imploring to be spared, until it could get itself decently out of the world.

In light of these facts, the Constitution was framed, and framed in conformity to it.

It may, however, be asked, if the Constitution were so framed that the rights of the people were naturally protected by it, how happens it that a large part of the people have been held in slavery ever since its adoption? Have the people mistaken the requirements of their own Constitution?

The answer is ready. The Constitution is one thing, its administration is another, and, in this instance, a very different and opposite thing. I am here to vindicate the law, not the administration of the law. It is the written Constitution, not the unwritten Constitution, that is now before us. If, in the whole range of the Constitution, you can find no warrant for slavery, then we may properly claim it for liberty.

Good and wholesome laws are often found dead on the statute book. We may condemn and practice under them and against them, but never the law itself. To condemn the good law with the wicked practice, is to weaken, not to strengthen our testimony.

It is no evidence that the Bible is a bad book, because those who profess to believe the Bible are bad. The slaveholders of the South, and many of their wicked allies at the North, claim the Bible for slavery; shall we, therefore, fling the Bible away as a pro-slavery book? It would be as reasonable to do so as it would be to fling away the Constitution. . . .

It may be said that it is quite true that the Constitution was designed to secure the blessings of liberty and justice to the people who made it, and to the posterity of the people who made it, but was never designed to do any such thing for the colored people of African descent.

This is Judge Taney's argument, and it is Mr. Garrison's argument, but it is not the argument of the Constitution. The Constitution imposes no such mean and satanic limitations upon its own beneficent operation. And, if the Constitution makes none, I beg to know what right has anybody, outside of the Constitution, for the special accommodation of slaveholding villainy, to impose such a construction upon the Constitution?

The Constitution knows all the human inhabitants of this country as "the people". It makes, as I have said before, no discrimination in favor

of, or against, any class of the people, but is fitted to protect and preserve the rights of all, without reference to color, size, or physical peculiarities.
. . .

In conclusion, let me say, all I ask of the American people is, that they live up to the Constitution, adopt its principles, imbibe its spirit, and enforce its provisions.

When this is done, the wounds of my bleeding people will be healed, the chain will no longer rust on their ankles, their backs will no longer be torn by the bloody lash, and liberty, the glorious birthright of our common humanity, will become the inheritance of all the inhabitants of this highly favored country.

C. TWO PARTYISM VS. THIRD PARTYISM

1. Two Partyism—"The Signs of the Times," by Samuel E. Cornish*

With the exception of an extremely small number who refused to vote or otherwise act politically under the Constitution, antebellum blacks were loyal supporters of the American political system. Their participation was limited because of the lack of voting rights in several states, but they worked in politics and were consistently petitioning for the franchise. In the late 1830s, the American Anti-Slavery Society was split between the Garrisonian moral suasionists and the politically-oriented abolitionists. Many blacks then assumed the unenviable position of trying to remain sympathetic to Garrison as a man and crusader for their cause while at the same time retaining their philosophy of working within the American political system. They were determined to act politically but the issue arose as to *how* their political actions should be channeled.

In August 1839, the political abolitionists held a "National Anti-Slavery Convention" at Albany in which they resolved to support only those candidates for public office who favored immediate abolition of slavery. This, of course, precluded most Whigs and Democrats.

Samuel Cornish attended the Albany Convention and opposed the idea of strictly limiting political support to immediate abolitionists. Cornish's

*Colored American, August 17 and 24, 1839.

influence among fellow blacks was strong. He had gone to Free African schools in Philadelphia and had later established the first Negro Presbyterian Church in New York City in 1822. In 1827, Cornish was co-founder of *Freedom's Journal*, the first black newspaper of the western world. He remained active in antislavery activities in New York City and became editor of the *Colored American* during the middle 1830s. After May 18, 1839, Cornish and James McCune Smith relinquished their official co-editorship of the *Colored American*. From that point, the editorial responsibilities were assumed by two of the newspaper's proprietors, Charles B. Ray and Philip A. Bell, both of whom were also from New York City.

In August 1839, Cornish wrote the following discourse in installments to the new editors, stating his case opposing the Albany Convention's resolution.

We attended the "National Anti-Slavery Convention" held week before last in the city of Albany. The virtue, influence, learning and talent in attendance, were worthy [of] the great objects of the meeting. Our soul was rejoiced in the doings of God and in the combinations and efforts of great and good men in behalf of the free colored man and the slave. . . .

We ourself had the misfortune or good fortune, to be in the minority on the subject of "Political Action," but though in the vocative we have the happiness of feeling that we are conscientiously so, and time and *time only*, can convince us that we are wrong. It is a matter to be demonstrated by experience and not by argument—(brother Lee's best syllogisms are altogether inefficient.) The brethren in the majority, we doubt not, are equally conscientious, and when they have been as long disfranchised and made, voluntarily, equally, politically contemptible, as we have been, involuntarily, we doubt not, but their conclusions will tally with our own.

The subject is an important one. Political power, subservient to moral power and influence, is a *mighty Anti-Slavery engine*—one too important to be sacrificed or to have its application neglected. We hold that all true abolitionists should go to the polls and *vote*, and that they should not, voluntarily forego nor place themselves under circumstances to be denied the privilege. . . . Should abolitionists stay from the polls and suffer the reign of political oppression, they will not be less guilty of maintaining our unrighteous laws, than the tyrants themselves.

Under this view of the subject, we shall show, in a series of numbers (that is, if words arguments and facts will do it,) that the following resolution is impolitic, inconsistent and injurious to the abolition cause; and that it must result in one of three things—a total delinquency to its injunctions, the disfranchisement of our friends (the abolitionists) or in the degradation of our cause from moral to political measures. . . .

Resolved, that we will neither vote for, nor support the election of any man for President or Vice President of the United States, or for Governor or Lieutenant Governor, or for any legislative office, who is not in favor of the immediate ABOLITION OF SLAVERY.

THE ABOVE RESOLUTION WE CONSIDER IMPOLITIC. It is a virtual disfranchisement of all who adhere to it—and there is nothing more calculated, with certain classes of the community, to break off the influence and lessen the respectability of abolitionists and their cause, than disfranchisement.—All intelligent colored men know this. Disfranchisement has been the source and means of their social and civil martyrdom. Had all the free States, in the spirit of our "Declaration of Independence," framed their several constitutions on equal principles and secured to all freemen, irrespective of complexion, the right of voting and eligibility to office, the influence colored men would have exerted in the politics of the nation, and the places they would have filled, long ere this, would have placed them above prejudice and beyond the reach of proscription, both in church and state. And were abolitionists, in the uncompromising spirit of their righteous principles, to inform the contending parties that regardless of their political prepossessions they should promptly and zealously sustain the party who conceded most to freedom and humanity, they would soon find each division seeking to emulate the other in liberality of principles and republicanism of action. Abolitionists would then hold the balance of power, command the respect and control the influence of both parties, in legislating the policy of the Nation.

But on the contrary, an adherence to the above resolution, on the part of abolitionists, requires but a compromise between the two political parties, who hate the principles of abolition much more than they do each other's politics, to disfranchise all the abolitionists in the land. Let the parties but agree with each other to place on neither ticket a candidate, who goes the creed of abolition and our good brethren of the "resolution" fall between two stools.

But says brother Stanton and others, we will vote for ourselves or vote our own ticket—yes good brethen, and this will avail as much as Pagan worship. With your abolition strengths in most States, to vote for yourselves . . . will be but as the Pagan adulation of an "alligator or an image." It will make your shorn and sacrificed influence ludicrous. . . .

But say some, this is better than sustaining slavery by our votes, for to vote for either party who do not go for immediate abolition is only choosing between [two] evils. We deny this. There may be a selection between two men who do not go the whole of our principles, which is not a choice between evils. For instance; should there be two candidates, the one much worse than the other, and whose election depended upon the neutrality of abolitionists, and his defeat upon their votes being placed in the other end of the scale, we ask, in such a case, would not abolitionists be bound to PREVENT THE GREATER EVIL by voting for the better man? Such precisely was the case in the election of Governor, in the State of New York, last autumn.

THE ABOVE RESOLUTION IS INCONSISTENT

1. Because it lets down our *noble cause* from the sacred basis upon which it was established—'*moral principles*,' and resorts to physical measures to accomplish a grand moral purpose. The brethren in the confusion of Babel, lost sight of the Polar star, and assumed the weapons of Saul, with which to fight the battles of David and Israel. Slavery if a political evil, is one which resulted from moral delinquency, and requires moral measures for its removal. But make the heart of this nation right with God, on the subject of American tyranny, and there will be no need of a resort to the ballot box. . . .

How inconsistent then for a Society, four fifths of whose members are professing christians, to overlook . . . those "weapons which are mighty, through God, to the pulling down of strongholds."

2. Because it carries with it features of distrust and impatience, unworthy our noble cause. The Bible tells us that—"He that believeth

shall not make haste.'' Why then should we resort to new and doubtful measures to carry our purposes. . . ? The ballot box may, without conviction of the heart, drive the nation to an involuntary emancipation, but moral suasion will, much sooner, lead to a voluntary, consistent and conscientious emancipation.

3. Because it is not consistent with their other resolutions which require all abolitionists to carry their principles to the polls. The others require them to vote, and the above, with a refinement . . . bordering on self-righteousness, ties up their hands so that, in half the States, they cannot vote, and in the other half, not more than one in every ten, can do it. How inconsistent, brethren!

THE ABOVE RESOLUTION IS INJURIOUS TO THE ABOLITION CAUSE.

If not conceived in the same spirit which led David to number Israel, yet the resolution wears much of the same aspect—*numerical strength the ballot box*—''MIGHT AND POWER.''

Brethren, why should we in this way, let down our cause to the level of its enemies. . . ? We are MORALLY abolitionists, and God is our vitality and hope. But the very assumption of political measures, even as mere auxiliaries to our heavenly machinery is a degradation of our cause. We ought to be conscientious politicians, but let our politics grow out of conscious duty to God and the slave, and always be *subservient means* in the prosecution of ''MORAL MEASURES,'' *but never the measures themselves*, in the prosecution of moral purposes. . . . The disfranchisement of the body of abolitionists or . . . the organization of a third political abolition party, . . . are to be deprecated as injurious, if not fatal to the abolition cause.

1. To pass such a resolution and not have sufficient fortitude and firmness to carry it out, will be dishonorable to abolitionists and reproach the abolition cause. . . . The body of abolitionists, who are politicians, will not be governed . . . by any resolutions which go to infringe upon their civil fights. . . . But

2. Should the good brethren . . . succeed in inducing all the abolitionists in the long to follow suit, the result will be injurious and fatal to abolition influence upon the corrupt politics of the country.

Abolitionists being a small minority in all the states, for years to come, must be virtually disfranchised and politically of *no account.* . . .

3. Should neither the first nor the second view be the result, but the third, the formation of a great anti-slavery party be resorted to; the consequence would be equal or more injurious. And we here raise our warning voice against any political organization of abolitionists whatever. . . . Slavery is A MORAL EVIL with an immoral basis and hinged upon political action. . . . The measures of its removal should therefore be emphatically *moral*—MORAL—MORAL.

That the formation of an anti-slavery political party by our friends would be injurious to the abolition cause might be maintained by many arguments and illustrated by many facts.—We could write a volume on this subject without the fear of its being gainsayed, though it might be resisted. Ask the honest, pure hearted anti-mason, what ruined his cause and he will tell you "political action." While he pushed principles upon the righteousness of his cause and the *immorality of masonry*—he was respected and prospered. But when he descended to physical contest, and political intrigue, he was despised and defeated.

Many who are in favor of political action are not aware of the corrupting influence of politics. . . . Experience teaches us that political success has always [gone] "hand in glove" with political corruption. It may be argued that this is not necessarily the case. . . We know not upon what principle of philosophy to account for these things [and] neither shall we attempt to argue them logically. It seems to be one of the eternal principles of fallen nature, for which we cannot account; political action has never yet taught moral duty.

To conclude, . . . we hope these remarks will be received in the spirit in which they are written. We have no other object in view but the good of the cause, and whenever we cease to point out in our brethren, what we think to be errors, we shall have ceased to love them.

2. *Third Partyism—"Political Action," by Charles B. Ray**

During the period in which Cornish's articles were appearing, Charles Bennett Ray had been traveling throughout the country and regularly

**Colored American*, November 9 and 16, 1839.

writing letters back to his paper stating his observations of meetings he attended. However, in November 1839, after his return to New York, Ray wrote the following essay in two installments, rebutting Cornish's arguments and supporting the establishment of a purely abolitionist third party.

Like Cornish, Charles B. Ray was a clergyman of the Presbyterian order. His undergraduate study was at Wesleyan University in Connecticut, and he had subsequently earned the reputation of being "a terse and eloquent writer." In 1839, Ray not only became editor of the *Colored American* but was chairman of the New York vigilance committee for the assistance and elevation of freemen and fugitives. His first article defending third partyism was published in the November 9, 1839 issue of his paper.

———————————

This subject has excited much attention for the months past, among the friends of abolition, and attracted greatly the attention of its enemies. This paper, perhaps, has produced more sensation upon this subject among friends of the slave, and caused more excitement than any of the other abolition papers. . . . Different opinions have been expressed through its columns, some of which in my opinion, have been erroneous. I now intend to give mine, and to such I shall give my influence through the paper and elsewhere.

I believe it a settled truth, that human governments are both right and proper. The Bible, in my opinion, not only suffers them to exist, but authorizes and directs their existence.—This opinion I first predicate upon the books of the Kings. Jesus Christ also, to say the least, directly approbated their existence. . . . If human government be right, and exist by the consent of the governed as the best system of government, the governed must vote, as the best mode to constitute government. The question now arises, by what rules ought men to be governed in casting their vote, or what motives should actuate them. . . .

Slaveholding is the giant sin of the land—a crime before God under all circumstances—an evil in all its effects and fruits. We are called upon to vote for a man, who, in his official station, *may* be called upon to act upon this subject, and we know beforehand, that he will give his influence directly or indirectly to sustain slaveholding; what right then, have we, by any law in the Bible (our rule,) to vote for such a man? No right. We are guilty for such an act.

But says Bro. Cornish, (in effect,) you are bound to vote for the [better] of two men, though they both may be bad, to prevent the greater evil; and he might strengthen his argument by saying, the good order of society requires it, for if you did not vote for the lesser, other men will vote for the greater and elect him. Be it so then. We have no right whatever, to involve ourselves in a little guilt by sustaining the smaller sin, because other men will involve themselves in the greater guilt by sustaining the greater sin. But if you vote for either, you disfranchise yourself, which you have no right to do. Granted that we have no right to disfranchise ourselves when we can vote and not involve us in guilt—when we cannot without sustaining moral evil as in slaveholding, we are bound to disfranchise ourselves. If other men will do wrong the guilt be upon their own heads.

Finally, so long as abolitionists disregard this rule in voting and vote for the party without regard to their abolition principles, so long will they be guilty, and so long shall we have slavery in some of its forms amongst us. We may create a universal conscience upon the moral bearings of slavery; but until that conscience directs or votes in strict accordance with our principles, we shall have slavery nevertheless. . . .

We believe also, that as abolitionists, we have got, hereafter, to take one of the three forms of the following dilemma; either to vote against our principles, and sustain slaveholding in all its abominations, either not to vote at all, or else to come out and form a third political party. We have not always entertained the latter opinion, but we now see no other course to be pursued.

Political abolition is the truth to put home to men already abolitionists, and not the doctrine to convert man with. The great mass of Ohio and Pennsylvania have yet got to be converted, to be indoctrinated, they are great wastes, *cities* and *villages* yet unmoved, and we have got to go there with the Bible, the sword of truth, and show them the conflicting principle of slavery, with the Bible. . . ; show them all its abomination, before they will ever see, feel, or act with us.

We hope this, because men never will act politically with us in the cause, until they act with us morally. It is vain to hope, that men will go to the polls and act with us, until they act with us morally. It is vain to hope that men will go [to] the polls and act with us, until they have seen slaveholding, in some of its iniquitous forms, a sin against God, a moral encroachment upon the rights of man, and those few who may, are not to be trusted, they go upon pretence, for interest or office, and not upon principle, they have no heart with us. They must first become morally incensed against the system, and then we may look for their cooperation.

Again we hope this, because we can reach the south, where the great battle is to be fought, with no other kind of abolition. Our political action has its limits, but our moral knows no bounds. They may tell us to cease our political abolition, we have no right, and shall not interfere with their laws, and so far we do cease; but when they say we shall not speak the truth about their system, and expose its iniquities, we expose so much the more. . . .

Again it is the moral feature of abolition, which regards the identity of the human species, *man as man*, which holds up the colored man, in common, and as the equal of other men; it is this which is at war with prejudice, and which if anything, will bring about that healthful state of feeling, which should be, and bring out those principles which should govern, and exist between man and man, without regard to color. This is the colored man's hope, for his sake then, we do hope all will go to work at moral abolition, and when we wish to prepare for another general election, then we will charge home political abolition, and try to make old converts and new ones, vote consistently.

D. VIOLENCE VS. NONVIOLENCE

1. Violence—"An Address to the Slaves of the United States of America," by Henry Highland Garnet*

Henry H. Garnet was born a slave in Maryland but escaped to freedom with his family in 1824 when he was nine years old. He studied at Oneida Institute in New York under Beriah Green. In 1840, Garnet went to Troy

*Walker's Appeal, With a Brief Sketch of His Life by Henry Highland Garnet, and also Garnet's Address to the Slaves of the United States of America (New York: Printed by J. H. Tobitt, 1848), p. 89-96.

to serve as pastor of the Negro Presbyterian Church. Along with Samuel Ringgold Ward, Garnet became one of the first members of the newly founded Liberty party in 1840, believing in working through political channels under the Constitution to accomplish the elevation of his people.

Garnet delivered his "Address to the Slaves" at the National Negro Convention in 1843. It reveals his growing impatience with slavery and his religious justification of violence. Garnet's "Address" was debated among delegates to the Convention before finally being rejected by one vote.

Brethren and Fellow Citizens:

Your brethren of the north, east, and west have been accustomed to meet together in National Conventions, to sympathize with each other, and to weep over your unhappy condition. In these meetings we have addressed all classes of the free, but we have never until this time, sent a word of consolation and advice to you. We have been contented in sitting still and mourning over your sorrows, earnestly hoping that before this day, your sacred liberties would have been restored. But, we have hoped in vain. Years have rolled on, and tens of thousands have been borne on streams of blood, and tears, to the shores of eternity. While you have been oppressed, we have also been partakers with you; nor can we be free while you are enslaved. We therefore write to you as being bound with you.

Many of you are bound to us, not only by the ties of a common humanity, but we are connected by the more tender relations of parents, wives, husbands, children, brothers, and sisters, and friends. As such we most affectionately address you.

Slavery has fixed a deep gulf between you and us, and while it shuts out from you the relief and consolation which your friends would willingly render, it afflicts and persecutes you with a fierceness which we might not expect to see in the fiends of hell. But still the Almighty Father of Mercies has left to us a glimmering ray of hope, which shines out like a lone star in a cloudy sky. Mankind are becoming wiser, and better—the oppressor's power is fading, and you, every day, are becoming better informed, and more numerous. Your grievances, brethren, are many. We shall not attempt, in this short address, to present to the world, all the dark catalogue of this nation's sins, which have been committed upon an innocent people. Nor is it indeed, necessary, for you feel them from day to day, and all the civilized world look upon them with amazement.

Two hundred and twenty-seven years ago, the first of our injured race were brought to the shores of America. They came not with glad spirits to select their homes, in the New World. They came not with their own consent, to find an unmolested enjoyment of the blessings of this fruitful soil. The first dealings which they had with men calling themselves Christians, exhibited to them the worst features of corrupt and sordid hearts; and convinced them that no cruelty is too great, no villainy, and no robbery too abhorrent for even enlightened men to perform, when influenced by avarice, and lust. Neither did they come flying upon the wings of Liberty, to a land of freedom. But, they came with broken hearts, from their beloved native land, and were doomed to unrequited toil, and deep degradation. Nor did the evil of their bondage end at their emancipation by death. Succeeding generations inherited their chains, and millions have come from eternity into time, and have returned again to the world of spirits, cursed, and ruined by American Slavery.

The propagators of the system, or their immediate ancestors very soon discovered its growing evil, and its tremendous wickedness, and secret promises were made to destroy it. The gross inconsistency of a people holding slaves, who had themselves "ferried o'er the wave," for freedom's sake, was too apparent to be entirely overlooked. The voice of Freedom cried, "emancipate your Slaves." Humanity supplicated with tears, for the deliverance of the children of Africa. Wisdom urged her solemn plea. The bleeding captive plead his innocence, and pointed to Christianity who stood weeping at the cross. Jehovah frowned upon the nefarious institution, and thunderbolts, red with vengeance, struggled to leap forth to blast the guilty wretches who maintained it. But all was vain. Slavery had stretched its dark wings of death over the land, the Church stood silently by—the priests prophesied falsely, and the people loved to have it so. Its throne is established, and now it reigns triumphantly.

Nearly three millions of your fellow citizens, are prohibited by law, and public opinion, (which in this country is stronger than law), from reading the Book of Life. Your intellect has been destroyed as much as possible, and every ray of light they have attempted to shut out from your minds. The oppressors themselves have become involved in the ruin. They have become weak, sensual, and rapacious. They have cursed you—they have cursed themselves—they have cursed the earth which they have trod. In the language of a Southern statesman, we can truly say, "even the wolf, driven back long since by the approach of man, now returns after the lapse of a hundred years, and howls amid the desolations of slavery."

The colonists threw the blame upon England. They said that the mother country entailed the evil upon them, and that they would rid themselves of it if they could. The world thought they were sincere, and the philanthropic pitied them. But time soon tested their sincerity. In a few years, the colonists grew strong and severed themselves from the British Government. Their Independence was declared, and they took their station among the sovereign powers of the earth. The declaration was a glorious document. Sages admired it, and the patriotic of every nation reverenced the Godlike sentiments which it contained. When the power of Government returned to their hands, did they emancipate the slaves? No; they rather added new links to our chains. Were they ignorant of the principles of Liberty? Certainly they were not. The sentiments of their revolutionary orators fell in burning eloquence upon their hearts, and with one voice they cried, LIBERTY OR DEATH. O, what a sentence was that! It ran from soul to soul like electric fire, and nerved the arm of thousands to fight in the holy cause of Freedom. Among the diversity of opinions that are entertained in regard to physical resistance, there are but a few found to gainsay that stern declaration. We are among those who do not.

SLAVERY! How much misery is comprehended in that single word. What mind is there that does not shrink from its direful effects? Unless the image of God is obliterated from the soul, all men cherish the love of Liberty. The nice discerning political economist does not regard the sacred right, more than the untutored African who roams in the wilds of Congo. Nor has the one more right to the full enjoyment of his freedom than the other. In every man's mind the good seeds of liberty are planted, and he who brings his fellow down so low, as to make him contented with a condition of slavery, commits the highest crime against God and man. Brethren, your oppressors aim to do this. They endeavor to make you as much like brutes as possible. When they have blinded the eyes of your mind—when they have embittered the sweet waters of life—when they have shut out the light which shines from the word of God—then, and not till then has American slavery done its perfect work.

TO SUCH DEGRADATION IT IS SINFUL IN THE EXTREME FOR YOU TO MAKE VOLUNTARY SUBMISSION. The divine commandments, you are in duty bound to reverence, and obey. If you do not obey them you will surely meet with the displeasure of the Almighty. He requires you to love him supremely, and your neighbor as yourself—to keep the Sabbath day holy—to search the Scriptures—and bring up your children with respect for his laws, and to worship no other God but him. But slavery sets all these at naught, and hurls defiance in the face of Jehovah. The forlorn condition in which you are placed does not destroy your moral obligation to God. You are not certain of Heaven, because you suffer yourselves to remain in a state of slavery, where you cannot obey the commandments of the Sovereign of the universe. If the ignorance of slavery is a passport to heaven, then it is a blessing, and no curse, and you should rather desire its perpetuity than its abolition. God will not receive slavery, nor ignorance, nor any other state of mind, for love, and obedience to him. Your condition does not absolve you from your moral obligation. The diabolical injustice by which your liberties are cloven down, NEITHER GOD, NOR ANGELS, OR JUST MEN, COMMAND YOU TO SUFFER FOR A SINGLE MOMENT. THEREFORE IT IS YOUR SOLEMN AND IMPERATIVE DUTY TO USE EVERY MEANS, BOTH MORAL, INTELLECTUAL, AND PHYSICAL, THAT PROMISE[S] SUCCESS. If a band of heathen men should attempt to enslave a race of Christians, and to place their children under the influence of some false religion, surely, heaven would frown upon the men who would not resist such aggression, even to death. If, on the other hand, a band of Christians should attempt to enslave a race of heathen men and to entail slavery upon them, and to keep them in heathenism in the midst of Christianity, the God of heaven would smile upon every effort which the injured might make to disenthral themselves.

Brethren, it is as wrong for your lordly oppressors to keep you in slavery, as it was for the man thief to steal our ancestors from the coast of Africa. You should therefore now use the same manner of resistance, as would have been just in our ancestors, when the bloody foot prints of the first remorseless soul thief was placed upon the shores of our fatherland.

The humblest peasant is as free in the sight of God, as the proudest monarch that ever swayed a sceptre. Liberty is a spirit sent out from God, and like its great Author, is no respector of persons.

Brethren, the time has come when you must act for yourselves. It is an old and true saying, that "if hereditary bondmen would be free, they must themselves strike the blow." You can plead your own cause, and do the work of emancipation better than any others. The nations of the old world are moving in the great cause of universal freedom, and some of them at least, will ere long, do you justice. The combined powers of Europe have placed their broad seal of disapprobation upon the African slave trade. But in the slave holding parts of the United States, the trade is as brisk as ever. They buy and sell you as though you were brute beasts. The North has done much—her opinion of slavery in the abstract is known. But in regard to the South, we adopt the opinion of the New York Evangelist—"We have advanced so far, that the cause apparently waits for a more effectual door to be thrown open than has been yet." We are about to point you to that more effectual door. Look around you, and behold the bosoms of your loving wives, heaving with untold agonies! Hear the cries of your poor children! Remember the stripes your fathers bore. Think of the torture and disgrace of your noble mothers. Think of your wretched sisters, loving virtue and purity, as they are driven into concubinage, and are exposed to the unbridled lusts of incarnate devils. Think of the undying glory that hangs around the ancient name of Africa:—and forget not that you are native-born American citizens, and as such, you are justly entitled to all the rights that are granted to the freest. Think how many tears you have poured out upon the soil which you have cultivated with unrequited toil, and enriched with your blood; and then go to your lordly enslavers, and tell them plainly, that YOU ARE DETERMINED TO BE FREE. Appeal to their sense of justice, and tell them that they have no more right to oppress you, than you have to enslave them. Entreat them to remove the grievous burdens which they have imposed upon you, and to remunerate you for your labor. Promise them renewed diligence in the cultivation of the soil, if they will render to you an equivalent for your services. Point them to the increase of happiness and prosperity in the British West Indies, since the act of Emancipation. Tell them in language which they cannot misunderstand, of the exceeding sinfulness of slavery, and of a future judgment, and of the righteous retributions of an indignant God. Inform them that all you desire, is FREEDOM, and that nothing else will suffice. Do this, and for ever after cease to toil for the heartless tyrants, who give you no other reward but stripes and abuse. If they then commence the work of death, they, and not you, will be responsible for the consequences. You had far better all die—die immediately, than live slaves, and entail your wretchedness upon your posterity. If you would be free in this generation, here is your only hope. However much you and all of us may desire it, there is not much hope of Redemption without the shedding of blood. If you must bleed, let it all come at once—rather, die freemen, than live to be slaves. It is impossible, like the children of Israel, to make a grand Exodus from the land of bondage. THE PHARAOHS ARE ON BOTH SIDES OF THE BLOOD-RED WATERS! You cannot remove en masse, to the dominions of the British Queen—nor can you pass through Florida, and over-run Texas, and at last find peace in Mexico. The propagators of American slavery are spending their blood and treasure, that they may plant the black flag in the heart of Mexico, and riot in the halls of the Montezumas. In the language of the Rev. Robert Hall, when addressing the volunteers of Bristol, who were rushing forth to repel the invasion of Napoleon, who threatened to lay waste the fair homes of England, "Religion is too much interested in your behalf, not to shed over you her most gracious influences."

You will not be compelled to spend much time in order to become inured to hardships. From the first moment that you breathed the air of heaven, you have been accustomed to nothing else but hardships. The heroes of the American Revolution were never put upon harder fare, than a peck of corn, and a few herrings per week. You have not become enervated by the luxuries of life. Your sternest energies have been beaten out upon the anvil of severe trial. Slavery has done this, to make you subservient to its own purposes; but it has done more than this, it has prepared you for any emergency. If you receive good treatment, it is what you could hardly expect; if you meet with pain, sorrow, and even death, these are the common lot of the slaves.

Fellow-men! patient sufferers! behold your dearest rights crushed to the earth! See your sons murdered, and your wives, mothers, and sisters, doomed to prostitution! In the name of the merciful God! and by all that life is worth, let it no longer be a debatable question, whether it is better to choose LIBERTY or DEATH!

In 1822, Denmark Veazie, of South Carolina, formed a plan for the liberation of his fellow men. In the whole history of human efforts to overthrow slavery, a more complicated and tremendous plan was never formed. He was betrayed by the treachery of his own people, and died a martyr to freedom. Many a brave hero fell, but History, faithful to her high trust, will transcribe his name on the same monument with Moses, Hampden, Tell, Bruce, and Wallace, Touissaint L'Overteur, Lafayette and Washington. That tremendous movement shook the whole empire of slavery. The guilty soul thieves were overwhelmed with fear. It is a matter of fact, that at that time, and in consequence of the threatened revolution, the slave states talked strongly of emancipation. But they blew but one blast of the trumpet of freedom, and then laid it aside. As these men became quiet, the slaveholders ceased to talk about emancipation: and now, behold your condition today! Angels sigh over it, and humanity has long since exhausted her tears in weeping on your acccount!

The patriotic Nathaniel Turner followed Denmark Veazie. He was goaded to desperation by wrong and injustice. By Despotism, his name has been recorded on the list of infamy, but future generations will number him among the noble and brave.

Next arose the immortal Joseph Cinque, the hero of the Amistad. He was a native African, and by the help of God he emancipated a whole ship-load of his fellow men on the high seas. And he now sings of liberty on the sunny hills of Africa, and beneath his native palm trees, where he hears the lion roar, and feels himself as free as that king of the forest. Next arose Madison Washington, that bright star of freedom, and took his station in the constellation of freedom. He was a slave on board the brig Creole, of Richmond, bound to New Orleans, that great slave mart, with a hundred and four others. Nineteen struck for liberty or death. But one life was taken, and the whole were emancipated, and the vessel was carried into Nassau, New Providence. Noble men! Those who have fallen in freedom's conflict, their memories will be cherished by the true hearted, and the God-fearing, in all future generations; those who are living, their names are surrounded by a halo of glory.

We do not advise you to attempt a revolution with the sword, because it would be INEXPEDIENT. Your numbers are too small, and moreover the rising spirit of the age, and the spirit of the gospel, are opposed to war and bloodshed. But from this moment cease to labor for tyrants who will not remunerate you. Let every slave throughout the land do this, and the days of slavery are numbered. You cannot be more oppressed than you have been—you cannot suffer greater cruelties than you have already. RATHER DIE FREEMEN, THAN LIVE TO BE SLAVES. Remember that you are THREE MILLIONS.

It is in your power so to torment the God-cursed slaveholders, that they will be glad to let you go free. If the scale was turned, and black men were the masters, and white men the slaves, every destructive agent and element would be employed to lay the oppressor low. Danger and death would hang over their heads day and night. Yes, the tyrants would meet with plagues more terrible than those of Pharaoh. But you are a patient people. You act as though you were made for the special use of these devils. You act as though your daughters were born to pamper the lusts of your masters and overseers. And worse than all, you tamely submit, while your lords tear your wives from your embraces, and defile them before your eyes. In the name of God we ask, are you men? Where is the blood of your fathers? Has it all run out of your veins? Awake, awake; millions of voices are calling you! Your dead fathers speak to you from their graves. Heaven, as with a voice of thunder, calls on you to arise from the dust.

Let your motto be RESISTANCE! RESISTANCE! RESISTANCE!—No oppressed people have ever secured their liberty without resistance. What kind of resistance you had better make, you must decide by the circumstances that surround you, and according to the suggestion of expediency. Brethren, adieu. Trust in the living God. Labor for the peace of the human race, and remember that you are three millions.

   2. Nonviolence—"Address on Non-Resistance to Offensive Aggression," by William Whipper*

A free black, William Whipper ran a lumber business in Columbia, Pennsylvania. He was a founder of the American Moral Reform Society, an organization designed to eliminate complexional distinctions and

*Colored American, September 9, 16, 23, 30, 1837.

concentrate on such general reforms as education, temperance, universal liberty, and peace. An integral part of the peace issue was the subject of physical nonviolence, particularly nonresistance. This address was delivered on August 16, 1837 at the First Annual Meeting of the American Moral Reform Society in Philadelphia. Proceedings of the meeting had been suspended so the address could be delivered. Afterwards, the organization unanimously resolved that "the principles of *peace* are worthy your attention, consideration, and adoption. Therefore, we do hereby tender to Mr. Wm. Whipper, our united thanks for his views, so ably delivered *thereon* this afternoon."

In contrast with Garnet's address of six years later, Whipper argued that the avoidance of physical violence could help the blacks. His address was in support of the resolution that: "The practice of non-resistance to physical aggression is not only consistent with reason, but the surest method of obtaining a speedy triumph of the principles of universal peace."

Mr. President: The above resolution presupposes that if there were no God to guide and govern the destinies of man on this planet, no Bible to light his path through the wilds of sin, darkness and error, and no religion to give him a glorious and lasting consolation while traversing the gloomy vale of despondency, and to light up his soul anew with fresh influence from the fountain of Divine grace—that mankind might enjoy an exalted state of civilization, peace and quietude in their social, civil and international relations, far beyond that which Christians now enjoy, guarded and protected by the great Author of all good and the doctrines of the Prince of Peace.

But, sir, while I am assuming the position that the cause of peace amongst mankind may be promoted without the scriptures, I would not, for a single moment, sanction the often made assertion that the doctrines of the holy scriptures justify war—for they are in my humble opinion its greatest enemy. And I further believe that as soon as they become fully understood and practically adopted, wars and strifes will cease. I believe that every argument urged in favor of what is termed a "just and necessary war," or physical self-defense, is at enmity with the letter and spirit of the scriptures, and when they emanate from its professed advocates should be repudiated, as inimical to the principles they profess, and a reproach to Christianity itself. . . .

The resolution asserts that the practice of non-resistance to physical aggression is consistent with reason. A very distinguished man asserts ''that reason is that distinguishing characteristic that separates man from the brute creation,'' and that this power was bestowed upon him by his Maker, that he might be capable of subduing all subordinate intelligence to his will. It is this power when exerted in its full force that enables him to conquer the animals of the forest, and which makes him lord of creation. There is a right and a wrong method of reasoning. The latter is governed by our animal impulses and wicked desires, without regard to the end to be attained. The former fixes its premises, in great fundamental and unalterable truths—surveys the magnitude of the objects and the difficulties to be surmounted, and calls to its aid the resources of enlightened wisdom as a landmark by which to conduct its operations.

It is self-evident that when the greatest difficulties surround us, we should summon our noblest powers. ''Man is a being formed for action as well as contemplation''; for this purpose there are interwoven in his constitution powers, instincts, feelings and affections which have a reference to his improvement in virtue, and which excite him to promote the happiness of others. When we behold them by their noble sentiments exhibiting sublime virtues and performing illustrious actions, we ascribe the same to the goodness of their hearts, their great reasoning powers and intellectual abilities. For were it not for these high human endowments, we should never behold men in seasons of calamity, displaying tranquillity and fortitude in the midst of difficulties and dangers, enduring poverty and distress with a noble heroism, suffering injuries and affronts with patience and serenity—stifling resentment when they have it in their power to inflict vengeance—displaying kindness and generosity towards enemies and slanderers—submitting to pain and disgrace in order to promote the prosperity of their friends and relatives, or the great interests of the human race. . . .

The great law of love forbids our doing aught against the interests of our fellow men. It is altogether inconsistent with reason and common sense for persons when they deem themselves insulted by the vulgar aspersions of others, to maltreat their bodies for the acts of their minds.

Yet how frequently do we observe those that are blessed by nature and education (and if they would but aspire to acts that bear a parallel to their dignified minds, they would shine as illustrious stars in the created throngs), that degrade themselves by practicing this barbarous custom, suited only to tyrants—because in this they may be justly ranked with the untutored savages or the animals of the forest that are impelled only by instinct. . . .

Human passion is the hallucination of a distempered mind. It renders the subject of it like a ship upon the ocean without ballast or cargo, always in danger of being wrecked by every breeze. Phrenologically speaking, a mind that is subject to the fluctuating whims of passion is without the organ of order, "which is nature's first law." Our reasoning powers ought to be the helm that should guide us through the shoals and quicksands of life.

I am aware that there are those who consider the non-resistance wholly impracticable. But I trust that but few such can be found that have adopted the injunction of the Messiah for their guide and future hope, for He commands us to "love our enemies, bless them that curse you, pray for them that despitefully use you, and persecute you." These words were peculiarly applicable at the period they were uttered, and had a direct reference to the wars and strifes that then convulsed the world, and they are equally applicable at this moment. If the Christian church had at her beginning made herself the enemy of war, the evil would doubtless have been abolished throughout Christendom. The Christians of the present day do not seem to regard the principles of peace as binding, or they are unwilling to become subject to the Divine government. Human governments, then, as well as now, were too feeble to stay the ravages of passion and crime, and hence there was an evident necessity for the imperious command, "Whomsoever shall smite thee on thy right cheek, turn unto him the other also."

And now, Mr. President, I rest my argument on the ground that whatever is *Scriptural* is *right*, and that whatever is right is reasonable, and from this invulnerable position I mean not to stray for the sake of any expediency whatever. The doctrine evidently taught by the Scriptural quotation evidently instructs us that resistance to physical aggression is wholly unnecessary as well as unrighteous, and subjects the transgressor to the penalty due from a willful departure from the moral and Divine law. Therefore every act of disobedience to the commands of Christian duty, in relation to our fellowmen may fairly be deemed unreasonable, as it is at enmity with our true interests and the welfare of human society. We are further instructed to turn away from the evil one, rather than waste our strength, influence and passions in a conflict that must in the end prove very injurious to both.

But someone perhaps is ready to raise an objection against this method of brooking the insults of others, and believe it right to refer to the maxim "that self-defense is the first law of nature." I will readily agree that it is the unbounded duty of every individual to defend himself against both the vulgar and false aspersions of a wicked world. But then I contend that his weapons should be his reasoning powers. That since a kind Providence has bestowed on him the power of speech and the ability to reason, he degrades his Creator by engulfing himself in the turmoils of passion and physical conflict. A mode of warfare practiced by barbarous tribes in their native forests and suited only to those animals that are alone endowed with the powers of instinct. Nor is it possible to suppose that men can pursue such a course without first parting with their reason. We often see men, while under the reigning influence of passion, as fit subjects for the lunatic asylum as any that are confined in the lunatic asylum on account of insanity.

In every possible and impartial view we take of the subject we find that physical conflict militates against the interest of the parties in collision. If I, in conflict with mine enemy, overcome him by my superior physical powers, or my skill in battle, I neither wholly subdue him, nor convince him of the justice of my cause. His spirit becomes still more enraged and he will seek retaliation and conquest on some future occasion that may seem to him more propitious. If I intimidate him I have made him a slave, while I reign a despot, and our relation will continue unnatural, as well as dangerous to each other, until our friendship has become fully restored. And what has been gained by this barbarous method of warfare when both parties become losers thereby? Yet this single case illustrates the value of all personal conflicts.

But let us pursue this subject in a more dignified view. I mean as it respects the moral and Divine government. Is it possible that any Christian man or woman that will flog and maltreat their fellow beings can be in earnest when they with apparent devotion ask their heavenly Father to "forgive their trespasses as they forgive others"? Surely they must be asking God to punish them—or when they say "lead us not into temptation, but deliver us from evil," do they mean that they should run headlong into both, with all their infuriated madness? Certainly not. Who would not be more willing to apply to them insincerity of motive, and that they knew not what they were doing, rather than suppose that intelligent minds would be capable of such gross inconsistency? Would it not prove infinitely better in times of trials and difficulties, to leave the tempter and temptation behind and pursue our course onward? But, says the objector, there will be no safety nor security in this method from the insults of the vulgar and the brutal attacks of the assassin. I am inclined to believe to the contrary, and will be borne out in that belief by the evidence of those that have pursued this Christian course of conduct.

A writer under the signature of Philopacificus, while "taking a solemn view of the custom of war," says, "There are two sets of professed Christians in this country, which, as sects, are peculiar in their opinions respecting the lawfulness of war, and the right of repelling injury by violence." These are Quakers and Shakers. They are remarkably pacific. Now we ask, does it appear from experience that their forbearing spirit brings on them a greater portion of injury and insults than what is experienced by people of other sects? Is not the reverse of this true, in fact? There may indeed be some such instances of gross depravity as a person taking advantage of their pacific character, to do them an injury with the hope of impunity. But in general it is believed their pacific principles and spirit command the esteem even of the vicious and operate as a shield from insult and abuse.

The question may be brought home to every society. How seldom do children of a mild and forbearing temper experience insults or injury, compared with the waspish, who will sting if they are touched? The same inquiry may be made in respect to persons of these opposite descriptions of every age, and in every situation of life, and the result will prove favorable to the point in question.

When William Penn took the government of Pennsylvania, he distinctly avowed to the Indians his forbearing and pacific principles, and his benevolent wishes for uninterrupted peace with them. On these principles the government was administered while it remained in the hands of the Quakers. This was an illustrious example of government on religious principles, worthy of imitation by all the nations of the earth.

I am happy to state that there are various incidents related by travelers, both among the native Africans and Indians, where lives have been saved by the presentation of a pacific attitude, when they would have otherwise fallen a prey to savage barbarity.

It has been my purpose to exhibit reason as a great safeguard, at all times capable of dethroning passion and alleviating our condition in periods of the greatest trouble and difficulty, and of being a powerful handmaid in achieving a triumph of the principles of universal peace. I have also thus far treated the subject as a grand fundamental principle, universal in its nature, and binding alike on every member of the human family. But if there be a single class of people in these United States on which these duties are more imperative and binding than another, that class is the colored population of this country, both free and enslaved. Situated as we are, among a people that recognize the lawfulness of slavery, and more of whom sympathize with the oppressor than the oppressed, it requires us to pursue our course calmly onward, with much self-denial, patience and perseverance.

We must be prepared at all times to meet the scoffs and scorns of the vulgar and indecent—the contemptible frowns of haughty tyrants and the blighting mildew of a popular and sinful prejudice. If amidst these difficulties we can but possess our souls in patience we shall finally triumph over our enemies. But among the various duties that devolve on us, not the least is that which relates to ourselves. We must learn on all occasions to rebuke the spirit of violence, both in sentiment and practice. God has said, ''Vengeance is mine, and I will repay it.'' The laws of the land guarantee the protection of our persons from personal violence, and whoever for any cause inflicts a single blow on a fellow being violates the laws of God and of his country and has no just claim to being regarded as a Christian or a good citizen. . . .

The power of reason is the noblest gift of Heaven to man, because it assimilates man to his Maker. And were he to improve his mind by cultivating his reasoning powers, his acts of life would bear the impress of the Deity indelibly stamped upon them. If human governments bore any direct resemblance to the government of God they would be mild in their operation, and the principles of universal peace would become implanted in every mind. Wars, fighting, and strifes would cease—there would be a signal triumph of truth over error—the principles of peace, justice, righteousness, and universal love would guide and direct mankind onward in that sublime path marked out by the great Prince of Peace.

And now, my friends, let us cease to be guided by the influence of a wild and beguiling passion—the wicked and foolish fantasies of pride, folly and lustful ambition—the alluring and detestable examples of despotism and governments—the sickly sensibility of those who from false notions of honor attempt to promote the ends of justice by placing ''righteousness under their feet,'' and are at all times ready to imbue their hands in a fellow creature's blood for the purpose of satisfying their voracious appetites for crime, murder and revenge. I say from them let us turn away, for a terrible retaliation must shortly await them, even in this life. The moral power of this nation and the world is fast wakening from the sleep of ages, and wielding a swift bosom that will sweep from the face of the earth error and iniquity with the power of a whirlwind. But a few years ago and dueling was considered necessary to personal honor, and the professional Christian, or the most upright citizen, might barter away the lives and happiness of a nation with his guilty traffic in ardent spirits with impunity. But now a regenerated public sentiment not only repudiates their conduct, but consigns them with ''body and soul murderers.'' Though the right to be free has been deemed inalienable by this nation from a period antecedent to the Declaration of American Independence, yet a mental fog hovered over this nation on the subject of slavery that had well-nigh sealed her doom were it not that in the Providence of God a few noble spirits arose in the might of moral power to her rescue. They girded on the power of truth for their shield and the principles of peace for their buckler, and thus boldly pierced through the incrustations of a false and fatal philosophy, and from the incision sprang forth the light of glorious liberty, disseminating its delectable rays over the dark chasms of slavery and lighting up the vision of a ruined world. And the effect has been to awaken the nation to her duty with regard to the rights of man—to render slaveholders despicable and guilty of robbery and murder—and in many places those that profess Christianity have been unchurched, denied the privilege of Christian fellowship. And the same moral power is now awakening in the cause of peace, and will bring disgrace and dishonor on all who engage in wars and fighting.

The period is fast approaching when church, as at present constituted, must undergo one of the severest contests she has met with since her foundation, because in so many cases she has refused to sustain her own principles. The moral warfare that is now commenced will not cease if the issue should be a dissolution of both church and state. The time has already come when those who believe that intemperance, slavery, war, and fighting are sinful, and it will soon arrive when those who practice either [sic] their rights to enjoy Christian fellowship will be questioned.

And now, Mr. President, I shall give a few practical illustrations, and then I shall have done. It appears by history that there have been many faithful advocates of peace since the apostolic age, but none have ever given a more powerful impetus to the cause of peace than the modern abolitionists. They have been beaten and stoned, mobbed and persecuted from city to city, and never returned evil for evil, but submissively, as a sheep brought before the shearer, have they endured scoffings and scourges for the cause's sake while they prayed for their persecutors. And how miraculously they have been preserved in the midst of a thousand dangers from without and within. Up to the present moment not the life of a single individual has been sacrificed on the altar of popular fury. Had they set out in this glorious undertaking of freeing 2,500,000 human beings with the war-cry of "liberty or death," they would have been long since demolished, or a civil war would have ensued; thus would have dyed the national soil with human blood. And now let me ask you, was not their method of attacking the system of human slavery the most reasonable? And would not their policy have been correct, even if we were to lay aside their Christian motives? Their weapons were reason and moral truth, and on them they desired to stand or fall—and so it will be in all causes that are sustained from just and Christian principles, they will ultimately triumph. Now let us suppose for a single moment what would have been our case if they had started on the principle that "resistance to tyrants is obedience to God"?—what would have been our condition, together with that of the slave population? Why, we should have doubtless perished by the sword, or been praying for the destruction of our enemies, and probably engaged in the same bloody warfare.

And now we are indebted to the modern abolitionists more than to any other class of men for the instructions we have received from the dissemination of their principles, or we would not at this moment be associated here to advocate the cause of moral reform—of temperance, education, peace and universal liberty. Therefore let us, like them, obliterate from our minds the idea of revenge, and from our hearts all wicked intentions towards each other and the world, and we shall be able through the blessing of Almighty God to do much to establish the principles of universal peace. Let us not think the world has no regard for our efforts—they are looking forward to them with intense interest and anxiety. The enemies of the abolitionists are exhibiting a regard for the power of their principles that they are unwilling to acknowledge, although it is everywhere known over the country that abolitionists "will not fight," yet they distrust their own strength so much that they frequently muster a whole neighborhood of from 50 to 300 men, with sticks, stones, rotten eggs and bowie knives, to mob and beat a single individual, probably in his " 'teens," whose heart's law is nonresistance. There is another way in which they do us honor—they admit the right of all people to fight for their liberty but colored people and abolitionists—plainly inferring that they are too good for the performance of such un-Christian acts—and lastly, while we endeavor to control our own passions and keep them in subjection, let us be mindful of the weakness of others; and for acts of wickedness committed against us let us reciprocate in the spirit of kindness. If they continue their injustice towards us, let us always decide that their reasoning powers are defective, and that it is with men as the laws of mechanics—large bodies move slowly, while smaller ones are easily propelled with swift velocity. In every case of passion that presents itself the subject is one of pity rather than derision, and in his cooler moments let us earnestly advise him to improve his understanding by cultivating his intellectual powers, and thus exhibit his close alliance with God, who is the author of all wisdom, peace, justice, righteousness, and truth. And in conclusion, let it always be our aim to live in a spirit of unity with each other, supporting one common cause by spreading our influence for the good of mankind, with the hope that the period will ultimately arise when the principles of universal peace will triumph throughout the world.

E. NONEXCLUSIVISM VS. EXCLUSIVISM

1. Nonexclusivism—"Letters to the Colored American,*" by William Whipper**

A steady controversy among blacks beginning in the mid-1830s concerned the extent to which their people should assemble exclusively and make efforts strictly in behalf of themselves. When the American Moral Reform Society was designed in 1834, William Whipper had been a major advocate of eliminating all racial exclusiveness and working to better the "family of man" without regard to color.

The exclusivism controversy became especially prominent during the three years preceding the 1843 National Negro Convention. There were calls for a national Negro convention by many black spokesmen in the country, but some blacks such as William Whipper and James McCune Smith thought that a special convention by and for the Negroes would only serve to perpetuate the complexional distinctions which it would assemble to eliminate.

In August 1840, the Colored Citizens of New York held a State Convention at Albany to devise means for elevation, such as the elimination of New York's discriminatory $250 property requirement which blacks had to meet before being allowed to vote. A response to the exclusive tone of the Albany Convention was issued by a black Pennsylvanian, William Whipper. As soon as he received a copy of the convention minutes, Whipper was prompted to write the following discourse in the form of two letters to Charles B. Ray, then the editor of the *Colored American*. Ray had served as Chairman of the Business Committee at the Albany Convention.

––––––––––––––

Friend Ray:—It is with a high sense of the goodness of Almighty God, in sparing and protecting us from many of the afflictions that have scourged the "human race," and swept from existence a portion of the distinguished advocates of human rights during the past year, that I take

*Colored American, January 30 and February 6, 1841.

up my pen to return your congratulations on the advent of "the new year," with the prospect and success that must attend an ardent, zealous, and untiring advocacy of the principles of our common cause.

Through the kindness of a friend I have just received for perusal, a copy of the "Minutes of the Albany Convention of Colored Citizens." It is a rich and valuable pamphlet. As I am opposed to the *manner* of its organization, I cannot, therefore, subscribe to the proceedings, as a whole, but I find in many of the reports and resolutions, principles and sentiments that are eternal and immutable. Principles that must and will dethrone slavery, and obliterate prejudice. . . . The first resolution will be admired by the friends of liberty and equality in all future generations, viz:

"Resolved: That ALL LAWS established for human government, and ALL SYSTEMS, of *whatever* KIND, founded in the SPIRIT OF COMPLEXIONAL CAST, are in *violation of the fundamental principles of DIVINE LAW, evil in their tendencies*, and should, therefore, be EFFECTUALLY DESTROYED."

Now, my dear sir, I believe the doctrines contained in the above resolution, have emanated from the sure fountain of heaven-born truth, and that all those that quench their thirst by partaking of that living stream will be governed by the principles it dictates. With the advocates of such principles, I delight to labor. The principles of this resolution are not only applicable to the "Church and government under which we live," but they reach to every organization for human improvement throughout the various ramifications of society. It seeks the entire destruction of all those invidious complexional distinctions, whether in institutions or "systems" that exclude by constitutional landmarks, any member of the human family from the common rights and privileges of membership, on account of complexional variations. I regard the resolution as a two-edged sword, that will divide as under those distinctive features in the various "systems" and constitutions throughout our country, that have been fostered by a spirit of hatred and selfishness, no matter by whom, or what complexion they were formed. The fiat of the convention has gone forth, and proclaimed their condemnation as being contrary to the spirit of the "Divine law, and the political principles of the frames of our republican government."

I hope your active and combined exertions may not only prove instrumental in giving New York a free constitution, but that the same genial influence may effect the much desired reformation in both our federal and state governments. But we should not stop here, civil tyranny is not more odious than religious despotism. Look at the incorporated feature of complexional distinction in our churches, schools, beneficial, and literary societies. Are these to be extended, tolerated, and supported in their present shape? Can we hope to be successful in reforming others before we procure a reformation among ourselves? Experience answers, no! while the resolution asserts that such institutions *ought to be destroyed*. The resolution saps the very foundation principle on which nearly all the institutions in our country are based. It is not confined to written constitutions, but utters forth its condemnation on "all systems," hence all those churches whose written constitutions are not defaced by the insertion of the terms, "white, colored or African," but whose practice, by the influence of a detestable prejudice, is such as to exclude persons of a certain complexion from a participation in the rights, privileges, and enjoyments of the same, are alike guilty of an infringement of the "divine law." Nor is this all, the very paper you edit [*Colored American*] bears upon its title the very distinctive feature, which is the object of the resolution to obliterate. I do, therefore, humbly hope that the principles of the resolution will fall on its distinctive title and grind it to powder. The convention, in passing this resolution, not only aided in bringing odium on the title of your paper, but it occupied a still higher ground, they ushered forth a withering condemnation on the form of their organization. For it is an indisputable fact, that the convention was formed by a system of representation, based on complexional cast, and, therefore, in the language of the resolution, "was in violation of the principles of divine law, evil in its tendency and should therefore have been effectually destroyed." I trust that all future conventions may guard against the errors of the past, and be governed by the spirit of this resolution, so that a consistency in principle, as well as unity of action, may be the legitimate means by which we shall be enabled to carry our cause onward to its final consummation. . . .

I must now proceed to the 2d resolution which is marked by a boundary line, but is equally strong in principle over the space it is intended to operate. It reads as follows:

"Resolved, That the toleration of complexional difference in the State of New York is a stain upon its constitution, and attaches it to the great system of oppression in the land, so vital to our national character, since it is upheld, not only in direct opposition to the common rights of humanity, but also runs counter to those very political principles asserted by the framers of our republican government." Now, sir, it is to be expected, that state action by the colored people of New York as a means of attaining their rights as Americans, will be followed by a state action, among the same class in other states. I do therefore appeal to them in behalf of their down-trodden situation—their love of republican principles—of civil and religious liberty to strictly examine the principles on which the "Albany Convention" was based, in order that they may discover whether its *model* claims their admiration, as the most righteous and successful method for the government of their future operations. Now I aver that the above resolution is either true or false. If it be true that the "toleration of complexional distinction in the state of New York, is a stain upon its constitution, and attaches it to the great system of oppression in the land, and in direct opposition to the rights of humanity" it is equally true of every other state constitution where that distinction exists, as well as the constitution of the United States. . . .

It is peculiarly appropriate for any people that have long been trodden under foot by the "iron heel" of any peculiar despotism that when they appeal to the rectitude of just principles in behalf of their deliverance, that they should first exhibit to the world, that they were not only prepared to act upon those principles themselves, but that they had hurled that principle of despotism from their own borders. . . . Now, sir, I respectfully ask if the amended constitution of the State of New York is "in opposition to the rights of humanity" on account of complexional difference, are not the Colored Churches, schools, benevolent and beneficial societies, formed and sustained in equal violation of the great fundamental principles of human rights? . . .

What I have said respecting the Albany Convention and what I regard as their very inconsistent course is equally applicable to our people in this state [Pennsylvania]. We too protested against the insertion of the term "white" in our State Constitution where we were nurturing and sustaining in our midst near one hundred institutions with "colored and African" charters, and the result was as might have been expected, I might *almost* say as we deserved.

There is no people on earth justly entitled to the commiseration of mankind on account of their peculiar situation until they are equally ready and willing to render the same justice to others. . . .

We must throw off the distinctive features in the charters of our churches, and other institutions. We have refused to hear ministers preach from the pulpit, because they would not preach against slavery. We must pursue the same course respecting prejudice against complexion. I verily believe that no man ought to be employed as a pastor of any Christian Church, that would consent to preach to a congregation where the "negro pew" exists; and I also believe it to be a violation of Christian principles for any man to accept the pastoral charge of a Church under a charter based on complexional distinction. You now see my friend, that I am willing to accept the resolution in its catholic spirit. I trust that it will not be asking too much of you, and those that voted for it, to aid in promoting its faithful application to all existing institutions within your control.

I remain yours in the cause of liberty and equality.

Wm. Whipper

*2. Exclusivism—"William Whipper Letters: A Response," by Thomas Sipkins Sidney**

A large number of blacks thought it was important to have a leadership role in elevating their people, even to the extent of having some activities exclusively conducted by and for themselves in combatting their uniquely oppressed condition. Blacks serving as officers at the Albany Convention, which Whipper had criticized, included such well-known persons as Henry Highland Garnet, Alexander Crummell, and Charles B. Ray. Ray himself had rebutted some of Whipper's criticisms, but perhaps the most thorough response to Whipper was written by Thomas S. Sidney, another delegate to the black convention in question. Little is known about Sidney, particularly about his adult life.

It is known, however, that Thomas S. Sidney was an orphaned New Yorker and a young classmate of Crummell and Garnet at Noyes Academy in Canaan, New Hampshire. As students, Sidney, Crummell,

Colored American, February 13, 20 and March 6, 1841.

and Garnet gave speeches at the 1835 Independence Day Celebration of the New Hampshire Anti-Slavery Society meeting in Plymouth. Sidney was reportedly a talented orator, with less stylistic sting than the other two speakers. In his 1855 autobiography, Samuel R. Ward referred to Thomas Sipkins Sidney as one of ten blacks who were examples of persons with ''high and distinguished achievements'' among his people.

In 1840, the three former classmates were all in attendance at the Albany Convention, the rationale for which is given below by Sidney in a series of three essays written to the *Colored American*.

I have noticed, of late, two letters in the *Colored American*, from Mr. Wm. Whipper, of Columbia, Pa., which contain sentiments, singular and unfortunate, though by no means novel and unheard of. They represent the views of a very respectable portion of our people. They are the sentiments which have characterized the controversy which has been carried between many of our brethren, and in which the *Colored American* and *National Reformer* have been interested. . . .

As a people . . . we entertain no chimeras concerning our *actual condition*; we feel, that though not chattels, yet we are slaves. The *necessity* of effort to extricate ourselves from the deep pitfalls, and the loathsome cells of the dark prison-house of oppression, is a common conviction. And the determination, we think, is fully made, to hurl from us every vestige of proscription and degradation. In all this, we all agree.

But there are differences among us. From whence do they proceed? Of what nature are they? They do not resolve themselves into *what* we shall do, neither *for whom* we shall do. The condition of our people, either in gentle or severe accents, incites us to effort, and for upraising the wronged, and pent up, and straitened humanity, as seen in the persons and condition of the *colored people* of this country. Do not the differences arise, then, let me respectfully ask, from the *mode of operation*—the *how* of the matter? This, *we* think, is the cause of the controversy.

Our purpose is not to animadvert upon all the different topics presented in Mr. Whipper's letters, but to notice this particular one, ''The mode of operation for the elevation of our people.'' In doing so, we shall most certainly vindicate the plan of the Albany Convention—the good old way of blessed memory—the time-sanctioned course of our sires, . . . and the living energy and undying fervor of youth—the mode in which our best men, the living and the dead, have labored—not ineffectually—for years, in behalf of the rights of the people. . . .

> Trust not the stale fallacious cry
>   Of foreign aid, or friendly dole,
> But timely will alone rely
>   On means within your own control:
> So shall success your efforts crown,
> And recreant friends your merits own.—Anon.

"Resolved, That the way to obtain rights that have been wrested from a depressed people is by the continual presentation of the first principles of political freedom, truth and justice, accompanied by corresponding efforts on the part of the proscribed."—*Albany Con*.

It is the irrevocable decree of nature, that our main hope of progress and elevation through life, shall depend upon our own energy and activity. The growth and development of our nature, rests mainly upon the putting forth of whatever powers we possess. We cannot make this exertion by the employment of foreign aid. Activity on the part of others though it may produce important results; yet neither brings forth our latent energies, nor can be imputed to us. . . .

Shall an outraged and insulted people, intent upon their disenthralment, come forth by themselves, express their convictions, and commence their operations? In reply, we adduce the general principle, as of primary import—self-exertion the great law of our being. And history in myriad forms, and enlivening hues, attests its truth and affirms its beauty.

We know not where to begin in availing ourselves of the rich and abundant testimonials with which its pages teem. They rise up before us, clothed in antique sanctity, or invested with modern truthfulness and grandeur. The great Exodus from Egypt, the atmosphere of patriotic inspiration which hangs around Marathon, and Bannockburn, and Bunker Hill,—every struggle for human rights, whether marked by sanguinary features, or purified by mental energy—the self-devotedness and patriotic nationality of Tell and DeWitt, of Washington and Bolivar, and L'Ouverture, give verity to our position, and elevate it above the changeful influence of temporary opinion, or dubitable disputation, and invest it with the purity, majesty and universality of a PRINCIPLE.

There is an illustration to which our mind now recurs which we think of peculiar and striking force—a people subjected to a deep and long-lasting prejudice, oppressed, disfranchised. We refer to the Irish. What has been the course of that long-insulted and deeply injured people? Have their leaders repudiated special, separate action? In their great contest for Catholic emancipation were associations among themselves condemned, and denounced as savoring of exclusiveness or as abandoning principle on their part? Nay, verily. The immortal patriots of Erin, from Fitzgerald to O'Connell, have sent forth their trumpet-calls, sounding over heath and bog, heard in antiquated castle and in lowly hut, by lord and peasant; invoking the entire people to organize themselves into associations for the freedom of Ireland. And by this system of operation they effected their emancipation. . . ,; and by this system of *exclusive effort* they will eventually throw off every hindrance to a free and unrestrained enjoyment of British law and British freedom. . . .

And look at our brethren in the British West Indies. How was the emancipation of the slave, and the enfranchisement of the free colored people effected there? We unhesitatingly affirm, that it was chiefly through the influence of the colored man—the oppressed. . . .

In these, and all similar cases, the legislation was effected, it is true, by those in power; but they were compelled, forced to it, by the combined exertions of the oppressed.

The testimony of history upon this point is distinctly harmonious, univocal . . . The stirring anxieties and deep intensities, the inflexible purpose, the indomitable will and the decided action of the oppressed; give indubitable evidence to the oppressor of a common nature in both, are an emphatic affirmation of like tendencies of soul, awaken a consciousness of those upward unquenchable aspirations that our mother humanity universally begets. . . .

Our friends, abolitionists, may redouble their efforts, they may lavishly expend their means, they may strew their pamphlets over the country, thick as the leaves in some primeval forest, where the soil is undistinguishable from their thickly bedded masses—they may add to their numbers, and fill up their ranks, until they become as numerous as that

——————————————————Pitchy cloud
Of locusts,
That o'er the realm of impious Pharoah hung
Like night.

Yet our condition will remain the same, our sufferings will be unmitigated, until we awaken to such a consciousness of a momentous responsibility, which we shall manifest by giving it actuality. We occupy a position, and sustain relations which they cannot possibly assume. *They* are our allies—OURS is the battle.

In coming forth as colored Americans, and pleading for our rights, we neither preclude the necessity, nor forbid the action of our friends, no more than the Americans forbade the help of their French allies . . . But they kept the idea of *American* resistance to oppression distinct and prominent. . . .

The necessity, nay, the DUTY of peculiar activity on the part of an aggrieved people, we conclude, is the dictate of reason and common sense, and the testimony of history. . . .

But lo! in the midst of our energetic and effectual exertions, we are called off from our efforts, when we have made considerable progress in undermining our great Bastille, a LEADER informs us, that not only we, but our fathers, yea, all mankind, have gone wrong, and that he has found out a better plan—a new *theory*.

He bids us disregard the voice of principle, to pay no heed to its historic affirmations, to repudiate the dictates of *reason* and common sense, to leave the path of our sires, and adopt a new theory, alike unsupported by reason, and unaffirmed by experience.

In speculating upon ''heaven-born truth,'' he comes to despising all specific actions or means, and can deal in nothing but generalities —universalities.

We differ from him. We do not think that by watering and preserving that plant that perfumes our room, that *therefore* we dislike all other plants in the world. We do not believe that in loving our own mother's sons, our brothers, that therefore we create a cord of caste, and exclude mankind from our rights. In fine, we have no sympathy with that cosmopoliting disposition which tramples upon all nationality, which encircles the universe, but at the same time theorises away the most needed blessings, and blights the dearest hopes of a people.

And pray, for what are we to turn around and bay the whole human family? In the name of common sense, we ask for what have we to make this great radical change in our operations? Why are we to act different from all others in this important matter? Why, because we *happen* to be—COLORED.

[Thomas S.] Sidney
A Member of the Convention

Appendix II

Black Abolitionism—
Denunciation and
Conciliation

*A. DENUNCIATION—"SPEECH AT ANTI-SLAVERY
CELEBRATION OF INDEPENDENCE DAY,"
BY CHARLES LENOX REMOND**

Free black spokesmen felt compelled to speak out against that institution which held their brethren in bondage. The black lecturing agents for antislavery societies were consistently more "radical" and denunciatory in their attacks on the slave system than most of their counterparts who remained in their respective localities.

In 1838, Charles Lenox Remond took the field as the first black antislavery lecturer under the auspices of the American Anti-Slavery Society. Remond was born a free black whose father had emigrated to Massachusetts from the West Indies. Given a good fundamental education in Salem, Remond developed into a much sought-after speaker during the movement. His philosophy remained similar to that of William Lloyd Garrison, though Remond made use of his elective franchise whenever he thought it expedient to do so. Moreover, Remond favored slave rebellion, in defiance of Garrison's nonviolent philosophy.

The following speech was delivered by Remond on July 4, 1857 at Framingham, Massachusetts before an assemblage of the Massachusetts

*Liberator, July 10, 1857, p. 110.

302

Anti-Slavery Society. Like Purvis in his speech of the same year, the transcript of which appears in the preceding appendix section, Remond called for disunion as a means of achieving liberty for the slave.

————————

Mr. President, and Ladies and Gentlemen: I hardly need inform those who are gathered together here to-day, that I take some satisfaction in responding to the kind invitation of the Committee of the Massachusetts A.S. Society, for more reasons, perhaps, than would at first appear to many who are present. We have been informed, by the gentleman who preceded our respected President (Mr. Jackson), that this is a repetition of eighty years' standing of the demonstration of the American people on the side of liberty and independence. The reason why I, above all others, take pleasure in coming to this platform, is not to exhibit, if I may so express myself, the commonplace idea of a colored man's speaking in public, nor is it the grateful associations that may appear to other minds, on another account, or for other reasons, but it is that I may have the satisfaction of saying, in a word, that I hold all demonstrations on this day, outside of the gatherings similar to the one of which we form a part, as so many mockeries and insults to a large number of our fellow-countrymen. To-day there are, on the Southern plantations, between three and four millions, to whom the popular Fourth of July in the United States of America is a most palpable insult; and to every white American also a mockery. Why, sir, I have been informed since I came into this grove, that on this platform sit one or two men recently from Virginia, known and owned there as slaves. I ask you, Mr. Chairman, and I ask this audience, what must be the emotions of these men, who are now on their way from Virginia, through the free State of Massachusetts, to Canada, where alone they can be free, happy, or out of danger? I ask you if I say too much when I say, that to the slave, the popular Fourth of July in the United States is an insult? And hence I was glad to hear our esteemed friend, Francis Jackson, inquire if we are willing to take our places here to-day upon the glorious motto of "No Union with Slaveholders"; if we are willing to subscribe to the declaration that shall affirm our purpose to be to dissolve this slaveholding Union. [Applause.] I do not know how others may feel; I do not expect to get a hearty response to that expression; but the time is coming when a larger number than is gathered here to-day will subscribe to the idea of a dissolution of the Union as the only means of their own safety, as well as of the emancipation of the slave.

Sir, I do not care, so far as I am concerned, to view even the deeds committed by the greatest men of the Revolution, nor the purposes which they achieved. I do not care whether the statue recently erected to commemorate the deeds of Joseph Warren be deserved or not; I do not care whether the great majority of the reminiscences that cluster around the history of this day be veritable or not; I do know, in my heart, that every slave, on every plantation, has the right from his God and Creator to be free, and that is enough to warrant me in saying, that we cannot come here for a better or a nobler purpose than to help forward the effort to dissolve the American Union, because, if the Union shall be dissolved, if for no other purpose than for the emancipation of the slave, it will be glory enough for me to engage in it. [Applause.] Hence, sir, I do not feel, as many may feel today, to make an appeal over the prostrate form of some slave mother; nor do I care to repeat the sayings of some noble slave father; nor do I ask the men on my right what they have to say. I have only to speak for myself; to speak for freedom for myself; to determine for freedom for myself; and in doing so, I speak and determine for the freedom of every slave on every plantation, and for the fugitives on my right hand; and in so speaking, I speak for those before me as emphatically as I can for the blackest man that lives or suffers in our country. I subscribe, Mr. Chairman, to the remark made by our esteemed friend, Mr. Foss, in the cars, while coming here to-day; that I have not a word to say about the evils of American slavery, as they are detailed on the one hand, and retailed on the other. The time has come for us to make the ground upon which we stand to-day sacred to the cause of liberty; and when we make the ground of Framingham thus sacred, we do away with the necessity for the disgraceful underground railroad of our country, that transports such men as these fugitives to the dominions of the British Queen, in order that they may secure their inalienable rights; we do away with the dishonor that now gathers around and over the State of Massachusetts, which makes it necessary for any man or any woman to pass beyond our border before he or she can be free. Talk to me of Bunker Hill, and tell me that a fugitive passed through Boston to-day! Talk about Lexington, and tell me a slave mother must be kept secreted in Boston!

Talk to me of commemorating the memory of Joseph Warren, while thirty thousand fugitive slaves are in Canada! I will not scout the memory of the Revolution, the memory of Washington, and Adams, and Hancock, until the soil of Massachusetts shall be as free to every fugitive, and as free to me, as it is to the descendants of any of them. [Loud applause.] And until we shall do this, we talk in vain, and celebrate in vain.

O, sir, I long to see the day when Massachusetts, and every New England State, shall be the only Canada needful to the American slave. I see CHARLES SUMNER, on the one hand, in Europe, trying to recover from illness and physical prostration, the result of American slavery; on the other hand, I see Kansas Prostrate and bleeding, the result of American slavery. Before me, I see HORACE GREELEY, kicked and cuffed in the city of Washington, as the result of slavery. I look at Massachusetts, and I see our State, as an entire State, silently acquiescing in the recent disgraceful decision given by Judge Taney in the United States Supreme Court, whereby it is declared that the black man in the United States has no rights which the white man is bound to respect! Shame on Judge Taney! Shame on the United States Supreme Court! Shame on Massachusetts, that she does not vindicate herself from the insult cast upon her through my own body, and through the body of every colored man in the State! [Loud cheers.] My God and Creator has given me rights which you are as much bound to respect as those of the whitest man among you, if I make the exhibitions of a man. And black men did make the exhibition of manhood at Bunker Hill, and Lexington, and Concord, as I can well testify. But in view of the ingratitude of the American people, in view of the baseness of such men as Judge Taney, in view of the dough-face character that degrades our State, I regret exceedingly that there is one single drop of blood in my own veins that mingles with the blood of the men who engaged in the strife on Bunker Hill and at Lexington. Better that any such man had folded his hands and crossed his knees, during the American Revolution, if this is the reward we are to derive from such hypocrites, such cowards, such panderers to American slavery, as Judge Taney and his co-operators.

Mr. Chairman, I will not dwell upon this theme. I am not the man to speak to a white audience on the Fourth of July. I am reminded by everything over me, beneath me, and all around me, of my shame and degradation; and I shall take my seat on this occasion by stating to every white man present, who does not feel that the time has come when the rights of the colored man should be restored to him, that I am among the number who would embrace this day, this moment, to strike the last fetter from the limbs of the last slave, if it were in my power to do so, and leave the consequences to those at whose instigation it has been fastened upon them.

I look around the country, and behold one other demonstration, and with the mention of that, I shall take my seat. During the last year, not a few exhibitions have been made, in various parts of our country, of the purposes of American slavery the year to come; but there was no stronger demonstration than that made during the late Presidential canvass by the American people; and whatever may have been said prior to that time of the general sentiment of our country, the election of James Buchanan to the Presidency has placed that question beyond doubt and cavil, and has determined that the American people, by an overwhelming majority, are on the side of slavery, with all its infernalism. Now, sir, it belongs to the true friends who are present to go forward, determined that this state of things shall be altered, and it can only be altered by the largest application and the freest promulgation of the doctrine set forth by the American and Massachusetts Anti-Slavery Societies. I am glad, therefore, to utter my testimony from a platform where they are represented; and let me say, friends, whether you believe it or not, that if the cause of universal liberty shall ever be established in our country, within our day and generation, it can only be by the promulgation to the country of the most radical type of Anti-Slavery, known as the "Garrison doctrine." [Applause]

B. CONCILIATION—"AN ADDRESS TO THE PEOPLE OF THE UNITED STATES," BY JAMES McCUNE SMITH*

In contrast to Remond, the antislavery appeals of many black leaders were geared toward gaining the cooperation of white society in applying laws and policies equally to whites and blacks. For instance, the

Proceedings of the Colored National Convention, Philadelphia, 1855 (Salem, New Jersey: Printed at the National Standard Office, 1856), p. 30-3.

National Negro Convention in 1855 featured such an appeal by James McCune Smith.

James McCune Smith received an M.D. degree with distinguished honors from the University of Glasgow in 1837, after which time he practiced medicine in New York City while actively working for the political and moral elevation of his people. Among Smith's contributions were essays on the comparative anatomy and mental capacities of the races which refuted the proslavery phrenological theories of the time.

The following address, vocally defended by Smith and Frederick Douglass and opposed by Purvis and Remond, was adopted by the 1855 Convention.

Fellow Citizens:—In behalf of three millions of our brethren, held in Slavery, in the United States:

In behalf of two hundred and fifty thousand, so called, free persons of color, occupying various grades of social and political position, from equal citizenship in most of the New England States, to almost chattel slavery in Indiana and the Southern States:

In behalf of three hundred thousand slaveholders, embruted with the lawlessness, and drunken with the blood-guiltiness of slaveholding:

In behalf of the Constitution of these United States, during sixty years perverted and misconstrued, so as to read things for persons, and Slavery for Liberty:

In behalf of the religion of Jesus Christ, brought into shame and disrepute by the evil constructions and worse practices fastened upon it by the American Church:

In behalf of the sacred cause of HUMAN FREEDOM, beaten down and paralyzed by the force of American Example—

The undersigned, delegates to a Convention of the People of Color, held in the city of Philadelphia, October 18th, 1855, beg leave, most respectfully, to address you:—

We claim that we are persons not things, and we claim that our brethren held in slavery are also, persons not things; and that they are, therefore, so held in slavery in violation of the Constitution, which is the supreme law of the land. For the Constitution expressly declares that all human beings, described under it, are persons, and afterwards declares, that "NO PERSON shall be deprived of liberty without due process of law;" and that the right of the people to be secure in their persons shall not be violated. And as no law has ever been enacted, which reduced our brethren to slavery, we demand their immediate emancipation, and restoration to the rights secured to every person under the Constitution, as the instant result of that personality with which the Constitution itself clothes them, and which it was ordained to protect and defend.

All human beings who may be born in this land, in whatever condition, and all who may come or may have been brought to this land, under whatever circumstances, are declared by the Constitution to be PERSONS: the idea that such may be property, or may become property, is no where recognized, but every where excluded by the Constitution.

The Constitution, moreover, endows Congress with the power, and calls on Congress to exercise the power to abolish Slavery in the Slave States, when it declares that "Congress shall provide for the general welfare;" and announces that "the United States shall guarantee to every State in this Union a republican form of government:" and that "this Constitution, and the laws of the United States, which shall be made in pursuance thereof, shall be the supreme law of the land; and the judges in every State shall be bound thereby, any thing in the Constitution or laws of any State to the contrary notwithstanding." (Art. 6, sec. 2.)

It is not needful to prove that slavery inhibits, obstructs and threatens to destroy the "general welfare," and is therefore an institution which Congress is competent, and in duty bound, to abolish everywhere where it may cause such obstruction. Nor is it necessary to show that slavery is a contradiction of the Republican form of Government, which the United States, that is Congress is constitutionally bound "to guarantee" to each and "every State in the Union:" which guarantee can only be accomplished by immediately abolishing slavery in every State where it may exist. These things contain their own proof in the very statement of them.

We claim, therefore, that the right and duty of Congress to abolish slavery in the slave States, is just as clear and well defined in the Constitution as the right to levy duties, declare war, or make a treaty.

To uphold a contrary view of the Constitution, requires that that instrument should contradict itself, and requires also that the idea of personal liberty, as defined by it, and on which you all, fellow-citizens, so confidently rely, shall be entirely erased therefrom. The personality of the negro and of the white man stand therein side by side; you cannot destroy the one without also destroying the other; you cannot uphold the one without also upholding both.

We solemnly believe, fellow-citizens, that a vast majority of you ardently wish that slavery may be abolished, and are willing to join in any lawful movement to accomplish this great purpose. We call upon you, therefore, at once to set about this glorious work in accordance with the provisions of the Constitution which is the ''supreme law of the land.'' Elect such a Congress, such a President, and thereby secure the appointment of such a Judiciary as will guarantee to each man, woman and child, in the land, the right to their own persons, which the Constitution guarantees. There is no other way, there never has been, there can be no other way to abolish slavery and the slave power throughout the land.

It is idle to talk of preventing the extension or circumscribing the limits of slavery: there is no foot of American Territory over which slavery is not already triumphant, and will continue triumphant, so long as there remains any foot of American Territory on which it is admitted that man can hold property in man. It is imbecile for you, fellow-citizens, with the gyves on your wrists, and your chains clanking audibly to the rest of mankind, any longer to boast the possession, or speak of the maintenance of your personal rights and franchises. During sixty-eight years you have suffered us to be robbed of these rights and franchises, in the belief that your own continued unimpaired. But now, after the experience of two generations, you find your own rights invaded and your own privileges taken away in like manner with ours. It is now, therefore, demonstrated, by incontrovertible History, that you cannot, by whatever neglect or suffered misinterpretation of the Constitution, imperil or abandon our rights, without, in like manner, imperiling and abandoning your own. It stands forth, in letters of living light, that there can be not one white free-man while there remains one black slave in the Union. And there can be no higher praise of the Constitution, than that its workings are absolute—if rightly interpreted, for Freedom—if wrongly, for Slavery—to all.

As at present misinterpreted and carried out, your own rights under the Constitution, fellow-citizens, are not a shade higher than those of the veriest slave in the South: your local elective franchises are exercised, your very territory occupied, your relations at home and abroad regulated at the bidding of the slave power; and you must either remain the willing victims of their atrocious institution, and hug the chains daily accumulating upon you, or you must at once rise and rend them, and regain your own liberties while you establish those of your brethren in bonds.

We earnestly call upon you, therefore, fellow-citizens, in behalf of the down-trodden slave, in behalf of your own imperiled liberties, in behalf of the cause of civil and Religious Freedom throughout the world, in behalf and in vindication of our glorious Constitution, we solemnly call upon you, peacefully, lawfully and constitutionally, to abolish slavery in the slave States.

Bibliography

BIBLIOGRAPHIES

African Bibliographic Center: Special Bibliographic Series. *Black History Viewpoints: A Selected Guide to Resources for Afro-American and African History: 1968*. Vol 7, No. 1. New York: Negro Universities Press, 1969.

Bibliographic Survey: The Negro in Print. Washington, D.C.: The Negro Bibliographic and Research Center, Inc., 1965—.

Dubois, W. E. B., and Guy B. Johnson. *Encyclopedia of the Negro*, Preparatory Volume. New York: The Phelps-Stokes Fund, Inc., 1964.

Dumond, Dwight Lowell. *A Bibliography of Antislavery in America*. Ann Arbor: University of Michigan Press, 1961.

Harlan, Louis R. *The Negro in American History*. Washington, D.C.: American Historical Association, 1965.

Joint Committee for Media Center Development. *The Heritage of the Negro in America; A Bibliography: Books, Records, Tapes, Filmstrips, Film and Pictures*. Michigan Department of Education, 1970.

Litwack, Leon F. "Bibliographical Essay," *North of Slavery*. Chicago: University of Chicago Press, 1961, p. 280-303.

Locke, Alain L. *The Negro in America*. Chicago: American Library Association, 1933.

Miller, Elizabeth W. *The Negro in America: A Bibliography*. Cambridge: Harvard University Press, 1966.

Porter, Dorothy B. *A Working Bibliography on the Negro in the United States*. Ann Arbor: University Microfilms, 1969.

————. "Early American Negro Writings: A Bibliographical Study,"
  Papers of the Bibliographical Society of America, XXXIX (Third
  Quarter, 1945) p. 192-268.
————. *The Negro in the United States; A Selected Bibliography*.
  Washington, D.C.: Library of Congress, 1970.
Schatz, Walter, ed. *Directory of Afro-American Resources*. New York:
  R. R. Bowker Company, 1970.
Welsch, Erwin K. *The Negro in the United States: A Research Guide*.
  Bloomington: Indiana University Press, 1965.
Work, Monroe N. (Compiler). *A Bibliography of the Negro in Africa and
  America*. New York: Octagon Books, 1965.

NEWSPAPERS AND PERIODICALS

Negro Publications

The Aliened American (Cleveland), 1853.
The Anglo-African Magazine (New York), 1859-1860.
The Colored American (New York), 1837-1839.
The Elevator (San Francisco), 1857-1861.
Douglass' Monthly (Rochester), 1861-1863.
Frederick Douglass' Paper (Rochester), 1851-1855.
Freedom's Journal (New York), 1827-1829.
National Reformer (Philadelphia), 1837.
North Star (Rochester), 1847-1851.
Northern Star and Freeman's Advocate (Albany), 1842.
Weekly Advocate (New York), 1837.
Weekly Anglo-African (New York), 1859-1860.

General Serial Publications

Anti-Slavery Bugle (Salem, Ohio), 1851-1858.
Anti-Slavery Examiner (New York), 1836-1845.
Anti-Slavery Record (New York), 1835-1837.
Anti-Slavery Tracts (New York), 1855-1861.
Emancipator and Republican (New York and Boston), 1833-1850.

The Friend of Man (Utica, N.Y.), 1836-1842.
Herald of Freedom (Concord, N.H.), 1836.
Liberator (Boston), 1831-1861.
Massachusetts Abolitionist (Boston), 1839-1841.
National Anti-Slavery Standard (New York), 1840-1865.
Pennsylvania Freeman (Philadelphia), 1840-1852.
Philanthropist (Cincinnati), 1836-1847.

DOCUMENTS

Appeal of Forty Thousand Citizens Threatened With Disfranchisement, to the People of Pennsylvania. Philadelphia: Printed by Merrihew and Gunn, 1838.

Brown, William W. *A Lecture Delivered Before the Female Anti-Slavery Society of Salem, at Lyceum Hall, November 14, 1847, by William W. Brown, a Fugitive Slave*. Boston: Massachusetts Anti-Slavery Society, 1847.

Calumny Refuted by Facts from Liberia, With Extracts from a Discourse by H. H. Garnet. London: Charles Gilpin, 1848.

Constitution of the African Civilization Society. New Haven: Printed by Thomas J. Stafford, 1861.

Constitution of the American Society of Free Persons of Colour, for Improving Their Condition in the United States. Also the Proceedings of the Convention with Their Address to the Free Persons of Colour in the United States, Philadelphia, 1830. Philadelphia: J. W. Allen, 1831.

Cornish, Samuel E., and Theodore S. Wright. *The Colonization Scheme Considered*. Newark: Printed by Aaron Guest, 1840.

Delany, M. R. *Official Report of the Niger Valley Exploring Party*. New York: Thomas Hamilton, 1861.

Douglass, Frederick. *Address on the Dred Scott Decision*. Rochester: Printed at the Office of Frederick Douglass, 1857.

Easton, Rev. Hosea. *A Treatise on the Intellectual Character and Civil and Political Condition of the Colored People of the United States*. Boston: Printed and Published by Isaac Knapp, 1837.

Forten, James, Jr. *An Address Delivered Before the Ladies' Anti-Slavery*

Society of Philadelphia, April, 1836. Philadelphia: Printed by Merrihew and Gunn, 1836.

Garnet, Henry Highland. *A Memorial Discourse; by Rev. Henry Highland Garnet, Delivered in the Hall of the House of Representatives, 1865 With an Introduction by James McCune Smith, M.D.* Philadelphia: Joseph M. Wilson, 1865.

―――. *The Past and the Present Condition, and the Destiny, of the Colored Race: A Discourse Delivered at the Fifteenth Anniversary of the Female Benevolent Society of Troy, N.Y., February 14, 1848*. Miami, Florida: Mnemosyne Publishing Inc., 1969.

―――. *Walker's Appeal, With a Brief Sketch of his Life. And Also Garnet's Address to the Slaves of the United States of America*. New York: Printed by J. H. Tobitt, 1848.

Hamilton, Robert S. *Discourse of the Scheme of African Colonization, Delivered before the Colonization Society, of Greene County Ohio at Xenia, July 4, 1849*. Cincinnati: Chronicle Book and Job Rooms, 1849.

Hamilton, William. *Oration Delivered in the African Zion Church, July 4, 1827*. New York: Printed by Gray and Bunce, 1827.

McCrummell, James, et al. *A Memorial to the Honorable Senate and House of Representatives of the Commonwealth of Pennsylvania, by the Colored Citizens of Philadelphia, 1834*. n.p., n.d.

Memorial of Thirty Thousand Disfranchised Citizens of Philadelphia to the Hon. Senate and House of Representatives. Philadelphia: Printed for the Memorialists at 22 South Third Street, 1855.

Minutes and Address of the State Convention of Colored Citizens of Ohio, Columbus, 1849. Oberlin: J. M. Fitch's Power Press, 1849.

Minutes and Proceedings of the First Annual Convention of the People of Colour, Philadelphia, 1831. Philadelphia: Published by Order of the Committee of Arrangements. 1831.

Minutes and Proceedings of the Second Annual Convention for the Improvement of the Free People of Color, Philadelphia, 1832. Philadelphia: Martin & Boden, Printers, 1832.

Minutes and Proceedings of the Third Annual Convention, for the Improvement of the Free People of Colour, Philadelphia, 1833. New York: Published by Order of the Convention, 1833.

Minutes of the Fifth Annual Convention for the Improvement of the Free

People of Colour, Philadelphia, 1835. Philadelphia: William P. Gibbons, 1835.

Minutes of the Fifth Annual Convention of the Colored Citizens of New York, Schenectady, 1844. Troy: J. C. Kneeland and Co., Printers, 1844.

Minutes of the Fourth Annual Convention for the Improvement of the Free People of Colour, New York, 1834. New York: Published by Order of the Convention, 1834.

Minutes of the National Convention of Colored Citizens, Buffalo, 1843. New York: Piercy & Reed, Printers, 1843.

Minutes of Proceedings of the Requited Labor Convention, Philadelphia, 1838. Philadelphia: Printed by Merrihew and Gunn, 1838.

Minutes of the State Convention of the Colored Citizens of Ohio, Columbus, 1851. Columbus: E. Glover, Printer, 1851.

Minutes of the State Convention of the Coloured Citizens of Pennsylvania, Harrisburg, 1848. Philadelphia: Merrihew and Thompson, Printers, 1849.

Minutes of the State Convention of the Colored Citizens of the State of Michigan, Detroit, 1843. Detroit: Printed by William Harsha, 1843.

Nesbit, William. *Four Months in Liberia or African Colonization Exposed*. Pittsburgh: Printed by J. T. Shryock, 1855.

Newsom, M. F., ed. *Arguments Pro and Con on the Call for a National Emigration Convention, by Frederick Douglass, W. J. Watkins, and J. M. Whitfield*. Detroit: Tribune Steam Presses, 1854.

Official Proceedings of the Ohio State Convention of Colored Freemen, Columbus, 1853. Cleveland: Printed by W. W. Day, Aliened American Office, 1853.

Pennington, J.W.C. *A Two Years' Absence, or a Farewell Sermon*. Hartford: H. T. Wells, 1845.

Proceedings of a Convention of the Colored Men of Ohio, Cincinnati, 1858. Cincinnati: Moon, Wilstach, Keys and Co., Printers, 1858.

Proceedings of the Colored National Convention, Philadelphia, 1855. Salem, New Jersey: Printed at the National Standard Office, 1856.

Proceedings of the Colored National Convention, Rochester, 1853. Rochester: Printed at the Office of Frederick Douglass' Paper, 1853.

Proceedings of the Connecticut State Convention of Colored Men, New Haven, 1849. New Haven: William H. Stanley, Printer, 1849.

Proceedings of the Constitution Meeting at Faneuil Hall, November 26, 1850. Boston: Printed by Beals and Greene, 1851.

Proceedings of the Convention of the Colored Freemen of Ohio, Cincinnati, 1852. Cincinnati: Printed by Dumas and Lawyer, 1852.

Proceedings of the First State Convention of the Colored Citizens of the State of California, Sacramento, 1855. Sacramento: State Journal Printing, 1855.

Proceedings of the National Convention of Colored People, and Their Friends, Troy, 1847. Troy: Steam Press of J. C. Kneeland and Co., 1847.

Proceedings of the National Emigration Convention of Colored People, Cleveland, 1854. Pittsburgh: Printed by A. A. Anderson, 1854.

Proceedings of the Second Annual Convention of the Colored Citizens of the State of California, Sacramento, 1856. San Francisco: J. H. Udell and W. Randall, 1856.

Proceedings of the State Convention of Colored Citizens of the State of Illinois, Alton, 1856. Chicago: Hays and Thompson, Book, Job, and Ornamental Printers, 1856.

Report of the Proceedings of the Colored National Convention, Cleveland, 1848. Rochester: Printed by John Dick, at the North Star Office, 1848.

Resolutions of the People of Color, at a Meeting Held on the 25th of January, 1831, With an Address to the Citizens of New York, in Answer to Those of the New York Colonization Society. New York: n.p., 1831.

Ruggles, David. *The "Extinguisher" Extinguished! or David M. Reese, M.D. "Used Up."* New York: Published and Sold by D. Ruggles, Bookseller, 1834.

Speeches and Letters of Robert Purvis. New York: Published by Afro-American League, n.d.

Statistical Inquiry into the Condition of the People of Color of the City and Districts of Philadelphia. Philadelphia: Printed by Kite and Walton, 1849.

The Minutes and Proceedings of the First Annual Meeting of the Ameri-

can Moral Reform Society. Philadelphia: Printed by Merrihew and Gunn, 1837.

BOOKS

Abels, Jules. *Man on Fire: John Brown and the Cause of Liberty*. New York: The Macmillan Company, 1971.

Adams, Russell L. *Great Negroes Past and Present*. Chicago: Afro-American Publishing Company, 1963.

Aptheker, Herbert. *Essays in the History of the American Negro*. New York: International Publishers, 1945.

———. *One Continual Cry: David Walker's Appeal to the Colored Citizens of the World, 1829-1830: Its Setting, Its Meaning*. New York: Humanities Press, 1965.

———. *The Negro in the Abolitionist Movement*. New York: International Publishers, 1941.

———. *To Be Free: Essays in American Negro History*. New York: International Publishers, 1948.

———, ed. *A Documentary History of the Negro People in the United States*. New York: The Citadel Press, 1951.

Auer, J. Jeffrey, ed. *Antislavery and Disunion, 1858-1861*. New York: Harper and Row, Publishers, 1963.

Ball, Charles. *Slavery in the United States: A Narrative of the Life and Adventures of Charles Ball*. New York: John S. Taylor, 1837.

Barbour, Floyd B., ed. *The Black Power Revolt*. Boston: Porter Sargent Publisher, 1968.

Bardolph, Richard. *The Negro Vanguard*. Westport, Conn.: Negro Universities Press, 1971.

Barnes, Gilbert H. *The Antislavery Impulse, 1830-1844*. New York: D. Appleton-Century Company, Inc., 1934.

Barnes, Gilbert H., and Dwight L. Dumond, eds. *Letters of Theodore Dwight Weld, Angelina Grimke Weld and Sarah Grimke, 1822-1844*. 2 vols. New York: D. Appleton-Century Company, Inc., 1934.

Bartlett, Irving H. *Wendell Phillips: Brahmin Radical*. Boston: Beacon Press, 1961.

Bell, Howard H. *A Survey of the Negro Convention Movement, 1830-1861*. New York: Arno Press, 1969.

————, ed. *Minutes of the Proceedings of the National Negro Conventions, 1830-1864*. New York: Arno Press, 1969.

Bennett, Lerone, Jr. *Before the Mayflower: A History of the Negro in America, 1619-1964*. Revised Edition. Baltimore: Penguin Books, 1966.

————. *Pioneers in Protest*. Chicago: Johnson Publishing Company, Inc., 1968.

Bernard, Jacqueline. *Journey Toward Freedom: The Story of Sojourner Truth*. New York: Norton, 1967.

Bibb, Henry. *Narrative of the Life and Adventures of Henry Bibb*, 3rd Edition. New York: Published by the Author, 1850.

Blaustein, Albert P., and Robert L. Zandrando, eds. *Civil Rights and the American Negro: A Documentary History*. New York: Trident Press, 1968.

Bontemps, Arna, ed. *Great Slave Narratives*. Boston: Beacon Press, 1969.

Bormann, Ernest G., ed. *Forerunners of Black Power: The Rhetoric of Abolition*. Englewood Cliffs, N.J.: Prentice-Hall, Inc., 1971.

Bracey, John H., et al., eds. *Free Blacks in America, 1800-1860*. Belmont, California: Wadsworth Publishing Company, Inc., 1971.

Brawley, Benjamin. *A Short History of the American Negro*, 2nd Rev. Ed. New York: The Macmillan Co., 1921.

————. *A Social History of the American Negro*. New York: The Macmillan Co., 1921.

————. *Early Negro American Writers*. Chapel Hill: The University of North Carolina Press, 1935.

Brotz, Howard, ed. *Negro Social and Political Thought, 1850-1920: Representative Texts*. New York: Basic Books, Inc., Publishers, 1966.

Brown, Sterling, et al. *The Negro Caravan*. New York: The Dryden Press, Inc., 1941.

Brown, William Wells. *Narrative of William W. Brown, a Fugitive Slave*. Boston: Published at the Anti-Slavery Office, 1847.

————. *The Black Man, His Antecedents, His Genius, and His Achievements*. New York: Thomas Hamilton, 1863.

————. *The Rising Son or, The Antecedents and Advancement of the Colored Race*. Boston: A. G. Brown & Co., Publishers, 1874.

Buckmaster, Henrietta. *Let My People Go: The Story of the Underground Railroad and the Growth of the Abolition Movement*. Boston: Beacon Press, 1963.

Burns, W. Haywood. *The Voices of Negro Protest in America*. London: Oxford University Press, 1963.

Chestnutt, Charles W. *Frederick Douglass: A Biography*. Boston: Small, Maynard and Co., 1899.

Cole, Arthur C. *The Irrepressible Conflict, 1850-1865*. New York: The Macmillan Co., 1934.

Crummell, Alexander. *Africa and America: Addresses and Discourses*. New York: Negro Universities Press, 1969.

Curry, Richard O., ed. *The Abolitionists: Reformers or Fanatics?* New York: Holt, Rinehart and Winston, 1965.

Curtis, James C., and Lewis L. Gould, eds. *The Black Experience in America: Selected Essays*. Austin: University of Texas Press, 1970.

Delany, Martin R. *The Condition, Elevation, Emigration, and Destiny of the Colored People of the United States. Politically Considered*. Philadelphia: Published by the Author, 1852.

Delany, Martin R., and Robert Campbell. *Search for a Place: Black Separation and Africa*. Ann Arbor: University of Michigan Press, 1969.

Dillon, Merton. *Benjamin Lundy and the Struggle for Negro Freedom*. Urbana, Ill.: University of Illinois Press, 1966.

Douglass, Frederick. *Life and Times of Frederick Douglass*, 1892 Edition. New York: Collier Books, 1962.

Douglass, Frederick. *My Bondage and My Freedom*. New York: Miller, Orton, and Mulligan, 1855.

Draper, Theodore. *Rediscovery of Black Nationalism*. New York: Viking Press, 1970.

DuBois, William E. Burghardt. *Black Folk Then and Now*. New York: Henry Holt and Company, 1939.

————. *John Brown*. Centennial Edition. New York: International Publishers, 1962.

Duberman, Martin, ed. *The Antislavery Vanguard: New Essays on Abolitionists*. Princeton: Princeton University Press, 1966.

Ducas, George, ed. *Great Documents in Black American History*. New York: Praeger, 1970.

Dumond, Dwight L. *Antislavery: The Crusade for Freedom in America*. Ann Arbor: University of Michigan Press, 1961.

Dumond, Dwight Lowell, ed. *Letters of James Gillespie Birney*, 2 vols. New York: D. Appleton-Century Co., 1938.

Essays and Pamphlets on Antislavery. Westport, Conn.: Negro Universities Press, 1970.

Farrison, William Edward. *William Wells Brown: Author & Reformer*. Chicago: The University of Chicago Press, 1969.

Fauset, Arthur H. *Sojourner Truth, God's Faithful Pilgrim*. Chapel Hill: University of North Carolina Press, 1938.

Filler, Louis. *The Crusade Against Slavery: 1830-1860*. New York: Harper Torchbook, 1960.

Fishel, Leslie H. and Benjamin Quarles, eds. *The Black American: A Documentary History*. Glenview, Ill.: Scott, Foresman, 1970.

Fisk University. *Unwritten History of Slavery*. Nashville: Social Sciences Documents, 1945.

Foley, Albert S. *God's Men of Color*. New York: Farrar Straus Company, 1955.

Foner, Eric. *Free Soil, Free Labor, Free Men*. New York: Oxford University Press, 1970.

Foner, Philip S. *Frederick Douglass*. New York: The Citadel Press, 1969.

———. *The Life and Writings of Frederick Douglass*, 4 vols. New York: International Publishers, 1950.

———, ed. *The Voice of Black America: Major Speeches by Negroes in the United States, 1797-1971*. New York: Simon and Schuster, 1972.

Foster, William Zebulon. *The Negro People in American History*. New York: International Publishers, 1954.

Franklin, John Hope. *From Slavery to Freedom: A History of American Negroes*, 2nd Edition, Revised and Enlarged. New York: Alfred A. Knopf, 1956.

Frazier, Thomas R., ed. *Afro-American History: Primary Sources*. New York: Harcourt Brace Jovanovich, 1970.

Frederickson, George M., ed. *William Lloyd Garrison*. Englewood Cliffs, N.J.: Prentice-Hall, Inc., 1968.

Fuller, Edmund. *Prudence Crandall: An Incident of Racism in Nineteenth-Century Connecticut*. Middletown, Conn.: Wesleyan University Press, 1971.

Garrison, William Lloyd. *Thoughts on African Colonization*, Part II. Boston: Printed and Published by Garrison and Knapp, 1832.

Gilbert, Olive. *Narrative of Sojourner Truth*. Ann Arbor, Mich.: University Microfilms Inc., 1966.

Golden, James L., and Richard D. Rieke. *The Rhetoric of Black Americans*. Columbus, Ohio: Charles E. Merrill Publishing Co., 1971.

Grant, Joanne, ed. *Black Protest*. New York: St. Martin's Press, 1970.

Green, William. *Narrative of Events in the Life of William Green*. Springfield: L. M. Guernsey, Book, Job, & Card Printer, 1853.

Griffiths, Julia, comp. *Autographs for Freedom*. Auburn, N.Y.: Alden, Beardsley and Co., 1854.

Gross, Bella. *Clarion Call: The History and Development of the Negro People's Convention Movement in the United States from 1817 to 1870*. New York: Published by B. Gross, 1947.

Hanes, Walton, Jr. *The Negro in Third Party Politics*. Philadelphia: Dorrance & Company, 1969.

Hart, Albert B. *Slavery and Abolition, 1831-1841*. New York: Harper and Brothers, 1906.

Herskovits, Melville J. *The Myth of the Negro Past*. Boston: Beacon Press, 1964.

Hill, Roy L., ed. *Rhetoric of Racial Revolt*. Denver: Golden Bell Press, 1964.

Hillis, Newell D. *The Battle of Principles*. New York: G. P. Putnam's Sons, 1905.

Katz, William L. *Eyewitness: The Negro in American History*. New York: Pitman Publishing Corporation, 1967.

Langston, John Mercer. *Freedom and Citizenship: Selected Lectures and Addresses*. Washington, D.C.: Rufus H. Darley, 1883.

Lincoln, S. Eric. *The Negro in America*. New York: Bantam Books, 1967.

Litwack, Leon F. *North of Slavery*. Chicago: The University of Chicago Press, 1961.

Logan, Rayford. *The Negro in the United States, A Brief History*. Princeton, N.J.: D. Van Norstrand Co., 1957.

Loggins, Vernon. *The Negro Author, His Development in America*. New York: Columbia University Press, 1937.

Loguen, Jermain W. *The Rev. J. W. Loguen, as a Slave and as a Freeman*. Syracuse, N.Y.: J.G.K. Truair and Co., 1859.

Lutz, Alma. *Crusade for Freedom: Women in the Antislavery Movement*. Boston: Beacon Press, 1969.

Mabee, Carleton. *Black Freedom: The Nonviolent Abolitionists From 1830 Through the Civil War*. New York: Macmillan Company, 1970.

Madden, Edward Henry. *Civil Disobedience and Moral Law in Nineteenth-Century Philadelphia*. Seattle: University of Washington Press, 1968.

Majors, Monroe A. *Noted Negro Women, Their Triumphs and Activities*. Chicago: Donahue and Hannesberry, 1893.

Malvin, John. *North Into Freedom: The Autobiography of John Malvin, Free Negro, 1795-1880*. Cleveland: Press of Western Reserve University, 1966.

Mathews, Marcia M. *Richard Allen*. Baltimore: Helicon Press, 1963.

May, Samuel J. *Some Recollections of our Antislavery Conflict*. Boston: Fields, Osgood, & Co., 1869.

McPherson, James M. *The Struggle for Equality*. Princeton: Princeton University Press, 1964.

Meier, August, and Elliott M. Rudwick. *From Plantation to Ghetto: An Interpretive History of American Negroes*. New York: Hill and Wang, 1966.

————, eds. *The Making of Black America: Essays in Negro Life and History*, 2 vols. New York: Atheneum, 1969.

Meltzer, Milton, ed. *In Their Own Words: A History of the American Negro*, Vol. 1, 1819-1865. New York: Apollo Editions, 1964.

Miller, Basil. *Ten Slaves Who Became Famous*. Grand Rapids: Zonderan Publishing House, 1951.

Miller, Ruth, ed. *Black American Literature: 1760-Present*. Beverly Hills, Calif.: Glencoe Press, 1971.

Narrative of Henry Box Brown. Boston: Published by Brown & Stearns, n.d.

Narrative of Sojourner Truth. Battle Creek, Mich.: Published for the Author, 1878.

Nell, William C. *The Colored Patriots of the American Revolution, with Sketches of Several Distinguished Colored Persons: To Which is Added a Brief Survey of the Condition and Prospects of Colored Americans*. Boston: Published by Robert F. Wallcut, 1855.

Nelson, Alice Moore Dunbar, ed. *Masterpieces of Negro Eloquence*. New York: Bookery Publishing Company, 1914.

Olcott, Charles. *Two Lectures on the Subjects of Slavery and Abolition*. Massillon, Ohio: Printed for the Author, 1838.

Oliver, Robert T. *History of Public Speaking in America*. Boston: Allyn and Bacon, Inc., 1965.

O'Neill, Daniel J., ed. *Speeches by Black Americans*. Encino, Calif.: Dickenson Publishing Company, Inc., 1971.

Osofsky, Gilbert, ed. *Puttin' on Ole Massa: The Slave Narratives of Henry Bibb, William Wells Brown, and Solomon Northrup*. New York: Harper & Row, 1969.

Pease, William H., and Jane H. Pease, eds. *The Antislavery Argument*. New York: Bobbs-Merrill, 1965.

Pennington, James W. C. *The Fugitive Blacksmith; or, Events in the History of James W. C. Pennington*. Second Edition. London: Charles Gilpin, 1849.

Pettigrew, Thomas J. *A Profile of the Negro American*. Princeton, N.J.: D. Van Nostrand, 1964.

Pinckney, Alphonso. *Black Americans*. Englewood Cliffs, N.J.: Prentice-Hall, Inc., 1969.

Porter, Dorothy, ed. *Negro Protest Pamphlets*. New York: Arno Press and the New York Times, 1969.

Quarles, Benjamin. *Black Abolitionists*. New York: Oxford University Press, 1969.

———. *Frederick Douglass*. Washington, D.C.: Publishers, Inc., 1948.

———. *Lincoln and the Negro*. New York: Oxford University Press, 1962.

———. *The Negro in the Making of America*. New York: Collier Books, 1964.

Ray, Florence. *Sketch of the Life of Rev. Charles B. Ray*. New York: Press of J. J. Little & Co., 1887.

Redding, J. Saunders. *The Lonesome Road*. Garden City, N.Y.: Doubleday and Company, Inc., 1958.

———. *They Came in Chains*. New York: J. B. Lippincott Co., 1950.

Richards, Leonard L. *Gentlemen of Property and Standing: Anti-Abolition Mobs in Jacksonian America*. New York: Oxford University Press, 1970.

Robinson, William H., Jr. *Early Black American Prose*. Dubuque: Wm. C. Brown Company Publishers, 1971.

Ruchames, Louis, ed. *Racial Thought in America: From the Puritans to Abraham Lincoln*. Amherst: University of Massachusetts Press, 1969.

———. *The Abolitionists: A Collection of Their Writings*. New York: G. P. Putnam's Sons, 1963.

Sillen, Samuel. *Women Against Slavery*. New York: Masses and Mainstream, 1955.

Simms, Henry H. *Emotion at High Tide: Abolition As a Controversial Factor, 1830-1845*. Richmond, Va.: W. Byrd Press, 1960.

Sloan, Irving J. *The American Negro: A Chronology and Fact Book*. Dobbs Ferry, N.Y.: Oceana Publications, 1965.

Smith, Arthur L. *Rhetoric of Black Revolution*. Boston: Allyn and Bacon, 1969.

———, ed. *Language, Communication and Rhetoric in Black America*. New York: Harper and Row Publishers, 1972.

Smith, Arthur L. and Stephen Robb, eds. *The Voice of Black Rhetoric: Selections*. Boston: Allyn and Bacon, 1971.

Sorin, Gerald. *New York Abolitionists: A Case Study of Political Radicalism*. Westport, Conn.: Greenwood Publishing Corp., 1971.

Staudenraus, P. J. *The African Colonization Movement: 1816-1865*. New York: Columbia University Press, 1961.

Steward, Austin. *Twenty-Two Years a Slave, and Forty Years a*

Freeman, 3rd Edition. Rochester, N.Y.: Allings and Cory, 1861.

Sunderland, LeRoy. *Anti-Slavery Manual*. New York: Percy and Reed, 1837.

The Narrative of Lunsford Lane, Published by Himself. Boston: Printed for the Publisher: J. G. Torrey, Printer, 1842.

Thomas, John L., ed. *Slavery Attacked: The Abolitionist Crusade*. Englewood Cliffs, N.J.: Prentice-Hall, Inc., 1965.

Thorpe, Earl E. *The Central Theme of Black History*. Durham, N.C.: Printed by Seeman Printery, 1969.

————. *The Mind of the Negro: An Intellectual History of Afro-Americans*. Baton Rouge, La.: Ortlieb Press, 1961.

Ullman, Victor. *Look to the North Star: a Life of William King*. Boston: Beacon Press, 1969.

Ullman, Victor, and Martin R. Delany. *The Beginnings of Black Nationalism*. Boston: Beacon Press, 1971.

Ward, Samuel Ringgold. *Autobiography of a Fugitive Negro*. London: John Snow, 1855.

Washington, Booker T. *The Story of the Negro*, 2 vols. New York: Doubleday, Page and Co., 1909.

Weisberger, Bernard A., ed. *Abolitionism: Disrupter of the Democratic System or Agent of Progress*. Chicago: Rand McNally and Co., 1963.

Wesley, Charles. *Richard Allen: Apostle of Freedom*. Washington, D.C.: The Associated Publishers, 1935.

Williams, George W. *History of the Negro Race in America*, 2 vols. New York: G. P. Putnam's Sons, 1883.

Williams, Jayme C., and McDonald Williams, eds. *The Negro Speaks*. New York: Noble and Noble, 1970.

Wilson, Armistead. *A Tribute for the Negro*. New York: W. Harned, 1848.

Woodson, Carter Godwin. *A Century of Negro Migration*. Washington, D.C.: The Association for the Study of Negro Life and History, 1918.

————. *Free Negro Heads of Families in the United States in 1830, Together With a Brief Treatment of the Free Negro*. Washington, D.C.: The Association for the Study of Negro Life and History, Inc., 1925.

———. *The Education of the Negro Prior to 1861*. New York: G. P. Putnam's Sons, 1915.

———. *The History of the Negro Church*. Washington, D.C.: The Associated Publishers, 1921.

———. *The Negro in Our History*. Washington, D.C.: The Associated Publishers, Inc., 1922.

———., ed. *Negro Orators and Their Orations*. Washington, D.C.: The Association for the Study of Negro Life and History, 1925.

———., ed. *The Mind of the Negro as Reflected in Letters Written During the Crisis*. Washington, D.C.: The Association for the Study of Negro Life and History, Inc., 1926.

Yatman, Norman R., ed. *Voices From Slavery*. New York: Holt, Rinehart and Winston, 1970.

JOURNAL ARTICLES

Abzug, Robert H. "The Influence of Garrisonian Abolitionists' Fears of Slave Violence on the Antislavery Argument, 1829-1840." *Journal of Negro History* 55 (January 1970): 15-28.

Aptheker, Herbert. "Militant Abolitionism." *Journal of Negro History* 26 (October 1941): 438-84.

Bell, Howard H. "Chicago Negroes in the Reform Movement, 1847-1853." *Journal of Negro History* 21 (April 1958): 153-65.

———. "Expressions of Negro Militancy in the North, 1847-1853." *Journal of Negro History* 45 (January 1960): 11-20.

———. "National Negro Conventions in the Middle 1840's: Moral Suasion vs. Political Action." *Journal of Negro History* 42 (October 1957): 247-60.

———. "Negro Nationalism: A Factor in Emigration Projects, 1858-1861." *Journal of Negro History* 47 (January 1962): 42-53.

———. "Negroes in California, 1849-1859." *Phylon* 28 (Summer 1967): 159-70.

———. "Some Reform Interests of the Negro During the 1850's as Reflected in State Conventions." *Phylon* 21 (Summer 1960): 173-81.

———. "The Negro Emigration Movement, 1849-1854: A Phase of Negro Nationalism." *Phylon* 21 (Summer 1959): 132-42.

Brewer, W. M. "Henry Highland Garnet." *Journal of Negro History* 13 (January 1928): 42-53.

———. "John B. Russwurm." *Journal of Negro History* 13 (October 1928): 413-22.

Dick, Robert C. "Negro Oratory in the Anti-Slavery Societies: 1830-1860." *Western Speech* 28 (Winter 1964): 5-14.

———. "Rhetoric of Ante-Bellum Black Separatism." *Negro History Bulletin* 34 (October 1971): 133-7.

Eaton, Clement. "A Dangerous Pamphlet in the Old South." *Journal of Southern History* 2 (August 1936): 323-34.

Farrison, William E. "William Wells Brown in Buffalo." *Journal of Negro History* 34 (October 1954): 298-314.

Foner, Eric. "Politics and Prejudices: The Free Soil Party and the Negro, 1849-1852." *Journal of Negro History* 50 (October 1965): 239-46.

Foster, Charles I. "The Colonization of Free Negroes in Liberia, 1816-1835." *Journal of Negro History* 38 (January 1953): 41-66.

Griffin, Clifford S. "The Abolitionists and the Benevolent Societies, 1831-1861." *Journal of Negro History* 44 (July 1959): 195-216.

Gross, Bella. "The First National Negro Convention." *Journal of Negro History* 31 (October 1946): 435-43.

Kennicott, Patrick C. "Black Persuaders in the Antislavery Movement." *Speech Monographs* 37 (March 1970): 15-24.

———. "Black Persuaders in the Antislavery Movement." *Journal of Black Studies* 1 (September 1970): 5-20.

Landon, Fred. "Henry Bibb, a Colonizer." *Journal of Negro History* 5 (October 1920): 437-47.

Lapp, Rudolph M. "Jeremiah Sanderson: Early California Negro Leader." *Journal of Negro History* 53 (October 1968): 321-33.

Levesque, George A. "Black Abolitionists in the Age of Jackson: Catalysts in the Radicalization of American Abolitionism." *Journal of Black Studies* 1 (December 1970): 187-202.

Litwack, Leon F. "The Federal Government and the Free Negro, 1790-1860." *Journal of Negro History* 43 (October 1958): 261-78.

Mann, Kenneth Eugene. "Nineteenth Century Black Militant: Henry

Highland Garnet's Address to the Slaves." *Southern Speech Journal* 34 (Fall 1969): 11-21.

Mehlinger, Louis R. "The Attitude of the Free Negro Toward African Colonization." *Journal of Negro History* 1 (July 1916): 276-301.

Myers, John L. "American Antislavery Society Agents and the Free Negro, 1833-1838." *Journal of Negro History* 52 (January 1967): 200-19.

Nichols, Charles H. "Who Read the Slave Narratives?" *Phylon* 20 (Summer 1951): 149-62.

Nichols, William W. "Slave Narratives: Dismissed Evidence in the Writing of Southern History." *Phylon* 32 (Winter 1961): 403-9.

Nogee, Joseph L. "The Prigg Case and Fugitive Slavery, 1842-1850." *Journal of Negro History* 39 (July 1954): 185-205.

Pease, Jane H., and William H. Pease. "Black Power: The Debate in 1840." *Phylon* 29 (Spring 1968): 19-26.

Pease, William H., and Jane H. Pease. "Negro Conventions and the Problem of Black Leadership," *Journal of Black Studies* 2 (September 1971): 29-44.

Perlman, Daniel. "Organizations of the Free Negro in New York City, 1800-1860." *Phylon* 32 (Summer 1971): 181-97.

Porter, Dorothy B. "Anti-Slavery Movement in Northampton." *Negro History Bulletin* 23 (November 1960): 33ff.

———. "David M. Ruggles: An Apostle of Human Rights." *Journal of Negro History* 28 (January 1943): 23-50.

———. "Sarah Parker Remond, Abolitionist and Physician." *Journal of Negro History* 20 (July 1935): 287-93.

———. "The Organized Educational Activities of Negro Literary Societies, 1828-1846." *The Journal of Negro Education* 12 (Spring 1943): 422-77.

Rosen, Bruce. "Abolition and Colonization, The Years of Conflict: 1829-1834." *Phylon* 33 (Summer 1972): 177-192.

Ruchames, Louis. "William Lloyd Garrison and the Negro Franchise." *Journal of Negro History* 50 (January 1915): 37-49.

Schriver, Edward. "Black Politics Without Blacks: Maine 1841-1848." *Phylon* 31 (Summer 1970: 194-201.

Shanks, Caroline L. "The Biblical Anti-Slavery Argument of the Decade 1830-1840." *Journal of Negro History* 16 (April 1931): 132-57.

Shiffrin, Steven H. "The Rhetoric of Black Violence in the Antebellum Period: Henry Highland Garnet." *Journal of Black Studies* 2 (September 1971): 45-56.

Smith, Arthur L. "Henry Highland Garnet: Black Revolutionary in Sheep's Vestments." *Central States Speech Journal* 21 (Summer 1970): 93-8.

———. "Socio-Historical Perspectives of Black Oratory." *Quarterly Journal of Speech* 56 (October 1970): 264-9.

Smith, Robert P. "William Cooper Nell: Crusading Black Abolitionist." *Journal of Negro History* 55 (July 1970): 182-99.

Strange, Douglas C. "Bishop Daniel Alexander Payne's Protestation of American Slavery, A Document." *Journal of Negro History* 52 (January 1967): 59-64.

Wagner, Gerard A. "Sojourner Truth: God's Appointed Apostle of Reform." *Southern Speech Journal* 27 (Winter 1962): 123-30.

Wahle, Kathleen O'Mara. "Alexander Crummell: Black Evangelist and Pan-Negro Nationalist." *Phylon* 29 (Winter 1968): 388-95.

Wander, Philip C. "Salvation Through Separation: The Image of the Negro in the American Colonization Society." *Quarterly Journal of Speech* 57 (February 1971): 57-67.

Warner, Robert A. "Amos Gerry Beman—1812-74, A Memoir on a Forgotten Leader." *Journal of Negro History* 22 (April 1937): 200-21.

Wesley, Charles H. "The Negro in the Organization of Abolition." *Phylon* 2 (Fall 1941): 223-35.

———. "The Negroes of New York in the Emancipation Movement." *Journal of Negro History* 24 (January 1939): 65-103.

———. "The Participation of Negroes in Anti-Slavery Political Parties." *Journal of Negro History* 29 (January 1944): 32-74.

Work, Monroe N. "The Life of Charles B. Ray." *Journal of Negro History* 4 (October 1919): 361-71.

UNPUBLISHED MATERIALS

Bell, Howard H. "A Survey of the Negro Convention Movement: 1830-1861." Ph.D. dissertation: Northwestern University, 1953.

Bennett, Dewitt C. "A survey of American Negro Oratory." M.A. thesis: George Washington University, 1933.

Bullock, Penelope Laconia. "The Negro Periodical Press in the United States." Ph.D. dissertation: The University of Michigan, 1971.

Collins, Sandra A. "A Rhetorical Analysis of Selected Speeches of Frederick Douglass: A Pre-Civil War Black Militant." M.A. thesis: Western Illinois University, 1970.

Dick, Robert C. "Rhetoric of the Negro Ante-Bellum Protest Movement." Ph.D. dissertation: Stanford University, 1969.

Fulkerson, Raymond Gerald. "Frederick Douglass and the Anti-Slavery Crusade: His Career and Speeches, 1817-1861." Ph.D. dissertation: University of Illinois, 1971.

George, Carol Ann. "Richard Allen and the Independent Black Church Movement, 1787-1831." Ph.D. dissertation: Syracuse University, 1970.

Hale, Frank W. "A Critical Analysis of the Speaking of Frederick Douglass." M.A. thesis: University of Nebraska, 1951.

Hite, Roger William. "The Search for an Alternative: The Rhetoric of Black Emigration, 1850-1860." Ph.D. dissertation: University of Oregon, 1971.

House, Graddenia O. "Anti-Slavery Activities of Negroes in New York, 1830-1860." M.A. thesis: Howard University, 1936.

Kennicott, Patrick C. "Negro Antislavery Speakers in America." Ph.D. dissertation: Florida State University, 1967.

Killian, Charles D. "Bishop Daniel A. Payne: Black Spokesman for Reform." Ph.D. dissertation: Indiana University, 1970.

Ladner, Cornelius Abraham. "A Critical Analysis of Four Anti-Slavery Speeches of Frederick Douglass." M.A. thesis: State University of Iowa, 1947.

Leonard, Rebecca. "The Rhetoric of Agitation in the Abolition and Black Liberation Movements." M.A. thesis: Purdue University, 1970.

Miller, Floyd John. "The Search for a Black Nationality: Martin R. Delany and the Emigrationist Alternative." Ph.D. dissertation: University of Minnesota, 1970.

Moseberry, Lowell T. "An Historical Study of Negro Oratory in the

United States to 1915.'' Ph.D. dissertation: University of Southern California, 1955.

Pipes, William W. ''An Interpretative Study of Old-Time Negro Preaching.'' Ph.D. dissertation: University of Michigan, 1942.

Schlobohm, Dietrich Hans. ''The Declaration of Independence and Negro Slavery: 1776-1876.'' Ph.D. dissertation: Michigan State University, 1970.

Sernett, Milton Charles. ''Black Religion and American Evangelism: White Protestants, Plantation Missions, and the Independent Negro Church.'' Ph.D. dissertation: University of Delaware, 1972.

Smith, Sidonie Ann. ''Patterns of Slavery and Freedom in Black American Autobiography.'' Ph.D. dissertation: Case Western Reserve University, 1971.

Wander, Philip. ''Image of the Negro in Three Movements: Abolitionist, Colonizationist, and Pro-Slavery.'' Ph.D. dissertation: University of Pittsburgh, 1968.

Whittaker, Helen Beatrice. ''Negroes in the Abolition Movement.'' M.A. thesis: Howard University, 1935.

Zucker, Charles Noye. ''The Free Negro Question: Race Relations in Ante-Bellum Illinois.'' Ph.D. dissertation: Northwestern University, 1972.

INDEX

332